Children's Literature

Volume 16

Volume 16

Annual of
The Modern Language Association
Division on Children's Literature
and The Children's Literature
Association

Yale University Press
New Haven and London
1988

Children's Literature

Editor-in-chief: Francelia Butler
Coeditors, Volume 16: Margaret R. Higonnet, Barbara Rosen
Book Review Editor: John Cech
Editorial Assistant: Paula L. Cardinal
Advisory Board: Robert Coles, M.D.; U. C. Knoepflmacher; Lois R. Kuznets; Alison Lurie; Sam Pickering, Jr.; Albert J. Solnit, M.D.
Consultants for Volume 16: Gillian Adams; Janice M. Alberghene; Rufus Blanshard; Rosemarie Bodenheimer; Ann Charters; Beverly Clark; Lee Copenhaver; Irving Cummings; Abbott Gleason; Selwyn Goodacre, M.D.; Martin Green; Constance Hieatt; Peter Hunt; Sylvia Iskander; Elizabeth Keyser; James R. Kincaid; Ruth MacDonald; Ira B. Nadel; Perry Nodelman; Judith Plotz; Compton Rees; Thomas M. Roberts; Glenn Edward Sadler; Mary Shaner; Michael Steig; Monika Totten
Conference Representative: Joy Anderson

The editors gratefully acknowledge support from the University of Connecticut.

Editorial correspondence should be addressed to:
The Editors, *Children's Literature*
Department of English, U-25
University of Connecticut
Storrs, Connecticut 06268

Manuscripts submitted should conform to the new *MLA* style. An original on non-erasable bond with two copies, a self-addressed envelope, and return postage are requested. Dot-matrix printouts cannot be accepted.

Volumes 1–7 of *Children's Literature* can be obtained directly from John C. Wandell, The Children's Literature Foundation, Box 370, Windham Center, Connecticut 06280. Volumes 8–16 can be obtained from Yale University Press, 92A Yale Station, New Haven, Connecticut 06520, or from Yale University Press, 13 Bedford Square, London WC1B 3JF, England.

Library of Congress catalog card number: 79–66588
ISBN: 0–300–04192–6 (cloth); 0–300–04193–4 (paper)

Set in Baskerville type by the Saybrook Press, Inc., Old Saybrook, Conn. Printed in the United States of America by Vail-Ballou Press, Binghamton, N.Y.

Published with assistance from the Kingsley Trust Association Fund established by the Scroll and Key Society of Yale College.

10   9   8   7   6   5   4   3   2   1

Contents

Musical Notes to The Annotated Alice

Cecily Raysor Hancock

When Alice Liddell Hargreaves in old age described those summer boating expeditions of 1862 when she and her sisters were
the first audience for the story that Lewis Carroll developed into
Alice's Adventures in Wonderland, she reported that they included
music: "On our way back we generally sang songs popular at the
time, such as 'Star of the evening, beautiful star,' and 'Twinkle,
twinkle, little star,' and 'Will you walk into my parlour, said the
spider to the fly,' all of which are parodied in the *Alice*" (Gray
276). The parodies mentioned by Mrs. Hargreaves are songs
rather than poems, sung rather than read or recited in *Alice's Adventures in Wonderland*; and the Liddell sisters were not the only
audience to which these parodies of familiar songs would have
suggested the tunes used by the fictional singers. The songs in
Through the Looking-Glass also seem to carry musical indications to
readers interested in such information. There have been many
tunes composed especially for the songs of Alice, and some of
them may be better tunes or more suited to the new words than
the ones the author and his first audience had in mind; but they
do not satisfy the curiosity excited by references to tunes known
to Carroll. The annotators who have provided the original words
parodied or references to them (Gardner; Gray; Green) have not
included the tunes, though they have made it easier to find them.

Some of these tunes are still familiar, though not necessarily to
everyone who would be glad to know them; but a few are now
obscure. The purpose of this article is to provide the tunes that
Lewis Carroll knew and, to the original audience of the Alice
books, suggested. Though for a general audience the practical
purposes of my study have been provided for by Alexandre Reverend's cassette and pamphlet, *Lewis Carroll and Music*, its schol-
arly and hortatory ones have not.[1] I wish to present the old tunes
together with something of their background. Tunes as well as
words have a place in cultural history.

Lewis Carroll's own preference for the tunes he originally had
in mind was expressed in several letters. When William Boyd, who

had composed new music for *The Songs from* Alice's Adventures in
Wonderland (1870), asked permission to set music to the poems
in the new *Alice* book, Carroll gave his permission but commented, "I am afraid, however, that you will find the same difficulty in your way as in the case of the former volume—namely,
that all verses at all like *songs* have well-known tunes already"
(*Letters* 168). In 1877 Carroll attempted to commission Arthur
Sullivan (not yet of Gilbert and Sullivan) to write tunes for a possible dramatic production of *Alice*. He wrote, "I should very much
like you to try one song in *Alice*—any that you prefer (except of
course those that were written for existing tunes, such as 'Will you
walk into my parlour?' and 'Beautiful Star')" (*Letters* 278). When
Henry Savile Clarke was preparing the very successful *Alice in
Wonderland* operetta with music by Walter Slaughter (it came out
in 1886 and had London productions in twenty Christmas seasons
between then and 1930 [Green 138]), Carroll specified several
tunes:

> One thing more occurs to me to request. Several of the songs
> are parodies of old Nursery songs, that have their own tunes,
> as old as the songs probably. I would much prefer, if you
> introduce any of these, that the *old* air should be used. The
> whole of the poetry, in both books, has been already pub-
> lished, with music, many times: people are constantly apply-
> ing for leave to do this: and they have simply spoiled such
> pieces as "Will you walk a little faster" by writing new airs. It
> would take a very good composer to write anything better
> than the sweet old air of "Will you walk into my parlour, said
> the Spider to the Fly." [*Letters* 637]

In response to a letter from Savile Clarke, Carroll wrote more
mildly, "As to retaining the tunes, it was hardly worth while to
trouble you. I find there are only *four* pieces that have known airs,
viz;—(in 'Alice') 'Twinkle, twinkle, little star.' 'Will you walk into
my garden" [*sic*]. 'Beautiful Star'— &, (in 'Looking-Glass')
'Bonnie Dundee' " (letter dated 6 September 1886, in the Alfred C. Berol Collection, Fales Library, New York University). After some weeks, Lewis Carroll sent three tunes, with comments:

> I went last night to one of my fellow students, who under-
> stands music. I whistled, & *he* wrote, & as the result I send

you the 3 airs, "I give thee all", "Twinkle, twinkle", & "Will
you walk into my parlour"—

"I give thee all" is Moore's poetry, written to a "National
Air" but of what Nation I know not. I like it, but am not so
deeply attached to it as to care much whether your Composer
uses it or his own setting—specially as my verses are not a
parody of the original. The *first* line is an imitation, but
after that I went off "on my own hook".

"Twinkle, twinkle" I *hope* will be used. It would be a *great* pity
not to do so—specially as it fits so well to the endless repetition of the words, by the sleeping Dormouse. They are certainly the notes which the *writer* attaches to the words, if any
weight may be given to that circumstance.

"Will you walk" is the only air I am really anxious to have
preserved. It is a favorite air with me, & the only one that
realises to me the idea of the dance. I should be sorry if any
other melody, however pretty in itself, were substituted for
it." [28 November 1886, Berol Collection]

It is an illustration of oral tradition among the literate that to
Lewis Carroll the tunes he preferred were inhabitants of the
memory rather than the printed page. He bought books of songs,
as the catalogue of the property sold after his death shows
(Stern); but when he wanted a written form of tunes that he knew
very well, he had them written down from his whistling. Like most
of us, Lewis Carroll heard a great deal more music than he saw. A
search for musical annotation is different from looking for books
an author might have read, though after a century there is not
much practical difference.

"Beautiful Soup" and "The Lobster Quadrille" have "Old
Tune" indicated in the 1886 and 1888 editions of Savile Clarke's
Alice in Wonderland, A Dream Play for Children in Two Acts, and
appear with the tunes of "Beautiful Star" and "Will you walk"
in the score printed in 1906. "Welcome, Queen Alice," the song
that goes to "Bonnie Dundee," also has "Old Tune" in the printed
play, but the tune is not printed in the score. "Twinkle, twinkle" is
said rather than sung in the play, and another song is substituted
for the White Knight's long song to the tune of "I give thee all."
(The operetta used traditional tunes for "The Mulberry Bush,"
"Humpty Dumpty," and perhaps "The Lion and the Unicorn,"

however, and "Tweedledum and Tweedledee" may also be a nursery tune.)

I

Taking the songs in the order in which they appear in the books, we begin with the three songs Alice Liddell Hargreaves remembered and we end with a good tune and one still well enough known to have the intended effect on some portion of today's audience. The first song, however, is the only one of those Lewis Carroll wanted in the operetta for which the tune he had in mind cannot be definitely determined. The difficulty is ironic, since this song is also the one for which there is now the most commonly associated and expected tune.

At least the first verse of Jane Taylor's "The Star," first published in 1806 and now generally identified by its first line as "Twinkle, Twinkle, Little Star," is so well known as a song now that for most readers of the Mad Tea-Party chapter of *Alice's Adventures in Wonderland* it will provide a good illustration of how the words of a parody can suggest the tune of the song parodied.

"—it was at the great concert given by the Queen of Hearts, and I had to sing

　'Twinkle, twinkle, little bat! How I wonder what you're at!'

You know the song, perhaps?"

"I've heard something like it," said Alice.

"It goes on, you know," the Hatter continued, "in this way:—

　'Up above the world you fly, Like a tea-tray in the sky.
　　Twinkle, twinkle—'"

Here the Dormouse shook itself, and began singing in its sleep *"Twinkle, twinkle, twinkle, twinkle——"* and went on so long that they had to pinch it to make it stop.

"Well, I'd hardly finished the first verse," said the Hatter, "when the Queen bawled out 'He's murdering the time! Off with his head!'"

"How dreadfully savage!" exclaimed Alice. [Gray 57–58]

Most English-speaking readers will echo internally Alice's "I've heard something like it," and for most of them the tune that comes to mind will be the familiar *do do sol sol la la sol* tune so useful to beginning instrumentalists—an international nursery tune with a printing history going back to eighteenth-century France,[2] now wedded (though not monogamously) to Jane Taylor's poem. This is not a tune that fits the references to the song in *Alice* by the author himself or by Alice Liddell Hargreaves. It does not provide especially well for the endless repetition of the words "twinkle, twinkle" by the sleeping dormouse, and it was not popular in 1862—at least not sufficiently popular to leave printed traces. Alice Hargreaves's comment "popular at the time" would seem to imply "popular then but not now."

"Twinkle, Twinkle, Little Star" was occasionally set to original tunes in sheet music and books of songs for children,[3] but none of these tunes seems to have been collected by other printers. The nineteenth-century collections of nursery rhymes with their traditional tunes did not include Jane Taylor's "Twinkle, Twinkle, Little Star" (its singing tradition was not sufficiently antique). When "Twinkle, Twinkle" achieved a position among rhymes printed with the tunes "which have always been associated with each particular rhyme" (Kidson, writing in 1904) or if not always, at least "for generations" (Graham, in 1911), it was Graham's example of the nursery rhymes "which are not fixed to one tune." Graham gives the tune almost universally printed with the rhyme now, but he names two other tunes locally associated with the same words—"Innocents" and "The Spanish Chant." Kidson printed "The Spanish Chant" as the traditional tune for "Twinkle, Twinkle, Little Star," and this pairing still turns up occasionally.[4] Disher in *Victorian Song*, mentions traditional association of "Twinkle, Twinkle, Little Star" with a hymn tune identified only by a snatch of words ("In the kingdom of Thy grace / Give a little child a place") and gives a lively account of its popularity in magic lantern shows (15–16).

"The Spanish Chant" (see fig. 1) is a sleepy tune with a good deal of scope for continued twinkles. I have found no printed evidence of the length of its nursery tradition,[5] but Kidson and Graham, both specialists in musical tradition, accepted the tune as traditional. The Savile Clarke operetta, which might have settled the matter, dodges the issue by not giving Carroll's tune or any tune at all. The sheet music in the British Library gives two set-

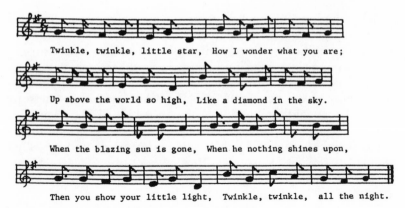

Figure 1. From Frank Kidson's *British Nursery Rhymes* [1904]. Kidson's note gives the author and date of the words and identifies the tune as "The Spanish Chant."

tings that are historically possible. Guylott's (1857) would have been in time for Alice Liddell's childhood but offers no special scope for repeated twinkles; Green's (see fig. 2) might have become a Dodgson nursery tradition and does have a plethora of repeated twinkles and a tune that would allow them to drone on and on. There have been so many tunes printed with the poem that even the least likely ones have a certain weight in depressing the chances that any particular one was Lewis Carroll's; we only know that he himself asociated a particular tune with the words and that it gave special scope to the dormouse. The use of the tune now familiarly associated with the song parodied does at least give some of the intended effect of parody.[6]

II

The next song, "The Lobster Quadrille" (" 'Will you walk a little faster,' said a whiting to a snail") uses another of the songs Alice Liddell remembered as having been sung with Lewis Carroll and parodied in the *Alice* books—and this is the one that Carroll especially insisted on for the operetta in his letter to Savile Clark, calling it "a favorite air with me, & the only one that realises to me the idea of the dance." It has been a dance tune in its time: under its older name of "Will You Come to the Bower?" it is among the fiddle tunes for country dancing copied down in the

Twinkle, twinkle, little Star,   How I wonder what you are,
When the blazing Sun is gone,   When his daily round is run--
In the dark blue sky you keep,&   often thro' my curtains peep, &

how I wonder what you are
when his daily round is run
often thro' my curtains peep,

Up above the world so high   Like a diamond in the sky
Then you show your little light-And twinkle, twinkle all the night;
For you never shut your eye   'Till the sun is in the sky

twinkle, twinkle, twinkle, twinkle, like a diamond in the sky
twinkle, twinkle, twinkle, twinkle, twinkle, twinkle all the night
twinkle, twinkle, twinkle, twinkle, 'Till the sun is in the sky

Figure 2. "The Little Star," from *Little Songs for Little Singers* (London: J. Green, 33, Soho Square, n.d.). The publisher and composer, John Green, had a music shop at the address given between about 1820 and 1848 (Humphries and Smith). Used with the permission of Mrs. Iona Opie.

1820s by the poet John Clare (Deacon). It may well have been used for quadrilles: their music was at first (early nineteenth century) country dance tunes and later (by Victorian times) arrangements of any tune that was currently popular (*Grove's Dictionary of Music*).

"Will You Come to the Bower?"—generally attributed to Thomas Moore as both author and composer—was very popular in the generation before Lewis Carroll's. Its tune, unnamed after the first citation, was used by several different comic songs entitled "The Spider and the Fly" (three of them beginning "Will you walk into my parlour?") that were popular throughout the nineteenth century. This tune was based on that of "Mrs. Bond," a somewhat earlier comic song also popular in the nineteenth century that maintains a nursery currency in England (Opie and

Opie, *Dictionary*; song in Rimbault, *Collection of Old Nursery Rhymes*; Crane, *Baby's Opera*; Graham; Kidson; Buck, *Nursery Songbook*; Mitchell and Blyton).[7]

The particular song that Lewis Carroll parodied in "The Lobster Quadrille" has been identified (Gardner; Gray; Green 282) as Mary Howitt's "The Spider and the Fly," without reference to the fact that Howitt's poem is also a song and appears with its traditional tune (with slight variations in words and tune, indicating a continuing singing tradition) in English nursery song books (Graham; Kidson; Buck; Mitchell and Blyton.)

As it happens, it was not a poem that was also a song that Lewis Carroll parodied, but a song that had no separate literary standing. Howitt's poem, which first appeared in 1829 (Opie and Opie, *Oxford Book of Children's Verse*,) was a reshaping with a female victim of a comic song with the same title by a singer and writer of music hall songs, Thomas Hudson, first printed by him in his 1824 annual collection of comic songs, without music but with the direction: *"Tune—'Will you come to the Bower?'"* Lewis Carroll's "Will you, won't you" refrain shows that it was Hudson's song rather than Howitt's that he had in mind. Hudson and Carroll adapted to their own use the twice repeated "Will you, will you, will you, will you Come to the bow'r?" refrain of "Will You Come to the Bower?" Howitt has no refrain in her poem; she uses the whole six lines of each verse for text. Hudson's song was, as Alice Liddell Hargreaves remembered, "popular at the time" in 1862; it had been taken up by another fashionable singer, Henry Russell. The British Library collection includes different versions published in London in 1855, 1858, and 1861. It was twice printed as a nursery song—by Helmore with the same tune he printed with "The Lobster Quadrille" and a refrain somewhat influenced by Carroll's, and by J. W. Elliott with one of his new tunes.

Hudson's "The Spider and the Fly," like the familiar Howitt one, ends with disaster and a moral. They are both about invitations that should not have been accepted. Mrs. Bond's "Dilly dilly dilly dilly come and be killed" call to her ducks is of the same inauspicious nature, and even the romantic solicitations of "Will You Come to the Bower?" might inspire caution in the worldly and practical mind.[8] The snail's reluctance to come and join the dance is temperamental, however; there is no apparent reflection on the motives of the whiting. The former associations of Lewis Carroll's "sweet old air" may not have occurred to him at all, though he had a wide acquaintance with frivolous songs and frequently parodied them; his medley, "Miss Jones," strings together bits of twenty-two familiar airs (*Collected Verse* 47–50).

Here are the first and last verses of Thomas Hudson's eight,[9] with the first refrain supplemented from other versions printed with the tune indicated:

"Will you walk into my parlour?" (said a Spider to a Fly,)
" 'Tis the prettiest little parlour sure that ever you did spy;
"You've only got to pop your head within side of the door,
"You'll see so many curious things you never saw before.
　"Will you walk in, pretty Fly?"
　["Will you, will you, will you, will you,
　　　walk in, pretty Fly?
　"Will you, will you, will you, will you,
　　　walk in, pretty Fly?"]

MORAL.

Now all young men take warning by this foolish little Fly,
Pleasure is the Spider, that to catch you fast will try;
For altho' you may think that my advice is quite a bore,
You're *lost* if you stand *parleying* outside of *Pleasure's door*.
　Remember, oh remember the foolish little Fly.

The tune as printed with the comic songs varies, especially in the cadences and the refrain—and not consistently, so that one can distinguish separate traditions. If the 1906 score of the Savile Clarke operetta did not include a form of the old tune (see fig. 3), it would be impossible to decide on a particular version as the one that Carroll had in mind. Those who have been happily singing "The Lobster Quadrille" with the first "Will you walk" tune that came to hand will find that the version printed in the 1906 score for Savile Clarke's *Alice in Wonderland: A Dream Play for Children*, though recognizable, is not precisely the version they know.[10] The air is much faster-moving than one would expect from the Mock Turtle's doleful singing,[11] well suited to its use with comic songs (incuding Carroll's parody) or as a dance tune for a qua-

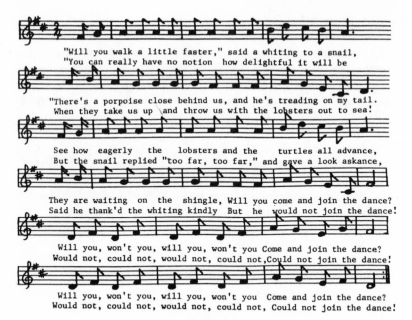

"Will you walk a little faster," said a whiting to a snail,
"You can really have no notion how delightful it will be

"There's a porpoise close behind us, and he's treading on my tail.
When they take us up and throw us with the lobsters out to sea!

See how eagerly   the   lobsters and the   turtles all advance,
But the snail replied "too far, too far," and gave a look askance,

They are waiting on the shingle, Will you come and join the dance?
Said he thank'd the whiting kindly But he would not join the dance!

Will you, won't you, will you, won't you Come and join the dance?
Would not, could not, would not, could not,Could not join the dance!

Will you, won't you, will you, won't you Come and join the dance?
Would not, could not, would not, could not, Could not join the dance!

Figure 3. Words and melody from the 1906 score of Savile Clarke's *Alice in Won-derland: A Dream Play for Children*, 1886.

drille. (The imploring lover of "Will You Come to the Bower?" was eager rather than languishing. Thomas Moore frequently set romantic words to lively tunes.)

III

The Mock Turtle's "Beautiful Soup" is another parody of a song sung with the Liddell sisters. "Beautiful Star," by James M. Sayles, introduced from America by the Christy Minstrels, was currently a very popular song—the British Library has thirteen vocal versions printed between 1857 and 1861, eight under Sayles's name and five anonymous, besides instrumental versions for that period and later. The parody would certainly have suggested the tune to a good many people. Even now, we can see that it is clearly a song rather than a poem that is parodied in chapter 10 of *Alice's Adventures in Wonderland* and that part of the joke must be musical. The typographical device of drawing out the vowels of the chorus in the Mock Turtle's song suggests that Carroll was thinking of, and mocking, the tune as well as the words—also that it must have been a suitably soupy tune. Complete words, as kindly provided by Gardner, give something of the general effect; but what was the tune?

The 1906 score does not follow exactly the texts of the original play (1886, 1888), which gave the words as they appear in *Alice's Adventures in Wonderland*, with the repetition of the last phrase of each verse (omitted in the score) and with the uppercase conclusion "Beautiful, beauti—FUL SOUP!", which suggests that the singer might be a little out of breath after holding all those long notes. Lewis Carroll may have been parodying a more strenuous form of the song than the one given here (see fig. 4), for I have chosen for the unprofessional singer an edition (not the only one) in the key of C and in 6/8 time. It is quite as authentic to set the song two notes higher, in E, and in 3/4 time with long notes held across bar lines. (The score of the operetta, Freiligrath-Kroeker, and Helmore all give the tune in C, Freiligrath-Kroeker in 6/8,

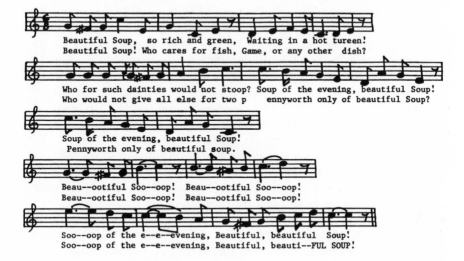

Figure 4. Tune from D'Almaine & Company's Standard Edition, "Beautiful Star in Heaven So Bright," Sung by Christy's Minstrels, Composed by S. M. Sayles [*sic*]. London [1858]. British Library, H. 1401.a(6.).

the other two in 3/4.) The Mock Turtle does not seem to repeat
the chorus after the first verse, and I have chosen sheet music that
does not have this repetition; but the Gryphon's demand of "Chorus again!" is quite right. One edition of the song directs "Chorus
to be Repeated after each Verse" the first time and "Repeat Chorus ad lib." after the second and third verses; others call for the
chorus *fortissimo* the first time, then again *pianissimo*. In *Alice's
Adventures Under Ground*, the Gryphon's demand came after the
first and only verse of the Mock Turtle's song; the second verse
was added later.

IV

In *Through the Looking-Glass*, chapters 4, 6, and 7—"Tweedledum
and Tweedledee," "Humpty Dumpty," and "The Lion and the
Unicorn"—introduce traditional rhymes and use characters and
incidents from them. Most readers today know these three
rhymes only as rhymes. The rhyming riddle "Humpty Dumpty"
seems to be simply a rhyme to Alice; but "Tweedledum and
Tweedledee" and "The Lion and the Unicorn" are both introduced as "the words of the old song," though they are not sung.

"Tweedledum and Tweedledee" is one of the rhymes that the
Opies were able to trace no farther than *Original Ditties for the
Nursery*, circa 1805. (The title's claim to originality, as they note in
A Nursery Companion, has not been refuted.) *Original Ditties* offers
its contents as songs, though it is a book of rhymes, with no music.
(One rhyme tells a story of "The Spider and the Fly." Its metrical
pattern does not fit "Will You Come to the Bower," and it ends in
triumph for the fly, with no explicit final moral.) Many of the
"original ditties" have refrains and suggest nursery songs by their
metrical pattern and an occasional verbal hint, as if they had been
written to definite tunes. Two are quite recognizably patterned
after nursery songs with good tunes.

Carroll's plea for giving nursery songs "their own tunes," his
mention of this rhyme as a song, and Slaughter's use of other
nursery tunes make it possible that the "Tweedledum and Tweedledee" tune in the operetta (see fig. 5) is traditional and one that
was familiar to Carroll. There was no strong singing tradition:
most nineteenth-century collections do not include a tune for this

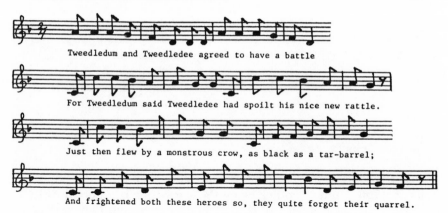

Tweedledum and Tweedledee agreed to have a battle

For Tweedledum said Tweedledee had spoilt his nice new rattle.

Just then flew by a monstrous crow, as black as a tar-barrel;

And frightened both these heroes so, they quite forgot their quarrel.

Figure 5. Words and melody from the 1906 score of Savile Clarke's *Alice in Wonderland: A Dream Play for Children*, 1886.

rhyme, and there are two different tunes published by Linley (1864) and Helmore.

V

The tune indicated in the dreamlike incident when Alice gives her hands to Tweedledum and Tweedledee and finds herself dancing around in a ring with them and singing "Here we go round the mulberry bush" to music that seems to come from the tree above them is rather more of an "old tune" than an old song. One might think it well enough established to offer no problems and really very little need for a note—except that the Norton critical edition of *Alice* soberly annotates the words as a *rhyme*! The Savile Clarke operetta includes a complete game, not just the tune. "This is the way we wash our hands" and "This is the way we go to school" verses are enacted standing in place, and the burden (the mulberry bush verse) is sung before and after each verse as the singers dance around in a ring—the familiar pattern that is also the pattern of the medieval dance, the carol or carole. The tune in the score (see fig. 6) is, I hope, still familar.

This tune goes to a number of singing ring games and is widely printed in books of games and children's songs.[12] Its name as a

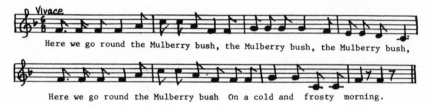

Here we go round the Mulberry bush, the Mulberry bush, the Mulberry bush,

Here we go round the Mulberry bush On a cold and frosty morning.

Figure 6. Words and melody from the 1906 score of Savile Clarke's *Alice in Wonderland: A Dream Play for Children*, 1886.

country dance tune, "Nancy Dawson," goes back to a song popular in 1760. Under another name the same tune is reported in J. Walsh's *Caledonian Country Dances*, published about 1740 (Opie, *Singing Games*). The words of the eighteenth-century song and of most of the games have the carol rhyme pattern with a repeated final tag (*aaar*). The fact that the tune is one of the two traditional tunes of a folk Christmas carol (carol in the later sense that derived from the older one) that had been printed with other music in the sixteenth century ("Sunny Bank" or "I Saw Three Ships Come Sailing In" [Dearmer, Williams, and Shaw, *The Oxford Book of Carols*, no. 3]) may reflect only its eighteenth- and nineteenth-century vogue; but there is a possibility that this tune is one of the really hardy perennials of popular lore. At any rate, it is a tune that has been well known since the eighteenth century and was current in Alice's day.

VI

"Humpty Dumpty" is neither sung nor referred to as a song in *Through the Looking-Glass*. Alice repeats it to herself, reflecting that "that last line is almost too long for the *poetry*" (italics added), and she tells Humpty Dumpty himself that the news about all the king's horses and all the king's men" is "in a book." Its tune, therefore, does not belong here except as part of the evidence that for *Alice in Wonderland* Slaughter did use tunes likely to be known to his (and Lewis Carroll's) audience, and not only the ones that we know that Lewis Carroll stipulated. The "Humpty Dumpty" tune in the operetta (see fig. 7) and one published by Linley in 1865 are enough alike and enough different to indicate a fairly established traditional association of tune and words,

Figure 7. Words and melody from the 1906 score of Savile Clarke's *Alice in Wonderland: A Dream Play for Children*, 1886.

though rhyming riddles are rhymes that may attract tunes rather than songs that may lose their tunes and become rhymes. Linley's form of the tune, in a version differing only enough to show that it was not copied but remembered, was printed by Kidson as traditional (with the note that "the air is the old Irish tune 'Off she goes' ") and can be found in more recent books of nursery songs (Buck; Mitchell and Blyton).

VII

"The Lion and the Unicorn" is a century older than "Tweedledum and Tweedledee" in the record, and there is little doubt that it is words to an old song (Opie and Opie, *Dictionary of Nursery Rhymes*). There are three nineteenth-century variants of a scattered and diversified traditional tune.[14] One of them (Linley, *Nursery Rhymes of England* [1860]) is still current in the Oxford and Faber nursery song books, (Buck, Mitchell and Blyton). The operetta tune (see fig. 8) begins like the traditional tunes but seems to have been altered and embellished. Those "rat-a-plans" sound French. English drums generally go "rub-a-dub-dub." Carroll did have Alice think of the words as belonging to an "old song" rather than to a rhyme, however; he probably knew a traditional tune.

VIII

Lewis Carroll was careful to indicate a tune for one song that parodied a poem with no associated tune. The parting song of the

The Lion and the Unicorn were fighting for the Crown.

The Lion beat the Unicorn all round the town!

Some gave him white bread and some gave him brown,

Some gave him plum cake and drum'd him out of town.

Rat-a-plan, rat-a-plan. Rat-a-plan, plan, plan, plan, plan.

Rat-a-plan, rat-a-plan. They drum'd him out of town.

Rat-a-plan, rat-a-plan. Rat-a-plan, plan, plan, plan, plan.

Some gave him plum cake and drum'd him out of town.

Figure 8. Words and melody from the 1906 score of Savile Clarke's *Alice in Wonderland: A Dream Play for Children*, 1886. Lewis Carroll's words had *them*, not *him*, and so do the words with the traditional tunes. "Him" does not fit Alice's problem dealing out the plum cake.

White Knight in chapter 8 of *Through the Looking-Glass*, "The Aged Aged Man" (also known, as the White Knight carefully and confusingly explains, as "Haddock's Eyes," "Ways and Means," and "A-sitting on a Gate"), is a reworked and amplified poem that Carroll had published earlier in a magazine, a parody of a long poem by Wordsworth. It is not recited but sung in the book, however, and its lack of internal verbal indications of any tune does not mean that Carroll leaves his readers to imagine the White Knight singing without imagining any particular tune.[15] Alice herself recognizes and identifies the White Knight's tune: "but the tune *isn't* his own invention," she said to herself: "it's *'I give thee all, I can no more'* " (Gray 187). She is described as being able to remember the whole scene years afterwards, with herself "listening, in a half-dream, to the melancholy music of the song" (Gray 188). Clearly the music is part of the appropriateness of this song to the singer.

Gardner identifies "I give thee all, I can no more" as Thomas Moore's "My Heart and Lute" and attributes the tune to Sir Henry Rowley Bishop.[16] (It is not, as Carroll thought, one of the "National Airs" to which Moore frequently wrote songs.) Then he gives not the tune but the original words to the tune, with those of the Wordsworth poem parodied. The mood of the melancholy ineffectual lover in "My Heart and Lute" suits the White Knight very nicely, and Gardner argues for the appropriateness of the song's words to Lewis Carroll himself. Moore's melancholy and sentimental words may also have affected Carroll's impression of the mood of the music associated with them, though I think the tune is musically a melancholy one.

Figure 9 gives the beginning of the White Knight's song, with

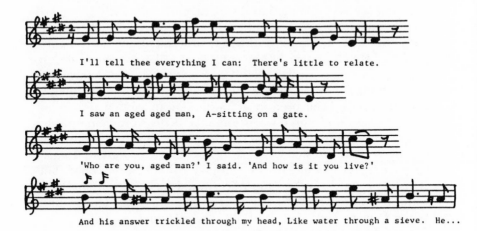

I'll tell thee everything I can: There's little to relate.

I saw an aged aged man, A-sitting on a gate.

'Who are you, aged man?' I said. 'And how is it you live?'

And his answer trickled through my head, Like water through a sieve. He...

Figure 9. Tune from "My Heart and Lute" ("I give thee all, I can no more") "Written by Thomas Moore, Esq. The Subject taken from a Melody composed by Mr. Bishop." London: J. Power, [1823]. British Library H.1980.mm(27.). The placement of the dotted notes and their following or preceding sixteenth notes varies within the two verses and two refrains.

the tune recognized by Alice. The first half of the first verse repeats as a refrain after both verses in the musical setting of
Moore's song, bringing us back to the original tonic. The White
Knight's song seems long for such repetitions, and the progress of
the narrative does not allow them. They can be worked in at the
conclusion, where there are no fewer than nine additional lines
before the final cadence.

The White Knight beat time, and the melancholy seesaw
rhythm of the tune makes it easy to imagine him doing it.

IX

The Red Queen's soothing lullaby for the White Queen in chapter
9 of *Through the Looking-Glass* is a parody of "Hushabye Baby,"
which has an established traditional tune that is still standard in
English books of nursery songs but has given way to a later American tradition in the United States. The "Hushabye Baby" tune
that was established in Alice's time and appears in the Oxford and
Faber books of nursery songs (Buck; Mitchell and Blyton) is a
form of the first strain of "Lilliburlero," a famous seventeenth-
century tune very common in the eighteenth century.[17] In American homes, this tune has often been displaced by "Rockabye
Baby" by "Effie I. Canning" (Effie I. Crockett, 1859–1940), published in 1884 but said by the composer to have been made up
about twelve years earlier when she was a young girl taking care
of a baby that needed lulling (Fuld). The tune is widely enough
known to have been used in a South African motion picture as
ironic background music when some terrorists were being put to
sleep with wildlife anesthetic (*The Gods Must Be Crazy*, 1980), and
it provides one attested example of a creative process that must
have occurred often in the history of nursery song; but
"Hushabye Baby" is the tune Alice would have known, and it is
better for the last line of Lewis Carroll's words—"Red Queen, and
White Queen, and Alice, and all!"—which does *not* call for any
slowing down at the end.

I present the tune as it appears in Rimbault's *Nursery Rhymes*
(n.d. but around 1846, with a printing in 1865), which may have
been in Lewis Carroll's library.[18] Charles Lutwidge Dodgson was
born in 1832 and probably learned the song before the age of
fourteen, and not from a book; but after the uncertainty about

"Twinkle," it is pleasant to be able to give a source for the Red Queen's lullaby from the first book that purported to print the traditional tunes to which nursery rhymes were "still sung in the nurseries of England." The tune appears in the same form in Rimbault's later (c. 1862) *Collection of Old Nursery Rhymes (Chappell's Nursery Rhymes)* and, with slight variations in the rhythm, in Linley's 1860 *Nursery Rhymes of England.* Its minor variations in later books show a continuing singing tradition. The Red Queen expects Alice either to know the tune or to pick it up on one repetition—though since we already know, and it is again demonstrated, that the Red Queen's expectations are quite unreasonable, we cannot deduce that Lewis Carroll expected more than that the tune would be generally recognizable.

"She's tired, poor thing!" said the Red Queen. "Smooth her hair—lend her your nightcap—and sing her a soothing lullaby."

"I haven't got a nightcap with me," said Alice, as she tried to obey the first direction: "and I don't know any soothing lullabies."

"I must do it myself, then," said the Red Queen, and she began:—

Hush-a-by lady, in Alice's lap!

Till the feast's ready, we've time for a nap.

When the feast's over, we'll go to the ball—

Red Queen, and White Queen, and Alice, and all!

Words as given in *Through the Looking-Glass* (Gray 197), tune given with "Hushaby, Baby" in Rimbault's *Nursery Rhymes* (1846).

And now you know the words," she added, as she put her
head down on Alice's other shoulder, "just sing it through to
me. I'm getting sleepy, too." [Gray 196–97]

X

The last song in *Through the Looking-Glass* has a particularly satis-
factory tune that adds a great deal to the words as read. Although
"Bonnie Dundee" is not obscure even now, Gardner earns gratitude as well as amazement by unearthing from Sir Walter Scott's
blank verse drama, *The Doom of Devorgoil* (1820), all eleven stanzas
of the original poem. The song, as printed with its tune, uses
four stanzas—the first, second, eighth, and ninth of the original
eleven. Carroll's parody goes no farther than the first line and the
chorus and the stanza form. It is clearly intended to indicate the
proper rousing tune for "Welcome, Queen Alice" rather than to
extract any comedy from the words normally associated with the
tune, except as singing comical words to any well-know tune gives
some effect of parody.

"Bonnie Dundee" is not hard to find in collections of Scottish
songs and college songs and old favorites. The tune, though
sometimes identified as an "Old Scottish Melody" (Buck, *Oxford
Song Book*) is the anonymous tune that made a popular song of
Scott's words as sung by Miss Dolby in 1840.[19] As a "Patrol" (music for the piano to be played at first softly, then louder and
louder, then dying away again, to give the impression of
approaching and then passing by), it had been known as "The
Band at a Distance" (Nettel). I give it here (see fig. 10) from
Freiligrath-Kroekers's *Alice Through the Looking-Glass* [1882], an acting version for children.

Knowledge of the right tunes can add a great deal to the pleasure of reading the parodies. People who know "Bonnie Dundee"
as a song must feel the swing of it as they read "To the Looking-
Glass world it was Alice that said . . ." and the rousing chorus,
"Then fill up the glasses as quick as you can, / And sprinkle the
table with buttons and bran: / Put cats in the coffee, and mice in
the tea— / And welcome Queen Alice with thirty-times-three!"
Once reminded, it is hard not to think the words to the tune, and
they are more exuberant sung than said.

To the Looking-Glass world it was Alice that said

"I've a sceptre in hand, I've a crown on my head.

Let the Looking-Glass creatures, whatever they be,

Come and dine with the Red Queen, the White Queen, and me!"

Then fill up the glasses as quick as you can,

And sprinkle the table with buttons and bran:

Put cats in the coffee, and mice in the tea--

And welcome Queen Alice with thirty-times-three!

Figure 10. As given, with the note *"Tune—* 'BONNIE DUNDEE,' " by Kate Freiligrath-Kroeker in *Alice Through the Looking-Glass and Other Fairy Plays for Children* [1882].

New tunes for the words may be as good as the old ones musically, or even much better than the originals, or more to the taste of a new audience (though Lewis Carroll did like some quite likable tunes). The old ones, however, are part of the original context. The sentimental tunes to "Beautiful Soup" and "The Aged Aged Man" have their own charm and appropriateness and contribute their modicum of humor to the text; and they have the same period interest as those moral poems for the young that Alice tries to recite with surprising results. Lewis Carroll quite plainly intended us to call these tunes to mind. They were not a purely private joke.

Dramatizations, home reading aloud, recorded versions, or stage productions could well use Carroll's tunes, if it were not easier to make up new ones than to find the original ones. Apart from these possible uses, it is pleasant to know the tune Alice referred to as "I give thee all, I can no more," and what Lewis Carroll had in mind when he drew out the vowels of "beau-tiful soo-oop." The tunes are part of the intended effect, adding bathos or zest to the splendid absurdity of the words.

Notes

1. Alexandre Reverend's cassette is primarily concerned with the new and attractive tunes written for Carroll's poems in the author's lifetime; the accompanying pamphlet gives a valuable account of Lewis Carroll's musical interests. I am particularly grateful to Reverend for references to published and unpublished letters of Carroll. My own research is a by-product of a continuing interest in the printed tradition of nursery song tunes.

2. Fuld's bibliographic note on "Twinkle, Twinkle, Little Star" traces "Ah! Vous Dirai'je, Maman" back to 1764 (Davenant has a 1740 reference) and gives the Köchel number (K265) of Mozart's variations on the melody. See also Baucomont (221), Böckheler.

3. *Little Songs for Little Singers*, by Lowell Mason (Boston: Perkins and Marvin, 1840); *The Little Songster*, by George J. Webb (Boston: Wilkins and Carter, 1840); and in England but after 1862, *Little Songs for Me to Sing*, illus. J. E. Millais [Sir John Millais], music by Henry Leslie (London: Cassell Petter & Galpin [1865]), and J. W. Elliott's book of original settings for nursery rhymes (1870). *The Catalogue of Printed Music in the British Library to* 1980 offers sheet music by John Green in his *Little Songs for Little Singers*, published by him in London, c. 1828 and c. 1840, and by Robert Guylott in his *Pretty Little Songs for Pretty Little Singers* (London [1857], 2d ed. [1857])—Guylott also set "How doth the little busy bee." There were also eight other settings, later than 1862 but tending to indicate that the words were not considered to have a firmly associated tune of their own at the end of the nineteenth century and well into the twentieth.

4. *Fifty Songs for Boys and Girls* (includes American tunes for several songs for which Kidson gives different tunes), compiled and arranged by Mary Nancy Graham (New York: Grosset & Dunlap, 1935); *The Big Book of Favorite Songs for Children*, selected and arranged by Dorothy Berliner Commins (New York: Grosset & Dunlap, 1951, 1978); *It's Easy to Play Nursery Rhymes* (tune marked "trad."), Cyril Watters (London; Wise, 1984). Alfred Moffat, who arranged the tunes in the collection annotated by Kidson and published several of his own collections of traditional tunes, used the same tune as Kidson's "Twinkle, Twinkle" in one of his collections illustrated by H. Willabeek LeMair, *Our Old Nursery Rhymes* (London: Augener [1911]).

5. *The Spanish Chant* was harmonized by Benjamin Carr in 1824 and published in 1826 in Philadelphia. It had a parlor vogue in the nineteenth century (*Catalogue of Printed Music in the British Library*) and was not used in *Hymns Ancient and Modern*, the hymn book that would have been best known to the Reverend Charles

Lutwidge Dodgson and was among those he owned (Stern). Smith's *Hymns and Tunes* lists a number of titles under which the tune is given in hymnbooks: "Spanish Chant," "Spanish Hymn," "Spanish Melody," "Spain," "Madrid," "Gethsemane," and "Litany."

6. I suppose the Dormouse might be sleepy enough to mutter in a monotone (though would that be "singing in his sleep"?) or might sing repeated twinkles even to a tune as ill-adapted to the use as the most popular current tune for "Twinkle, Twinkle." A purely practical and unscholarly solution to the problem of fitting the Dormouse's twinkles to the international tune would be to go off into the kindred but sleepier tune that Haydn used as the theme of the second (Andante) movement of his Surprise Symphony (No. 94). It fits nicely, and the variations would suppy any dormouse until he was suppressed. Freiligrath-Kroeker used this tune for a parody of "Twinkle, Twinkle, Little Star" in *Alice Through the Looking-Glass and Other Fairy Plays for Children* (in "The White Wolf," not in the *Alice* play).

7. The British Library music collection includes sheet music of "The Favorite Song of Mrs. Bond as sung by Mr. Bannister, Junr. in the Mayor of Garratt" (London: Longman and Broderip [c. 1790], shelf list g.1277.a.[25.]), and of "Will you come to the Bow'r, A Much Admired New Song . . . Written and Composed by T. M Esqr." (Dublin: Hime [1798] [g.356]). Longman and Broderip failed in 1798 (Humphries and Smith); and aside from the question of priority of publication, the tune of the "New Song" has a slide of two successive half steps at the cadence that seems like a sophistication. The "Mrs. Bond" tune of 1790 and in a later song book, *The Nightingale* (London: Thomas Tegg [1728]), which gives the same tune and words, has the repetition of its two-line stanza marked by repetition signs in the music. These have been ignored by later tradition, so that the nursery "Mrs. Bond" has stanzas half the length of the nursery "The Spider and the Fly," although otherwise absorbed into the "Will You Come to the Bower?" musical tradition. Thomas Moore did not publish "Will You Come to the Bower?" among his songs or its words in his collected works, and the many printings of the song with his name were not published by the original publishers of his other songs. Many publishers of the song attributed it to him, and Walter Savage Landor wrote a "Sensible Girl's Reply" to the song of which the longer version (1863) begins "Tommy Moore, Tommy Moore"; Landor, *Complete Works*, vol. 4, ed. T. Earle Welby (New York: Barnes and Noble, [1962]), 66−67.

8. The tune of "Will You come to the Bower?" has another grim association, of interest to Americans rather than to Carrollians but with some possible relevance to the character of the tune. Carmer gives the song (two verses of its three) with the note that "Davy Crockett is said to have begun singing this when the Mexican attack on the Alamo began. A few months later Texan forces going into battle at San Jacinto [1836] were spurred to revenge by a single fife and drum playing 'Will You Come to the Bow'r?' " Was Davy Crockett's mind on romantic dalliance? I should say that his summons probably and that of the fifer at San Jacinto certainly were no more benevolently intended than Mrs. Bond's call to her ducks. Is it only evil associations, or is there musically something ominous about this lively tune?

9. All eight verses of the words are given, with the tune and a comment on the popularity of the song around 1850, in Levy, *Flashes of Merriment*. (There is a misprint in the fourth verse: "with sorrow and to sign" should be "with sorrow sad to sigh.") Mr. Levy very generously sent me photoreproductions of all copies of the different songs of "The Spider and the Fly" in his sheet music collection (now in the Johns Hopkins Library), including three printings of Hudson's song and three of two American versions, one later and to a new tune. The sheet music he reprinted was published in Boston by Oliver Ditson at 115 Washington Street, his address from 1844 to 1857 (Wolfe). Though the tune is an accurate version of

"Will You Come to the Bower?" it is identified by the publisher as "Composed by O. H. Normino." O. H. Normino is also given as the composer of a different version (words and tune both show signs of oral transmission) in the *Franklin Square Song Collection*, 1881 (McCaskey). Oliver Ditson did buy up and reprint old music plates, and he might have had some now-uncheckable source of information; but the claim of O. H. Normino (and even his or her existence) has no confirmation that I could find.

10. The only really striking difference from current nursery tradition is the *do mi do mi* will you won't you's in the refrain. That is not one of the many variations of the refrain that I have seen in other forms of the tune. The current nursery survivors give *do mi mi mi* (as in "Will You Come to the Bower?") and *do mi mi sol*. The passing note that makes the jump at "*whiting*" only a third (*la do*) is from the original "Mrs. Bond." "Will You Come to the Bower" goes up a fourth, *sol do*, like most current nursery versions of "Mrs. Bond" but unlike the nursery tunes for Howitt's "Spider and the Fly."

11. The Mock Turtle sang, "very slowly and sadly," but that was his nature, not the nature of the song. In the first version of the story, *Alice's Adventures Under Ground*, the Mock Turtle sang, also "slowly and sadly," another song "Salmon Come Up," for the quadrille. Since my own curiosity has extended to looking up the original of this—a minstrel song, "Sally Come Up," words by T. Ramsey, music by E.W. Mackney—in the Houghton Library at Harvard (sheet music published in Boston by Oliver Ditson, copyright 1863) and in the British Library (*Seventeen Songs by E. W. Mackney*, London: Musical Treasury [1862] G.460), I give the tune here to Carroll's words (see fig. 11). The words of the original are like them only in having a chorus beginning "Sally come up! oh, Sally go down!", unless possibly "My lubly, charming Sally!" in the second verse and "Dar's not a face like Sally's" in the fourth may be distantly echoed. Parody here functions essentially as a guide to a tune. Carroll had heard the Linley sisters sing "Sally, Come Up" "with great spirit" the day before the famous expedition in 1862 (*Diaries*, 3 July, 1862).

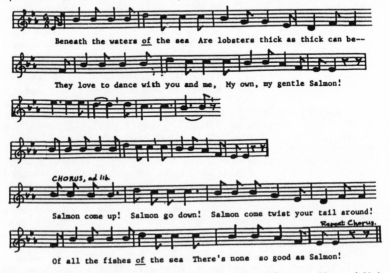

Figure 11. Tune from sheet music in the Houghton Library at Harvard University. An earlier edition in the British Library (G.460) gives the same tune.

12. There are eleven references in the index of Iona and Peter Opie's *Singing Game*, and twenty-one under "Nuts in May." In their introduction, the Opies point out that " 'Here We Go Round the Mulberry Bush' has a significant place in Chesterton's *Manalive* and Eliot's 'The Wasteland'." Additional information on the tune can be found in Fuld's *Book of World-Famous Music*, Chappell's *Popular Music of the Olden Time*, Simpson's *British Broadside Ballad and Its Music*, and one little note on its use in the British Navy in Wood's *Oxford Song Book*, vol. 2.

13. Lewis Carroll had projected and even begun an essay on "Nursery Songs" several years before the writing of the *Alice* books (*Diaries* 80, 93, 129).

14. Perhaps, "related tunes" would be a better expression than "variants." The three tunes seem to belong to the same tradition but are not, like most forms of "Will You Come to the Bower?" clearly the same tune with variations. As two of them are now quite obscure, I give the three here for comparison (see fig. 12). I have the word of Bruce Bellingham, of the University of Connecticut Department of Music, that it is not mere wishful thinking on my part that these tunes are related. The song sheet, which is in the Opie Collection and is used here by Iona Opie's kind permission, gives an address to which the publisher moved around 1837 (Humphreis and Smith). All three tunes are given twice, to make up a tune of normal length; but these short-quatrain rhymes fit half a normal tune, and fit it as four-stress couplets.

Figure 12. Three nineteenth-century tunes for "The Lion and the Unicorn" copied in parallel for comparison. Marks for line endings have been added. The short measure in the song sheet is a mere oversight; the accompaniment has a full measure.

15. There is only one song actually sung in the *Alice* books for which Lewis Carroll does not seem to suggest a tune—the Duchess's reverse lullaby in the "Pig and Pepper" chapter of *Alice's Adventures in Wonderland*. "Speak roughly to your little boy, / And beat him when he sneezes" parodies a poem, not a song, but is of course sung, with a chorus, "Wow! wow! wow" "in which the cook and the baby joined" (Gray 48–49). The chorus suggested a tune known as "Bow, Wow, Wow" (among other titles) to Frederick Helmore. (See Chappell 717; the tune is also given by Wood with Hudson's "Guy Fawkes.") This tune, however, requires the repetition of the second half of each of Lewis Carroll's quatrains to make a six-line verse, and the refrain is not simply "Bow, wow, wow" but "Bow! wow! wow! Tol de rol di ri-dy i-dy, bow! wow! wow!" Carroll did not suggest a tune for "Speak roughly" among those he associated with his songs and wanted used in the play of *Alice in Wonderland*; the tune in the play is presumably by Slaughter. Freiligrath-Kroeker did not hear a suggestion in the Wow! wow! wow! chorus, but she gave the tune of "Will you walk into my parlour?" (the "Lobster Quadrille" tune) for "Speak Roughly"—an effective choice, though it adds a good many "wow"s to the

chorus and requires a repetition of the quatrain that could have been avoided by using the form of the tune now known with "Mrs. Bond."

16. Henry Bishop (1786–1855) set many of Moore's later poems. He was also the composer of the tune to John Howard Paine's "Home, Sweet Home."

17. It was a theme song of the Glorious Revolution of 1688, which displaced James II, the last Stuart king of England. Robert Louis Stevenson has a pirate whistle the tune dismally in chapter 15 of *Treasure Island*. Besides being historically appropriate, it is an excellent whistling tune and would produce the effect Stevenson describes very well. The complete form is common in nursery song books with "There was an old woman toss'd up in a basket." For its history, see Simpson, *The British Broadside Ballad and Its Music*.

18. The *Nursery Rhymes* in Lot 594 of the auction catalogue "Nursery Rhymes, Traditonal Tunes (a collection of ballad airs [by Kidson]), The National Music of the World, Trevelyan's Ladies in Parliament" would seem to have been a song book by the company it keeps (Halliwell's *Nursery Rhymes of England* and *Nursery Rhymes and Tales* and some other books containing rhymes as rhymes appear elsewhere in the list); but "Nursery Rhymes," though it is the short title of Rimbault's collection, is too general a title for certainty. It is a curiosity of the printing tradition of the tunes associated with nursery rhymes that books containing them often reveal the fact only in a subtitle (and not always there), whereas many books of rhymes without tunes have titles that suggest books of songs.

19. It is a Scots tune in style—those sixteenth notes followed by dotted eighths at "Red Queen" and "White Queen" are called "Scots snaps" and considered a musical Scotticism (Fiske 14, 23), though they can also be noticed in "My Heart and Lute." Its remoter history is unknown. For the seventeenth century, "Bonny Dundee" (air lvii in *The Beggar's Opera*) that Scott indicated, see Chappell and Simpson.

Works Cited

Baucomont, Jean. *Les Comptines de langue française*, Recueillies et commentées par Jean Baucomont, Frank Guibat, Tante Lucile, Roger Pinon, et Philippe Soupault. 1961. Paris: Seghers, 1970

Böckheler, Lotte. *Das englische Kinderlied*. Leipzig, 1935.

Boyd, William. *The Songs from* Alice's Adventures in Wonderland. Music composed by William Boyd. London: Weeks [1870].

Buck, Percy, ed. *The Oxford Nursery Songbook*. 1933. 3d ed., London: Oxford UP, 1984.

———. *The Oxford Song Book*, vol. 1. 1916. London: Oxford UP, 1973.

Carmer, Carl, ed. *Songs of the Rivers of America*. New York: Farrar & Rinehart, 1942.

Carroll, Lewis. *Alice in Wonderland*. Ed. Donald J. Gray. Norton Critical Editions. (Includes *Alice's Adventures in Wonderland* and *Through the Looking-Glass* [illus. John Tenniel], and *The Hunting of the Snark*.) New York: Norton, 1971. (Quotations from the *Alice* books in this article are from this edition.)

———. *Alice's Adventures in Wonderland*. Ed. Selwyn Goodacre. Illus. Barry Moser. Preface and notes by James R. Kincaid. Berkeley: U of California P, 1982.

———. *Alice's Adventures under Ground* (a facsimile of the original Lewis Carroll manuscript). Ann Arbor, Mi.: University Microfilms, 1964.

———. *The Annotated Alice*. Ed. Martin Gardner. Illus. John Tenniel. 1960. New York: New American Library, 1974.

————. *The Collected Verse of Lewis Carroll*. London: Macmillan, 1932.

————. *The Diaries of Lewis Carroll*. Ed. Roger Lancelyn Green. 2 vols. London: Oxford UP, 1954.

————. *The Letters of Lewis Carroll*. Ed. Morton N. Cohen with the assistance of Roger Lancelyn Green. 2 vols. London: Oxford UP, 1979.

————. *Through the Looking-Glass and What Alice Found There*. Ed. Selwyn Goodacre. Illus. Barry Moser. Preface and notes by James R. Kincaid. Berkeley: U of California P, 1983.

Chappell, William. *The Ballad Literature and Popular Music of the Olden Time*. 2 vols. London, 1859. New York: Dover, 1965.

Clarke, H[enry] Savile. *Alice in Wonderland: A Dream Play for Children in Two Acts*. Music by Walter Slaughter. London: "The Court Circular" office, 1886. (This and the 1888 version and the edition below [the score] were consulted at the Houghton Library at Harvard University.)

————. *Alice in Wonderland* (Vocal Score). London: Aschenberg, Hopwood & Crew, 1906. In *English and American Drama of the Nineteenth Century—English*. Readex Microprint, 1969. Courtesy of New York Public Library.

[Crane, Lucy]. *The Baby's Bouquet: A Fresh Bunch of Old Rhymes and Tunes*. Tunes collected and arranged by L. C. [Lucy Crane; see *DNB*]. Illus. Walter Crane. London: Warne [1879].

————. *The Baby's Opera: A Book of Old Rhymes with New Dresses by Walter Crane. The Music by the Earliest Masters*. London: Warne [1877].

Davenson, Henri. *Le Livre des Chansons*. Paris, 1944. Neuchâtel (Suisse): Editions de la Baconnière, 4me éd., revue, corrigée et augmentée, 1977.

Deacon, George. *John Clare and the Folk Tradition*. London: Sinclair Brown, 1983.

Dearmer, Percy, R. Vaughan Williams, and Martin Shaw. *The Oxford Book of Carols*. 1928. London: Oxford UP, 1961.

Disher, Maurice Willson. *Victorian Song from Dive to Drawing Room*. London: Phoenix House, 1955.

Elliott, James William. *Mother Goose; or National Nursery Rhymes and Nursery Songs*. Set to original music by J. W. Elliott. New York: n.d. First printed 1870. *Mother Goose* is the title of American editions, *National Nursery Rhymes and Songs* the original English title. This lavishly illustrated and much reprinted book has contributed a number of melodies that are now the expected tunes in the United States and one ("Hey Diddle Diddle") that is anonymously reprinted in *The Oxford Nursery Songbook*. Rpt. *Nursery Rhymes and Nursery Songs*. New York: Hart, 1977.

Fiske, Roger. *Scotland in Music: A European Enthusiasm*. Cambridge: Cambridge UP, 1983.

Freiligrath-Kroeker, Kate [Käthe in library listings]. *Alice and Other Fairy Plays for Children*. With original and adapted music. [1879] 2d ed. London: W. Swan Sonnenschein, 1880. (Harvard University, Houghton Library. A later, undated American edition adds "in Wonderland" to the title, though this first play draws on both *Alice* books.)

————. *Alice Through the Looking-Glass and Other Fairy Plays for Children*. London: Swan Sonnenschein [Christmas 1882].

Fuld, James J. *The Book of World-Famous Music*. Rev. ed. New York: Crown, 1971.

Gardner, Martin, ed. *The Annotated Alice*. 1960. New York: *New American Library*, 1974.

Graham, John, ed. *Traditional Nursery Rhymes*. 13th ed. [printing]. London: J. Curwen, 1911. (This is a song collection for children, with traditional tunes and some historical notes on the tunes.)

Gray, Donald J., ed. *Alice in Wonderland*, by Lewis Carroll. Norton Critical Editions. (Includes *Alice's Adventures in Wonderland, Through the Looking-Glass*, and *The Hunting of the Snark*, as well as biographical and critical selections.) New York: Norton, 1971. (Quotations from the *Alice* books in this article are from this edition.)

Green, Roger Lancelyn, ed. *The Lewis Carroll Handbook*, by Sidney Herbert Williams and Falconer Madan. 1931. London: Oxford UP, 1962.

Grove's Dictionary of Music and Musicians, 5th ed. Ed. Eric Blom. London: Macmillan, 1954.

Hately, T. L., ed. *The Illustrated Book of Nursery Rhymes with Music*. Illus. Keely Halsewelle. London, Edinburgh, and New York: T. Nelson and Sons [1865]. (Another edition 1882. Both in British Library.)

Helmore, Frederick, comp. and ed. *The Little One's Book, Containing the Songs in "Alice in Wonderland" and "Through the Looking Glass," Also a Selection of Nursery Rhymes to the Old Tunes, and Other Easy Songs and Rounds*. Frederick Helmore's Singing Method, no. 1. London: Weekes [1903]. (Later edition of a book that was in Lewis Carroll's library. Morris L. Parrish Collection of Victorian Novelists, Princeton University Library.)

Hudson, Thomas. *Comic Songs* [6th collection]. London: Thomas Hudson, 1824. Printed by Walton and Mitchell, 24 Wardour Street. (New York Public Library.)

Humphries, Charles, and William C. Smith. *Music Publishing in the British Isles from the Beginning until the Middle of the Nineteenth Century*. New York: Barnes and Noble, 1970.

Kidson, Frank, ed. *75 British Rhymes (And a Collection of Old Jingles)*. Accompaniment by Alfred Moffat. London: Augener [1904].

Levy, Lester S. *Flashes of Merriment: A Century of Humorous Songs in America, 1805–1905*. Norman: U of Oklahoma P, 1971.

Linley, George, ed. *Fifty Nursery Songs and Rhymes, Adapted to Familiar Tunes by George Linley*. 2d series. London: Metzler, 1864. (Most of the tunes are traditional but not traditionally associated with the rhymes with which they are given. British Library.)

———. *Nursery Rhymes of England, Adapted to Familiar Tunes by George Linley*. London: Brewer, 1860. (There were editions published by F. Pitman Heath c. 1920 and c. 1925. The tunes are generally versions of those traditionally associated with the words. British Library.)

McCaskey, J. F., comp. *The Franklin Square Song Collection: Favorite Songs for School and Home*, vol. 1 [of eight]. New York: Harper, 1881. (New York Public Library.)

Mitchell, Donald, and Cary Blyton. *The Faber Book of Nursery Songs*. London: Faber, 1963. American edition, *Every Child's Book of Nursery Songs*. New York: Crown, 1968.

Nettel, Reginald. *Sing a Song of England: A Social History of Traditional Song*. London: Phoenix, 1954.

Opie, Iona, ed. *Ditties for the Nursery*. New illus. ed. of *Original Ditties for the Nursery*, c. 1805. London: Oxford UP, 1954.

Opie, Iona. *The Singing Game*. London: Oxford UP, 1985.

Opie, Iona, and Peter Opie, eds. *A Nursery Companion*. London: Oxford UP, 1980.

———. *The Oxford Book of Children's Verse*. London: Oxford UP, 1973.

———. *The Oxford Dictionary of Nursery Rhymes*. 1951. Rev. ed. Oxford: Clarendon, 1952.

Reverend, Alexandre. *Lewis Carroll and Music*. With cassette tape of "Lewis Carroll's Songs." Paris: Syndicat du Wonderland, 1987. (The address is 79, Rue Damrémont, 75018 Paris, France.)

Rimbault, Edward F. *A Collection of Old Nursery Rhymes, with Familiar Tunes.* [*Chappell's Nursery Rhymes* on the cover.] London: Chappell, n.d. [1862]. (Harvard University Library, New York Public Library.)

————. *Nursery Rhymes, with the Tunes to Which They Are Still Sung in the Nurseries of England* (Obtained Principally from Oral Tradition). London: Cramer, n.d. [1846]. (Harvard University Library.)

Simpson, Claude M. *The British Broadside Ballad and Its Music.* New Brunswick, N.J.: Rutgers UP, 1966.

Stern, Jeffrey, ed. *Lewis Carroll's Library: A Facsimile Edition of the Catologue of the Auction Sale following C. L. Dodgson's Death in 1898, with Facsimiles of Three Subsequent Booksellers' Catalogues Offering Books from Dodgson's Library.* Edited with an introduction by Jeffery Stern. Silver Spring, Md.: Lewis Carroll Society of North America [Charlottesville: UP of Virginia] 1981.

Wolfe, Richard J. *Secular Music in America, 1801–1825: A Bibliography.* 3 vols. New York: New York Public Library, 1964.

Wood, Thomas, ed. *The Oxford Song Book,* vol. 2. 1928. London, Oxford UP, 1963.

Signs from the Imperial Quarter: Illustrations in Chums, *1892–1914*

Robert H. MacDonald

The boys' magazine *Chums* carried on the spines of its bound annual volumes from 1893 to 1908 an illustration of two soldiers, one standing firing a revolver, the other kneeling. The soldiers were holding hands. A source and explanation for this image can be found in *Chums* itself, where in volume 2 (1893–94), the frontispiece is a more explicit version of the same scene (fig. 1). Here the two soldiers, clearly officers, are defending themselves in a fight to the death. The erect figure, his foot braced against a rock, fires at a horde of natives, dimly seen waving spears in the background. His sword is in his right hand. His companion has collapsed, stricken, and leans his head on the other's thigh. The caption of this picture is "Chums."

A tiny unit in the vast myth of Empire, this illustration has a dramatic and immediate meaning. The officers in their "Last Stand" offer a complex sign of imperial manhood. Manhood consists in fighting, fighting means dying, dying is sanctified by brotherhood. Courage, loyalty, duty, and patriotism are given iconographic form as the discourse of last stands is invoked in the magazine: a dusty spot in the desert, a unit ambushed on the frontier, the fortuitous but ironic meeting of old school friends— or enemies—water gone, ammunition expended, horses killed, the murderous natives closing in, the last thoughts of school, queen, and country as the assegais fall. Yet there will be a happy ending: in the code of the boys' adventure story a rescue is possible. Somewhere in the background of this visual narrative lies the ethos of the imperial task, resistance to the spear-waving natives, to those forces of barbarism for whose suppression or benefit the sacrifice is made.

It is my intention in this article to examine the use of illustrations in *Chums*, both historical and fictional. My thesis is that by repetition and emphasis, a vocabulary of patriotic images was developed and exploited, which for a generation of British males dramatized the myth of Empire. The primary motifs of these il-

Figure 1. "Chums." *Chums* 2 (1893–94): frontispiece.

lustrations defined manhood, race, and individual action: manhood shown in the heroics of courageous soldiers or brave frontiersmen; lessons of race demonstrated by the examples of barbarous natives or uncivilized Dutchmen; and the complicated relationship between choice and duty set forth as an insistent expectation that the wars of school led to the games of war. A close relationship was established between the world of boys and the world of men.

Previous studies have concentrated on the fiction of the boys' magazines, and on the imperial message of such writers as G. A. Henty (Turnbaugh; James; Dunae, "Boys' Literature"); my focus here will be on the visual rather than the narrative, and specifically on the ways in which one magazine exploited an iconography of power. The patriotic illustrations as a whole provide an example of the ways in which ideology is translated into an accessible though complex code. The ethos is almost exclusively masculine—women are noticeable only by their absence. Glory, strength, and violence are made dramatic and meaningful, yet rendered innocent by boyish high spirits. The program is the social reproduction of aggressive virility.

I

"Popular" imperialism was a dominant force in British social life during the twenty-five years before the First World War; it pervaded public consciousness through a dozen media (MacKenzie 15–38). The boys' magazines in general reflected the imperial doctrine faithfully; even the *Boy's Own Paper*, which was guided by a strong evangelical tradition (Duane, *"Boy's Own Paper"* 123–32) and which was usually hostile to militarism, was careful to support England's place in the world. The ideology of imperialism (see, for instance, Field 83–117) was announced to boys in straightforward and obvious terms: might was right, England was strong, what she had she held. The moral justifications followed behind, with the bringing of Christ to the pagans and the imposition of law on the unruly. After the missionary and the soldier came the merchant; trade created prosperity. All things English were superior to all else. Across the seas from the mother country were the daughter colonies establishing British rule, and beyond them, strange lands of outer darkness, places of disorder or impurity. In time the Empire might claim even these: in the words Baden-Powell ascribed to that heroic Elizabethan empire-builder, Captain John Smith, "our mission is to *clean* the world" (*Scouting for Boys* 65; Baden-Powell's handbook, in fact, might serve as an epitome of juvenile imperialist propaganda).

Chums was founded in 1892 as a commercial rival to the immensely successful *Boy's Own Paper* (1879–1967); after a shaky start it captured a large share of the same audience. The readership of both magazines was mainly middle-class, though as the years went on *Chums* extended its range downward. Its formula was the familiar mixture of fiction, information, and sports, together with "quality" illustrations, many of them in color. *Chums* was chattier and racier than the *Boy's Own Paper*—it printed many more jokes and anecdotes—but it subscribed to the same public school ethic, which it appropriated for its largely non–public school audience. The main innovation made by *Chums* was a consistent and forthright devotion to imperialism; it discovered what Alfred Harmsworth was discovering for the adult press (Field 106–11), that the conquest and defense of the Empire could be presented as an exciting and even sensational drama. Where *Chums* led, the other boys' magazines were eventually forced to follow (Carpenter 41–47), for—as with the *Daily Mail*—jingoism sold papers. By the turn of the century patriotic fervor had invaded other middle-class magazines (such as *Young England,* founded 1880, and the newcomer *The Captain,* founded 1899) and was full-fledged in the "cheaper" papers that Harmsworth was now publishing for errand boys and office boys (Carpenter 51–55). When the war began in 1914 even the *Boy's Own Paper* was compelled to publish patriotic military pictures.

Two narrative examples illustrate contrasting aspects of the imperial moment. In a story by Professor J. F. Hodgetts, serialized in volume 6 (1883–84) of the *Boy's Own Paper,* the history of the Anglo-Saxon conquest of the Celtic Britons is described, and the irresistible force of an English imperial character announced. King Arthur and his "band of heroes," though brave men, succumbed—in accordance with social-Darwinian theory—to the barbaric virility of a stronger race. "We were invaders with no more right to the soil of Britain than we have to that of Spain or

Austria." "English-like," we helped ourselves, "driving out, cutting down, and in every way destroying the wretched inhabitants. If this is a strange assertion to my reader, let him turn to the history of New Zealand, America, and Australia" (6:450). The history of "this fair island" is a history of conquest; it is the very nature of the English to claim, take, and possess; the Anglo-Saxon is the lord of the earth, not by right but by the sword. This is imperialism defined by the myths of national character and historical destiny; the mood is confident, no irony is intended, and surprisingly, given the evangelical principles of the *Boy's Own Paper,* moral judgment defers to racial imperatives.

A less confident note is struck in Frank Cleveland's futuristic "The Great Mutiny of 1911," a serial which ran in *Chums* volume 8 (1909–10). The second Indian Mutiny is planned, "striking a deadly blow at the heart of the Empire," as the lascars in every British port prepare for mutiny. "The British had educated the native. They had taught him that he was a man, instead of an inanimate clod. They had fed him, when otherwise he would have starved. They had clothed him, when but for them he would have gone naked. But gratitude had small place in the Aryan *[sic]* mind." Thus the Hindus, the Muslims, and the Chinese begin their terror of the civilized world: they run "silent-footed" through the "terrible" night, they slash right and left with their fearful knives; "to wear a white skin . . . was a sure signal for death" (8:783–85). Here history "repeats" itself—the traumatic horror of the Indian Mutiny is reimagined—and the world is not yet "clean." The imperial mission must go on.

Isolated though they are here from their context as boys' adventure stories, these two examples sufficiently illustrate three typical characteristics of imperial ideology: the mythologizing of history, the use of the language of power, and a theory of racial superiority. They typify the difference in mood between the moral assurance of the 1880s and the xenophobic nervousness, linked to fears of national decadence, of the prewar years. Perhaps most important for an analysis of the illustrations in *Chums,* they point to the shift toward more violent expressions of popular nationalism, in which militarism was given a prominent role. For its juvenile audience, the patriotic iconography of *Chums* helped set in place an assertive image of virile manhood.

II

The historical illustrations of *Chums* cannot be understood without reference to their journalistic context. The weekly *Boy's Own Paper* (published by the Religious Tract Society) had established the "quality" illustrated boys' magazine in the 1880s; both it and its monthly competitor *Young England* (published by the Sunday School Union) dramatized their stories with pictures of significant action. Both also printed full-page pictures, usually in color, which were not attached to their fiction: some of these were sentimental ("Sabbath Bells"—two girls and a puppy), some historical ("A Charge of Witchcraft"—villagers accusing an old woman), some romantic (highwaymen, pirates, or smugglers), and some military ("Our National Decorations"). Each periodical frequently illustrated certain moral themes of the imperial enterprise, such as the Royal Navy's capture of a slaver or a heroic rescue at sea.

History was often illustrated in the *Boy's Own Paper,* especially if it were Roman, Anglo-Saxon, or medieval, but the patriotic subject was typically distanced and the treatment of military glory restrained or even critical. Thus, to take some examples from volume 12 (1889–90), "An Episode of the Battle of Waterloo" (137), in which a "brawny Highlander" carries off the standard of the Young Imperial Guard, standard-bearer and all, is mock-heroic; but a scene with the caption "Afterwards" (441), showing a riderless horse standing on a battlefield amid the dead and the dying, reflects on the futility and costs of war. A cartoon with the title "War—A Moral Tale in Six Tableaux" is even more suggestive: two cocks fight, defeather each other—and end up hanging in the poulterer's window (543).

Both the *Boy's Own Paper* and *Young England* praised patriotism, but they were careful to associate it with the higher moral virtues, such as brotherhood, manliness, and unselfish sacrifice. When they illustrated it, they did so with circumspection, with emphasis on personal behavior rather than the justification of the military enterprise as a whole. The *Boy's Own Paper,* for instance, did describe the slaughter of the army under the Zulus at Isandlana, and it drew from that defeat two moral examples, the "saving of the colours" by Lieutenants Melvill and Coghill, and the Hon. Standish Vereker's sacrifice of his own life in favor of a native trooper. Significantly, both incidents were placed into a historical frame: "saving the colours" was dignified with a reproduction of "the famous painting by L'Hardivillier," and Vereker's death was associated with that of Philip Sidney. Like the legend of Sidney giving his water to the dying soldier, Vereker's act became a type of "unselfish generosity," ensuring his entry into the pantheon of heroes and demonstrating that historic English chivalry might be extended to the native races (1:269; 1:317). During the South African War the *Boy's Own Paper* lost circulation as a consequence of its refusal to run military stories (Dunae, "Boys' Literature" 115); one of its few concessions to the patriotic fever of 1899 was to show a medieval knight riding to battle "For Queen and Country," his shield carrying the letters "B.O.P." (cover illustration, vol. 21, no. 1,081).

In opposition to this spirit of evangelical morality and restrained imperialism, *Chums* almost from its first numbers joined the mood of the New Journalism (Field 119—51) in celebrating the glories of war in its fiction, its articles, and its illustrations. Heroic boys fought with Wellington or Wolseley, and "Glorious Deeds of the Empire" or "Real Tales of Action" were regularly documented. "The Charge of the Light Brigade" and "Shooting the Zulu" became the choice for color illustrations. The subjects of the twelve monthly color plates for volume 7 (1898—99), included, typically, four military scenes and one naval picture, showing the Empire at work on the North-West Frontier, in Matabeleland (twice), historically (in the Peninsular War), and at sea (a fight between a battleship and a torpedo boat).

These pictures, though in their contemporaneity and emphasis new for the boys' magazines, were not invented by *Chums*; rather, they were adaptations of the drawings in the popular illustrated papers. In the pages of the *Illustrated London News* and its competitors, the campaigns of the Empire were recorded, and artists attached to the imperial army dramatized war in the Sudan or Southern Africa. (The hero of Kipling's *Light That Failed* was just such an artist.) Behind the topical art of popular journalism were the serious painters of patriotic canvases, creating for Victorian society icons of military glory. Thus General Gordon was forever seen at the moment of his death, standing at the top of the steps of the governor's palace at Khartoum, proudly defying the

crouching fanatics of the Madhi; Colonel Baden-Powell, caught in
lonely vigil, the "Wolf That Never Slept," was shown guarding the
outposts of Mafeking from the sneaking Boer.

Perhaps the most successful of the image-makers was Lady
Butler,[1] the mark of her acceptance the queen's purchase of a
picture for St. James's Palace. Priestess of the British army, Lady
Butler memorialized it in its moments of crisis, triumph, or defeat: "The Roll Call" (1874, the Crimea), "The Remnants of an
Army" (1879, Afghanistan), "The Defence of Rorke's Drift"
(1880, the Zulu war), "Scotland for Ever" (1881, the charge of the
Scots Greys at Waterloo), "Floreat Etona" (1882, the first Boer
War). Each picture became a pregnant sign of Empire, giving
form and resonance to the military ethic, to esprit de corps, to
duty, to endurance, to desperate courage, and to coolness in the
face of barbaric fury. Victory and defeat equally were triumphs of
will. Success was but the just tribute of fate, and disaster,
redeemed by the chivalric gesture, only proved that the superior
race would eventually prevail; the Eton officer's charge to the
death at Laing's Nek turned a rout into a celebration of the nation's spirit and qualified the subsequent shock of Majuba. A considerable literature, both adult and juvenile, supported and con-
solidated this iconography (see, for instance, Cynthia Behrman's
bibliography in *Victorian Legends of the Sea).*

In joining itself to this imperial enthusiasm and its conventions
of illustration, *Chums* belonged at once to the mood of the 1890s.
While it shared many of the same values as the *Boy's Own Paper* it
carried less moral cargo; though it printed articles on "good"
causes such as Dr. Barnardo's Homes or the heroics of firemen,
its main intention was clearly to entertain and thrill. Drawing on
the same vocabulary of the public schools and the school story as
the older magazines, it managed to exploit a more demotic vein,
using current slang and slogans, words and phrases which themselves defined, naturalized, and embodied the imperial ethic. The
heroic officer was only "playing the game"; facing the fanatic enemy, he was "in a tight corner." He was one with the Chum who
hid his feelings, who knew what English "coolness" meant, who
was led by instinct and by pluck to defend the minority. Like a
true Englishman, he took pleasure in the presence of danger, and
he rejoiced in the perils of the sea. This discourse lent itself read-

ily to the adventure of Empire and served to caption the iconography of imperial might.

In the patriotic pictures of *Chums* a series of motifs emerges. There is, first of all, a display of power. The navy has the new panoply of technological might, the army the glory of uniforms and horses. A picture of the latest battleship or the fastest torpedo boat will have a caption like "Steel Walls of Britain," which links the image to an imperial past. Regiments are always shown ceremonially—on parade, at a march-past, or returning from a field day. Thus volume 9 (1900–01) contains a color picture of the Royal Lancers returning to quarters (414) and another of the Coldstream Guards "breaking out into skirmishing order" (614). Even the humor that sometimes lightened the stirring solemnity of these images contributed to their idealization—for instance, the comic contrast between a cheeky urchin and the soldiers he marches alongside suggests that all red-blooded boys will want to join the troops. The impulse of these pictures, of course, was to glorify "Our Soldiers," whose colorful uniforms lent themselves so well to dramatic illustration. The *Boy's Own Paper*, with its self-given task of instruction, had often printed illustrations of regimental uniforms and regimental badges; *Chums*, with its need to involve readers more directly in the drama of Empire, liked to show its troops on the move.

The conventional scene carrying the clearest and most unequivocal message was that of the charge, the impetuous ride of the cavalryman or the desperate assault of the foot soldier. This was the moment of "cold steel," the triumph of lance or the bayonet in the hands of a hero. (Interestingly the machine gun, though useful and even crucial in warfare, was not the weapon of heroes and was assumed to be out of action: "the Gatling's jammed and the Colonel dead.") The charge, as sign, was pure emotion, signifying the nation defended by personal death or glory.[2] "For Queen and Country: the 21st Lancers at Omdurman," in volume 8 of *Chums* (1899–1900), depicting the charge of the cavalry—including Lieutenant Winston Churchill—is a typical example (342). The caption is significant in its use of the generalized patriotic slogan alongside the specific identification.

Real military or naval combat offered the possibility of an emblematic act, a deed which could stand as symbol, in itself defining

the essence of virtue, of courage, endurance, or sacrifice. On the
North-West Frontier in 1897 British forces were opposed by Afridi tribesmen at Dargai; first the Gurkhas, then the Dorsetshires,
and then the Gordon Highlanders assaulted the heights. Piper
Findlater, playing the charge, was shot through both legs; though
he could not stand, he braced himself against a rock and continued piping, all the while under heavy fire. "Gallant Gordons, gallant troops all," *Chums* said (7:134), printing a full-page color picture of the action (fig. 2). This scene was also reproduced in the
illustrated papers, and it was the subject of a tableau in Madame
Tussaud's. In the same vein was "Dawn at Last" in volume 8
(1899–1900), a picture of wounded soldiers under Boer fire
(684). These symbols of heroic endurance and sacrifice echo that
Victorian favorite, the Roman soldier in the ashes of Pompeii,
faithful at his post to the death.[3] An important variant of duty
under fire was the last stand; *Chums'* "Major Wilson's Last Ride" is
a resonant example: Major Wilson rides out with his companions
to meet the Matabele; he would be surrounded and speared
down, as the legend had it, with "God Save the Queen" on his lips
at the end (7:70). The sand of the desert might be sodden red,
but as Sir Henry Newbolt's "Vitae Lampada" reminded the dying
Chums, the torch of life would be handed on "to the host behind"
in the schoolboy cry of "Play up! play up! and play the game!"

The iconography of power insisted upon Anglo-Saxon domin-
ion; the superiority of the English conqueror was reiterated in
image after image. The young imperial officer, striking down the
Indian sepoy with "one terrific slash across the face" ("How Lord
Roberts Won the V.C.," 9:15), is remembered in a historical act—
but the incident from the Indian Mutiny, commemorated, made
emblematic, dramatically represents the symbolic positions of
colonizer and colonized (fig. 3). The mounted Englishman is upright; beneath him writhes the mutinous sepoy. The controlled
energy of his great black horse signals Roberts's strength. Beside
him, the Sikh "sowar" he has saved and the sowar's horse both
defer to his power. Violence is legitimated.

Through a succession of such pictures, the readers of *Chums*
were made familiar with British imperial ideology, in which history was shown as a glorious and inevitable progress. Each hero
stood by metonymy for the manhood of the nation; each young
reader was asked to thrill to the heroic action. The iconography

Figure 2. "Storming the Heights at Dargai." *Chums* 7 (1898–99).

Figure 3. "How Lord Roberts Won the V.C." *Chums* 9 (1900−01).

represented, in the Barthian sense, coherent, sanitized speech, a feature of a myth in which war became "natural" (Barthes 142–43), a myth which was able to make its point through the insistent power of the sign. Seeing comes before words. The illustrations carried their own rhetoric: fighting was reduced to a code in which reflection was absent, bravery instinctive, suffering rendered as endurance, and death presented only as dignified sacrifice. Even pain was as nothing in the heat of the moment, as *Chums* explained in one article on "Hardship and Heroism at the Front,"[4] illustrating the point with a dramatic image of a cavalryman stopped in mid gallop (fig. 4). The caption read "Hit!" (10:413).

III

In its presentation of fictional material *Chums* was able to duplicate the motifs of the "real" world: displays of military power, colonial "scraps," or heroic rescues all translated easily to the conventions of the adventure story. As the queen's soldiers stood fast against the queen's enemies, so the hero of romance, with pluck and great high spirits, confronted his adversaries. The iconography not only makes the connection between fact and fiction— often blurring the two—but places the young reader at the center of the drama. As in the historical pictures, the essential version of the illustrative theme is the personal encounter between hero and antagonist. The moment chosen for illustration is usually the crisis, just before the act that will resolve the hero's fate. The image must amaze the reader without giving knowledge of the outcome of the action. Captions, usually from the text, reinforce the suspense: "I was looking down the barrel of the Frenchman's revolver"; "The natives raised their assegais"; "The huge beast prepared to spring." The layout most often isolates and centers the hero, his threatening inferiors crowding dangerously close, often behind or beneath him. If he is not alone, he is with a Chum, and here the meaning points to the theme of the embattled comrades—like the Chums on the magazine's spine.

The success of *Chums* in exploiting patriotism lay as much as anything else in the incorporation of the boy reader into the "story" of patriotism, especially through a youthful protagonist. The old conventions of fairy tale and romance helped shape the imperial plot: a set of adventures forming a sequence of tests,

Figure 4. "Hit!" *Chums* 10 (1901–02).

trials, and noble tasks; a noble hero facing a dangerous and evil foe. The testing ground might be the playing field or the battle-front. The models of manhood might be the scout, the imperial officer, the frontiersman, or the big-game hunter; the enemy a working-class lout, German spy, or savage native. Just as the brave English hero stood in for the "Chum," so all who were not "English-like" became the "Other"—foreign, alien, threatening, and inferior. The ideology of power depended upon this simplis-tic and reductive identification, as the reader was repeatedly asked to distinguish between "us" and "them."

In this binary world the enemies of the Empire are treated ac-cording to their lights. Blacks advance murderously on the hero: "Keep your distance, you rascals!" the frontiersman shouts (fig. 5). The "Dutchmen" skulking and scheming—threats to upright imperial order—are characterized as low "vermin" ("How Jake Saved the Guns: An Incident of the Johannesburg Rising" [the Jameson raid]; cover illustration, vol. 4, no. 193). The Zulu who proves his gratitude to the "young white boss" ("Mombasi the Zulu Exile;" cover illustration, vol. 4, no. 168) is an example of the instinctual virtue of the warrior races—whether Maori, Gurkha, or Afridi—and a confirmation of the appropriateness of colonial feudalism.

The discourses of imperial ideology named or hailed the reader first on the covers and title pages, as *Chums* called out to "Chums" (Benveniste 225–26; cf. Williamson). The paired figures on the spine of the annual volumes—the "Chums" in their "last stand" —were soldiers; they were what the "Chum" might become. Framing the annual covers were the figures of boys dressed in sports clothes and surrounded with sports gear, who nominated what "Chums" ideally were, middle-class public school boys with a "normal" interest in games.[5] Inside the magazine, the number head again hailed the "Chum." The first number head showed two boys, one dressed in school clothes, sitting with a book on his knees, the other in sportswear, leaning on the title *Chums* (fig. 6). The sitting boy—the younger—defers to the standing boy, and a ball, gloves, a racket, a fisherman's creel, and a fencing mask lie at their feet. These details name and define the boy: he reads, but he is no muff—at heart he is a sportsman. In the corner behind the boys waves a Union Jack: the "Chum" is a patriot.

In March 1908 this number head was significantly revised. The

Figure 5. "Keep your distance, you rascals!" *Chums* 14 (1905−06). Reproduced by permission of the Osborne Collection of Early Children's Books, Toronto Public Library.

Chums, a little older, were moved to the right-hand corner (fig. 7). Now seated before their school, the games player, in short trousers, is reading a book beside a youth in a suit. Except for a fencing mask—a sign of both class and perhaps militarism—the sports equipment has disappeared. Balancing their image on the left is a mounted bugle boy who is leading a charge or calling the nation to arms; a warship serves as background to this figure. The gaze of the youth leads both to the book, the world of school, and to the scene opposite, the world of the Empire. The centered title *Chums* links the battles of the playing field to the glorious sport of war, repeating the familiar theme of Newbolt's "Vitae Lampada," with its twinned scenes of the cricket match and the last stand in

Figure 6. Number head,
used until March 1908.

Figure 7. Number head,
used after March 1908.

the desert. And the stories' titles again name the boy reader as subject, centered in the role of plucky Jack, honest Jim, or manly Dick.

The title pages of the annual volumes also hail the reader, nominating him as the subject in a cycle of adventure and imperial romance. In volume 2 the title *Chums: An Illustrated Paper for Boys,* set in a central oval, is flanked on the right by a boy sailor in a ship's rigging and on the left by two Chums in sports clothes. At the top of the oval is the U.S. Overland Mail coach, attacked by Indians; below, men in a rowboat are shooting seals and an Indian with a dagger pursues a running figure. Already the new theme—the contrast of man to nature, civilization to savage—is visible, and by volume 3 war joins the frontier as subject. In volume 7 (1898–99), for instance, the oval *Chums* is intruded upon with drawings of an escape from prison, a soldier about to dynamite a fort, a frontiersman avoiding a charging buffalo, and another watching a baboon. The title pages and number heads set the scene for the stories within, inviting the boy reader to enter their world of colonial adventure.

This ideological incorporation of the young reader is straightforward and obvious, but with other illustrations the patriotic meaning is more subtle—though none the less present. The cover illustration of the first number of *Chums* (14 September 1892) shows a boy in eighteenth-century garb on a rearing horse, at whose neck lunges a furry beast. A look of horror on his face, the boy swings a dagger. The caption, "A huge something, gaunt, grisly, and terrible," refers to the onset of the hero's nearly fatal fight with a "great grey wolf," in the serial narrative "For Glory and Renown." This illustration, chosen for the cover centerpiece of the first bound volume and repeated on the covers of the next sixteen volumes, typifies a simple kind of encounter, the confrontation of the hero with a wild beast. In his period costume, the hero belongs clearly to the world of romance; he is mounted, his attacker is mysteriously "a huge something." This indeterminate beast could stand for any Other, even a human one. Significantly, the boy is called Harry, that most English of names, and his personal adventure is to be "read" in terms of the patriotic theme "For Glory and Renown."

The full impact of this image is drawn from the two iconographical traditions of boys' romances and imperialism. The fight with a wild beast, a typical crisis of the adventure story, was the frequent subject of illustrations in all the boys' magazines. Wild animals frequently appeared in pictures unattached to a story line, where they were used to shock. Thus the *Boy's Own Paper* in volume 3 (1880–81) rather startlingly reproduced "the celebrated picture" "The Lion's Bride," showing a caged lion pawing a dead[?] woman. The aftermath of a big-game hunt could be redolent of danger: "Bringing Ashore the Big White Bull," in *Young England* (10:98), showed the white hunter and his native assistants landing a hippo. The jungle in itself gave a thrill, though its danger often remained implicit: the *Boy's Own Paper* portrayed lions watching a sleeping camp (5:409). Even without confrontation between man and beast, these illustrations of exotic settings tacitly evoked danger in difference.

Chums from its early years treated this material in its own way, placing its boy heroes into immediately life-threatening struggles with animals, dramatized in color pictures: "In the Nick of Time" (rescued from the coils of a boa constrictor), "Battling with an Eagle," "A Rude Awakening" (surprised by lions)—all in volume 2. By volume 7 a third of the monthly color illustrations were devoted to fights with animals, ranging from the classical (a cowboy knifing a buffalo) to the unusual ("Gripped by a Cuttle-fish"); for ten years or so these contests with the Other were as frequent as the military scenes.

At first sight these images seem innocent of any ideological intent; they belong to the tradition of romance, to the hero's fight with the dragon. They confront the reader by proxy with an obvious, primal opponent; wild animals are dangerous, but natural. Yet placed in the context of the imperial world view of the boys' magazines, the wild animal is not "natural"—it is a charged and potent emblem of savagery and the demonic (cf. Ritvo).

In these periodicals the landscape of romance is not neutral territory. It draws meaning from the myth of imperial geography, in which the world is divided into those lands which are in order and those which remain to be colonized. The imperial adventure takes place on the frontier, in Canada, in South Africa, in India, and most typically of all, in the jungle. An example from *Chums* shows this dramatically (fig. 8), as the hero, with knife in hand on a spit of land in the river, stands between a crouching tigress and the waiting crocodiles (cover illustration, vol. 10, no. 509). He is in the

Figure 8. "The Tigress . . . Was Crouching for Her Spring." *Chums* 10 (1901–02).

tightest of "tight corners." His back is straight, his expression
stern, his lips closed. His clothes identify him as a young frontiersman, for he is dressed in the outfit made familiar by the imperial
scouts (such as Baden-Powell). He faces, dramatized simply, the
Dark Continent, a stereotype of savagery and violence (Brantlinger 182–98). His mission is to destroy or transform this jungle. As representative imperial soldier, frontiersman, or adventurer, the English hero belongs here; he has rights.

   The savage animal became an obvious symbol of the untamed,
and by its very aggression justified its own destruction: the amor-

ality of the law of the jungle confirmed the ideology of power, that might was right. The deeds of the great white hunters, as related in detail to boys, wrote a text for this adventure. Mr. F. C. Selous and Mr. Herbert Ward both "shot elephants by the score, and lived among cannibals, and witnessed slaughter, and brutality, and ignorance in their worst forms" (2:73)—and returned to be lionized in the pages of *Chums.* Invited to admire and join in, the Chum could now play the role of the white hunter, the adventurer who confronted and "bagged" the tiger, the lion, and the boa constrictor, and who in bringing back his "heads" had claimed and appropriated the savage world. At the same time, paradoxically, by juxtaposition with traditional military notions of chivalric equality, "big game" were noble enemies and merited the respect of their hunter, just as the warrior races, Afridis, Zulus, or "Fuzzy-Wuzzies" [the Sudanese], were in their courage worthy opponents of the imperial officer.

In a society increasingly fearful of decadence and of the threat from within (see *Scouting for Boys,* passim), the jungle might be a model for industrial England, and hyenas, jackals, or baboons images of the hooligan. The nuances of class were also a part of imperial discourse, as the adventure story and the school story shared themes and conventions. The boy hero outwitting the skulking Boers and the schoolboy resisting the town toughs are both fighting the same fight; both are manly, plucky, and patriotic. The Chums who defend themselves in a street brawl fight cleanly with a left to the jaw; their working-class opponents use clubs and boots (cover illustration, vol. 2, no. 81). The illustrations make these points visually by signs easily recognized by the confirmed Chum (fig. 9). The hero or heroes are center stage. They stand upright, straightbacked, in the impeccable dress of frontiersman, officer, or gentleman. Their faces are oval, foreheads broad, jaws firm. Their expressions are stern, but fearless. Their opponents, whether town toughs or wild beasts, scowl and snarl, baring their teeth.

These illustrations are in the same mold as the rest of the iconography; they merely return the patriotic theme to its perceived social matrix: the public school, with its emphatic class values. (As readers of P. G. Wodehouse's public school stories would have been aware, being "patriotic" was showing good form on the cricket field, supporting the side, and playing the game.) Versions

Figure 9. "He Joined Heartily in the Fray." *Chums* 2 (1893–94).

of public school duty, loyalty, and pluck are announced again and again to *Chums'* non–public school readers, reaching an insistent climax in stories which twin school and Empire and which authenticate the struggles of the boy by linking them to the courage of the soldier. Thus, in a story of September 1914, "Telling how a Boy Everyone thought 'No Good' proved his Bravery in Battle," "Dormouse, the War Boy" uses his brains to outwit school bullies, circus roughs, and, finally, a German zeppelin. Dormouse leaves school (improbably) to become a member of the gallant French Aviation Corps, where he fights, as an illustration indicates, "For the Sake of the Allies" (cover illustration, vol. 23, no. 1,148).

From 1909 on, *Chums* modified its format under competitive pressure from the popular Harmsworth papers (such as the *Marvel*, the *Boys' Friend*, and the *Union Jack*): most of the "departments" disappeared, the emphasis was placed on fiction, and the color plates were dropped. At this time the cover and spine of the annuals reverted to more traditional images of boyhood and romance, to a cowboy on a rearing horse, a young boy leaping for a football. The mustachioed maturity of the two "Chums" in their last stand was replaced by a clean-limbed sportsman reaching for the prize.[6] At the same time, the material inside the magazine grew even more direct in its patriotism. As early as 1906 *Chums* had caught the invasion fever (cf. French), and until 1914 ran story after story of England threatened by the armies and navies of Germany, France, and Russia. Boy heroes saved the day. With the invention of the Boy Scouts in 1908 *Chums* joined in the Scouting craze; in the year beginning June 1909 it ran as many as ten Scouting stories, with Boy Scout heroes helping the police put down working-class rioters, thwarting foreign invaders, and catching German spies: "Dick thrust his staff between the legs of the pretended artist and brought him heavily to the ground" (cover illustration, vol. 17, no. 875). As the title of this 1909 story indicated, even the home front presented patriotic opportunities to Chums: "Scouts to the Front!"

Once the war actually began in 1914, the enemy as Other was clearly identified and the patriotic image became unambiguously simple. The confident superiority of the two "Chums," an emblem of loyalty, courage, and duty—the civilized ethic—gave way to aggressive xenophobia. With the war, the growing pessimism visible in Cleveland's story of the "Mutiny of 1911," foreshadowing the last stand of Empire, led into the redemptive and defensive vision of a final confrontation between nations. Though images of imperialist expansion were to reappear in the 1920s and 1930s (MacKenzie 218), nationalism for the moment took over in both the adult and juvenile press. No illustration makes this point with a more brutal directness than the one printed on 20 February 1915 (cover illustration, vol. 23, no. 1,171), which showed the Kaiser's head centered in a rifle target and invited Chums to compete in a shooting match.

Notes

My research is based on the Osborne Collection in Toronto Public Library, where I received the informed help of Jill Shefrin and Dana Tenny. I am grateful to my colleagues Alan McLay and Ben Jones, and to Stephen Henighan for advice.

1. Elizabeth Southerden Thompson, born 1846. "The Roll Call," exhibited in 1874, caused a sensation and made her reputation. Engravings of her paintings—almost exclusively military subjects—were very popular. She married General Sir William Butler in 1877. Ruskin described her picture "Quatre Bras" (1875) as "Amazon's work."

2. In *The Wind in the Willows* (1908) Kenneth Grahame catches the tone of military heroics (without too much parody), as the Mole, disguised as a washerwoman, alarms the stoats holding Toad Hall with stories of the forces coming to get them: "a hundred bloodthirsty badgers, armed with rifles . . . six boat-loads of rats, with pistols and cutlasses . . . a picked body of toads, known as the Die-Hards, or the Death-or-Glory Toads."

3. In the First World War the example of this heroic type was Jack Cornwall, V.C., the boy sailor, ex–Boy Scout, who stood by his gun to death at the Battle of Jutland. His action became an icon of sacrifice (see the reproduction in the *Boy's Own Paper* 39:112).

4. The accompanying article, while giving realistic or humorous details of battle, paints war as the ultimate male experience: "the fierce impatience of all delay, the tugging at the nerves that is not fear, the deepening excitement as the crisis of the fight draws nigh, and the last mighty, delirious madness of the charge, that sends men shouting and cheering wildly onward to victory or death—what words can tell the power of those supreme moments."

5. This cover was used for the annual volumes until 1908, when, for one cover only, a female tennis player was added to the sportsmen. Whatever message was intended—and girls did read the boys' magazines—this feminine intrusion into a strictly masculine world bore no relationship to the content of the magazine, and the experiment was not repeated.

6. It is tempting to give even these signs an imperial meaning. During the defense of Mafeking, Baden-Powell was called "The Goalkeeper" (he had played in goal at school), keeping the Empire's goal safe from attack. *Chums* is silent on this point, but with the 1908 founding of Boy Scouting, Baden-Powell was once again in the news. The cowboy on the front cover was of course a Canadian cowboy.

Works Cited

Baden-Powell, Robert S. S. *Scouting for Boys*. London: Horace Cox, 1908.

Barthes, Roland. *Mythologies*. Trans. Annette Lavers. St. Albans, Eng.: Paladin, 1973.

Behrman, Cynthia F. *Victorian Myths of the Sea*. Athens: Ohio UP, 1977.

Benveniste, Emile. *Problems in General Linguistics*. Miami: U of Miami P, 1971.

Boy's Own Paper. London: Religious Tract Society [weekly 1879–1914; monthly thereafter to 1967].

Brantlinger, Patrick. "Victorians and Africans: The Genealogy of the Myth of the Dark Continent." *Critical Inquiry* 12 (1985): 166–203.

The Captain. London: Newnes. [monthly 1899–1914]

[Carpenter, Kevin.] *Penny Dreadfuls and Comics*. London: Victoria and Albert Museum, 1983.

Chums. London: Cassell [weekly 1892–1932].

Dunae, Patrick A. "Boys' Literature and the Idea of Empire, 1870–1914." *Victorian Studies* 24 (1980): 105–21.

———. "*Boy's Own Paper*: Origins and Editorial Policies." *Private Library* 2d ser. 9 (1976): 123–58.

Field, H. John. *Toward a Programme of Imperial Life.* Westport, Conn.: Greenwood, 1982.

French, David. "Spy Fever in Britain, 1900–1915." *Historical Journal* 21 (1978): 355–70.

James, Louis. "Tom Brown's Imperialist Sons." *Victorian Studies* 17 (1973–74): 89–99.

MacKenzie, John M. *Propaganda and Empire: The Manipulation of British Public Opinion, 1880–1960.* Manchester: Manchester UP, 1984.

Ritvo, Harriet. "Learning from Animals: Natural History for Children in the Eighteenth and Nineteenth Centuries." *Children's Literature* 13 (1985): 72–93.

Turnbaugh, Roy. "Images of Empire: George Alfred Henty and John Buchan." *Journal of Popular Culture* 9 (1975): 734–40.

Williamson, Judith. *Decoding Advertisements.* London: Marion Boyars, 1978.

Young England. London: Sunday School Union / Melrose [260 weekly numbers, thereafter monthly; 1880–1937].

Allegory, Orthodoxy, Ambivalence: MacDonald's "The Day Boy and the Night Girl"

Cynthia Marshall

"Since polarization dominates the child's mind," writes Bruno Bettelheim, "it also dominates fairy tales" (9). The characterization in George MacDonald's fairy tale "The Day Boy and the Night Girl" evinces such polarization: Photogen knows and loves only light, Nycteris can survive and flourish only in darkness. But the story, the last fairy tale MacDonald ever wrote,[1] subverts numerous expectations a reader might bring to the genre. Not only does the split between Photogen and Nycteris lack any obvious ethical significance, but the final point of the tale is the necessary joining of the realms of darkness and light. Ordinarily in fairy tale, a plot in which the good, beautiful, and clever triumph affirms a basic antinomy, but in this case the tale confronts, questions, and ultimately destroys its own distinctions. Despite an initially apparent polarization, "The Day Boy and the Night Girl" reveals intense moral ambivalence. Uncovering this ambivalence, through consideration of the tale as allegory, helps explain the poor critical reception of the tale. More generally, it illustrates how allegory, still too often considered rigid or reductive, can live potently within another genre such as the fairy tale, blending realistic and symbolic techniques usually thought alien to the mode. Finally, such an examination shows how allegory's traditions and techniques inform and complicate an apparently naive narrative, giving it resonance. A fresh examination of these generic issues will enhance our understanding of MacDonald's work in the fairy tale mode.

I

MacDonald himself was careful to maintain the distinction between the two modes of allegory and fairy tale. In his essay "The Fantastic Imagination," he declares that fairy tales can, indeed must, have "some meaning" (*Orts* 316). However, different readers may perceive different meanings, for "a fairytale is not an

allegory. There may be allegory in it, but it is not an allegory"
(*Orts* 317). In a letter written soon after the publication of *Phantastes,* which he calls "my fairy tale," MacDonald blusters, "I don't
see what right the *Athenaeum* has to call it an allegory and judge or
misjudge it accordingly—as if nothing but an allegory could have
two meanings!" (Greville MacDonald 297).[2] These remarks need
to be considered in the context of nineteeth-century critical dialogue, however. Romantic critics distinguished symbol, which they
saw as imaginative and organic, from allegory, considered dull,
closed, and mechanical. Coleridge, like Goethe, believed allegories
were translatable, while symbols were supralinguistic and "imper-
vious to local limitations" (Fletcher 17*n*). This distinction, pro-
ceeding as it did from the central Romantic perception of a split
between reason and imagination, hinged on a covert evaluation:
allegory was bad, symbol good. MacDonald was making a generic
place for his work within this Romantic framework. As Stephen
Prickett observes, "What he wants to do is to differentiate between
the mechanical rigidity of 'strict allegory' and what he calls a
'fairy-tale,' which uses allegory as one of a number of modes of
symbolic narration" (173−74).

Twenty years ago Rosemond Tuve wondered at "the number of
words spent defining and delimiting allegory in this decade," an
effort which had then largely failed to clarify the matter, since
"certain well-inculcated nineteenth-century assumptions about interpretation cloud the language of theory, and rebellions against
them cloud the theory itself" (3). "Allegory" is still widely used as
a term of disapproval in critical dialogues—one indication of how
much we feel the influence of the Romantic movement in literature. These debates have borne significantly upon some readings
of MacDonald, for most readers quickly realize that his narratives
are symbolic yet find the texture of associations far richer than
that normally encountered in parable, moral exemplum, or even
most allegories.[3] Some oddly narrow generic assumptions have
resulted. As late as 1982, one critic who speaks of allegory as "a
very transparent and mechanical one-to-one relation of meaning
to symbol" labels MacDonald's work "mythic" (Hein 111, xvii).
Richard H. Reis maintains that "multiplicity and indefiniteness
distinguish genuine symbolism from mere allegory" (78) and
therefore calls MacDonald's fantasies "symbolic works" (29). C. S.
Lewis emphasizes the "mythopoeic" (*Anthology* 17) and preverbal

power of Macdonald's work. Even Prickett, having recognized the constraints on MacDonald's theoretical assumptions, limits himself to antiquated generic codes when he asserts that "an allegory can, by definition, have no more meaning than the author originally put into it" (173), a difficult hypothesis to test. Prickett attributes the power of MacDonald's work to its "highly developed mysticism" (186).

MacDonald believed that fairy tales convey meaning through the imagination, in defiance of logical explanations. He advises against telling children "what the fairy tale means" (*Orts* 317). A related resistance to double consciousness, to interpretation of symbols, and to anything "phony or moralistic" (86) in children's literature can be found in W. H. Auden's afterword to *The Golden Key*. Auden assimilates fairy tale to myth when he describes "stories about a Secondary world" (82) that follows its own peculiar laws. (Auden seems in fact to paraphrase MacDonald, who wrote that "man may, if he pleases, invent a little world of his own, with its own laws" [*Orts* 316]). Such a work, Auden claims (again echoing MacDonald), "demands of the reader total surrender" (84). "To hunt for symbols in a fairy tale is absolutely fatal. In *The Golden Key*, for example, any attempt to 'interpret' the Grandmother or the air-fish or the Old Man of the Sea is futile: they mean what they are" (85). Auden's remarks perpetuate MacDonald's theoretical directives; his phrasing betrays the New Critic's hostility not only to psychoanalytic translation but also to allegory.

The largest problem for MacDonald's critics may have been the recalcitrant association between allegory and didacticism. Repelled by those nineteenth-century children's stories that offer moral precept set unconvincingly in a frame of wooden narrative, and distrustful of allegory as a mode, they have sought some other label for MacDonald's work. Certainly it can be disconcerting to recognize, as Gillian Avery does, that "MacDonald wanted nothing less than that children should be perfect, not only as children, but all through their lives" (60−61). But didacticism is a red herring. All literature is ideological (Suleiman 2) in that it conveys moral values, and all children's literature is in some sense didactic.

What distinguishes allegory, as we now understand the mode, is not didacticism, but rather reflexivity: allegorists, to ensure the communicability of their message, must give themselves away. Allegory exists, according to Northrop Frye, "when a poet explicitly indicates the relationship of his images to examples and precepts, and so tries to indicate how a commentary on him should proceed" (90). From this perspective it appears ironic that Auden, defending his attack on interpretation, cites an instance of metanarrative in *The Golden Key*—the moment in which the Old Man of the Earth's instructions to Tangle constitute MacDonald's reflexive advice to the reader: "You must throw yourself in. There is no other way" (85). Paradoxical as it may seem, such explicit indications of the unknowable "way" typify the allegorical cues to which visionaries have traditionally resorted as they wrestle to convey through metaphor, symbol, and other forms of displacement or other-speaking their ineffable insights. The stress on codes is a sign of the difficulty rather than the poverty of moral ideas. The automatic, even compulsive, quality of allegory's vehicular systems bears no innate resemblance to the themes delivered. The medium, in this case, is not the message.

In fact, apparent simplicity of structure may reflect complexity of theme. Allegory's rigid systems can impose aesthetic control on powerfully threatening or disruptive ideas. Angus Fletcher finds allegories to be "symbolic power struggles" far more often than they are "the dull systems that they are reputed to be" (23). Fletcher contends that the mode's typically polarized characters, its obvious moral valuations, its predictable plots, all proceed from an author's own profound awareness of ambivalence. If the allegorist is anxious to show forces of good vanquishing those of evil, the drive may be inspired less by ethical didacticism than by the author's consciousness of internal ambivalence. Writing allegory can signal retreat from the vagaries of moral commitment into an ordered, structured world, a world like that in fairy tales from which ambiguity is banished. Hence Joel Fineman's belief that "allegory arises in periods of loss, periods in which a once powerful theological, political, or familiar authority is threatened with effacement. Allegory arises then from the painful absence of that which it claims to recover" (Greenblatt viii). One dialectic informing the allegorical mode is that of loss and recovery: the mature author recognizes the oversimplification of a scheme like that of "The Day Boy and the Night Girl"; he simultaneously yearns for its clarity. And as modernists such as Virginia Woolf or Bertolt Brecht have taught us, authors may tip their hands, pointing to their use of codes and thus betraying the artificiality of such a scheme, in order to force us as readers to reassess certain values we unthinkingly embrace.

II

MacDonald's concern to distinguish good from evil does in fact lead to moralizing interventions in his realistic novels and in certain of his children's books. *At the Back of the North Wind,* for instance, contains passages in which the narrator explains or states moral value. More generally, one might say that MacDonald's juxtaposition of worlds and of narratives in his literature for children functions in a way that calls for interpretation of the one in the light of the other. In *North Wind,* the "dream" experience of the North Wind is not kept separate from "real" experience: Diamond reflects that Nanny "must have been to the back of the north wind!" (192). And not only does Diamond look for "meaning" in his books, but his mentors challenge him to find it. Furthermore, MacDonald points to his own intertextual allusions, as when he notes the debt of "Little Daylight" to "Sleeping Beauty" (*Fairy Tales* 168–69), a reference that in turn underscores the importance of spiritual sleeping and waking in the larger narrative. (And it is just such stress on signs and their interpretation that we have identified as characteristic of allegory.) What distinguishes *At the Back of the North Wind* from MacDonald's fairy tales, I would argue, is the clarity of the novel's system of moral values.

In general, MacDonald is freer to express ambivalence in his fiction for children than he is in other forms of writing. In the allegorical fairy tale, where he moves "out of the area of imitated literal life into an area where universals rather than particulars seem to be met" (Tuve 26), moral certainty gives way to a more complex demonstration of the author's psychomachia, his inner conflict. In "The Light Princess," for instance, complexity and ambivalence are manifested in "the double use of the word *light*" (*Fairy Tales* 22). With the King's denouncement of punning ("the most objectionable form duplicity can assume" [22]), MacDonald points to his allegorical code, which nevertheless remains untranslatable: multiple meanings are intrinsic to the story. So too a golden plate discovered late in the story contains not one but two inscriptions. And finally, the agent of evil in this story is the White Snake of Darkness, whose name suggests the antithetical quality of allegory.

Moral ambivalence is by no means immediately apparent in "The Day Boy and the Night Girl." The tale is instead remarkable for its polarized characterization. Lacking the playfulness of "The Light Princess" or the rich developmental symbolism of "The Golden Key," "The Day Boy and the Night Girl" traces a witch's scientifically conducted experiment in severing light from dark as components of human experience. The simplicity of the narrative scheme barely conceals a strange tension in the tale, however, a clue that something lies beneath its surface. For instance, in a fairly typical authorial intrusion, the narrator describes an incidental set of wall hangings "intended to represent various of the powers of Nature under allegorical similitudes"; he then remarks how "nothing can be made that does not belong to the general scheme" (248). Such insistence on representation and the "scheme" of nature underscores verbal creation and displacement. It leads to the question of how this particular story's schematization relates to an artistic "general scheme." We may come to suspect that the tale's polarized symbolism aims "to recover" some certainty whose "painful absence" its author felt.

There is, in fact, strong internal evidence for MacDonald's ambivalent relationship to the story. "The Day Boy and the Night Girl" begins with a description of the witch Watho, whose desire "to know everything" became "a wolf in her mind" (241). Watho, as the tale goes, conceives of the scheme of splitting day and night. But in the world of faery, a witch is by no means necessary to account for a boy who knows only light and a girl who knows only darkness. The witch is to a certain degree extraneous to the narrative. She evidently exists as MacDonald's fictional surrogate, a unique sort of doubling device, enacting in the tale his experimental fission of life's components. When, at the tale's conclusion, Watho is shot and killed, the author is, I think, clearly "indicating how a commentary on him should proceed"—allegory's main office, according to Frye. Through the witch's destruction, MacDonald effectively destroys himself as author of the tale. That she is shot through her own agency is particularly appropriate for an artist depicting his own demise. The text thus offers a biographical allegory of conclusion, one validated by fact: "The Day Boy and the Night Girl" was the last fairy tale MacDonald wrote. What motivated this allegorical self-destruction? In what way was the tale struggling against its author, as Photogen and Nycteris struggled against Watho?

Assuming that Watho represents some aspect of the tale's author, we might logically proceed to establish symbolic identities for the other main characters, Photogen and Nycteris, as well. Doing so is not easy. In his other works, MacDonald uses "light" in the manner traditional for Christian writers—as a symbol for divinity and spiritual truth. In an early letter to his fianceé, MacDonald writes, "Is God's sun more beautiful than God himself? Has he not left it to us as a symbol of his own life-giving light?" (Greville MacDonald 122). In one of his "unspoken sermons," MacDonald draws the conventional metaphorical identification between divinity and light with the words, "I am saved—for God is light"; the sermon continues, "whatever seems to me darkness, that I will not believe of my God" (*Sermons* 167, 167−68). In another sermon, entitled "The Mirrors of the Lord," he sees Christians as striving "until at length the glory of our existence flashes upon us, and . . . [we] know that our existence is not the moonlight of a mere consciousness of being, but the sun-glory of a life justified by having become one with its origin, thinking and feeling with the primal Sun of life" (*Sermons* 53−54).

In MacDonald's fairy tales, the symbolism of light at first glance appears to be just as straightforward. Thus Little Daylight shrivels under the dark of the moon and grows to full beauty in confluence with its light. The numinous grandmother of *The Princess and the Goblin* opposes the dark underworld of the goblins. But we should note that it is often specifically the moonlit realm which functions as a transition to true enlightenment. Thus the Light Princess's nightly swims with the prince humanize her; their subliminally erotic play prepares her for the experience of love. Similarly Mossy and Tangle leave the sunlit world of reality for the moonlit land of faery, where they may pass through the land of shadows to the rainbow and up to the Platonic source of all light ("The Golden Key"). And Little Daylight attains day only after she and her rescuing prince have passed through the fairies' night world. In these stories MacDonald constantly uses a narrative trajectory involving changing forms of light; typically moonlight governs a threshold of initiation, a realm where education takes place, but the goal lies beyond in some higher, brighter realm, which is often represented as daylight. "Is that the sun coming?" asks Little Daylight at her tale's conclusion (*Fairy Tales* 186).

"The Day Boy and the Night Girl" is more problematic. The tale defies the coherent dualities of MacDonald's religious symbolism, for Photogen and Nycteris, as light and dark, by no means correspond simply to God and his enemies. Hein usefully refers us to Romantic nature symbolism to explain the positive value of moonlight and the imagination as these are linked to Nycteris. But this symbolic equation must be extended to include the religious dimension of the fairy tale. The mother of Nycteris, for instance, is "born for the second [time]" as she gives birth, and she passes " into a world . . . unknown" (244). At the conclusion Nycteris refers explicitly to afterlife in a punning reference: "but who knows," she says to Photogen, "that when we go out, we shall not go into a day as much greater than your day as your day is greater than my night?" (288). These final lines suggest the Pauline notion of life on earth as a dark shadow of the reality beyond. But they also suggest the Augustinian idea that night and day are mere gradations of light, that darkness is the lowest rung on a ladder of light extending ultimately into heavenly incandescence. The lines of symbolic identification do not necessarily coincide with other uses of similar systems; moreover, identifications (or meanings) can shift even as one moves from level to level within the allegory.

A certain ambiguity becomes evident between the possible connotations of light—and even more problematically, of darkness. Nycteris is associated not just with the night but with death. Her mother, "a young widow whose husband had lately died" (241), herself dies in childbirth; the pregnancy is passed in chambers modeled on "the tomb of an Egyptian king" (242), containing a sarcophagus. Nycteris's own first recognition of death comes when the dim lamp suspended from the roof of her chamber falls and shatters. When she steps on a shard, "it flashed upon her that the lamp was dead, that this brokenness was the death of which she had read without understanding, that the darkness had killed the lamp. . . . It was not the lamp any more now that it was dead, for all that made it a lamp was gone, namely, the bright shining of it. Then it must be the shine, the light, that had gone out!" (250. Here darkness is clearly connected with death ("the darkness had killed the lamp"). Moreover, the passage presents allegorically a Christian view of mortality: the light ("all that made it a lamp") represents the soul, whose departure leaves only the "broken-ness," the darkness, of the body. We might distinguish between Nycteris's naive view of death, however, and the informed under-standing of the narrator, who describes the death of Nycteris's mother as a second birth.

But, even given the reference to death as passageway to life beyond, it is odd that the tale portrays Nycteris, the "creature of the darkness" (265) so sympathetically. Her sensitive and em-pathic qualities enable this escaped "troglodyte" (252), imprisoned from birth in a dimly lit tomb, to comprehend nature's mysteries—shadows, wind, cycles of the moon—with reverence and a pagan religious awe. She endures the tortures of the witch, who exposes her to the sunlight she cannot endure; and she bravely assists Photogen, paralyzed by fear of the dark, in escaping the witch's castle. Nycteris is, according to the narrator, "the greater, for suf-fering more, she feared nothing" (284). The moonlit realm associ-ated with Nycteris is one of education and initiation, as in other stories by MacDonald. But, atypically, the brightness of the sun is Nycteris's nemesis rather than her goal, and the creature associ-ated with the sun is rigorously devalued.

Photogen, though "radiant as Apollo" (271), lacks the powers of a sun god. He deserts Nycteris when she is terrified by the day-light; "seven times in all" he tries "to face the coming night" (274) and each time he fails. Photogen describes the sun as "the soul, the life, the heart, the glory of the universe. . . . The worlds dance like motes in his beams. The heart of man is strong and brave in his light, and when it departs his courage grows from him—goes with the sun" (268). But MacDonald qualifies this glorious Apol-lonian description by acerbically remarking on Photogen's arro-gance, "the arrogance of all male creatures until they have been taught by the other kind" (271).[4] Photogen's daily practice of hunting becomes value-laden through contrast with Nycteris, who responds to nature's creatures "not in the spirit of the hunter, but of the lover" (264).

In the characterization of Photogen and Nycteris, the tale per-haps privileges (as Hein realizes) the Romantic valuation of imagi-nation, creativity, and female virtue over an Apollonian prefer-ence for light and reason. But the narrative point of the story is the necessary *joining* of Photogen's daylight realm with Nycteris's moonlight one. Both poles are shown to be valuable, both crucial for spiritual wholeness. As Photogen states near the conclusion, "If ever two people couldn't do the one without the other, those two are Nycteris and I" (287). This final synthesis transcends the Romantic value scheme, which for the most part simply inverts the religious significance MacDonald attaches to the same set of symbols (light and darkness) in his more orthodox prose.

Context clearly influences the use of a specific symbol or set of symbols. Yet when an author uses his or her symbol for divinity inconsistently, a reader might well note the discrepancy and question its significance. Moreover, MacDonald insists that "what we mean by light, God means by light" (*Sermons* 169). While maintaining the divinity and unity of light in "The Day Boy and the Night Girl" ("all light is one" [251]), he also embraces the value of darkness here more radically than in any of his other fairy tales. For he glorifies a girl of shadows and asserts the final necessity of joining together day and night. The tale needs to be interpreted allegorically to account for this apparent authorial inconsistency. As modern theorists suggest, allegory's polar antagonisms may initially suggest orderly and firm commitments on the part of an author, but the key actually lies in the author's ambivalence. Allegorists' attitude toward their work is, according to Fletcher, like Schiller's toward the sublime—"a mixed feeling," both "painful" and "joyous" (Fletcher 267). Allegorists who set good and evil (or light and dark) characters in opposition give birth to both from their own minds.

Indeed, reading the allegorical fairy tale may heighten our awareness of MacDonald's ambivalence in other texts. MacDonald's "unspoken sermon" on light, when read from this perspective, evinces less than perfect moral certainty. Two biblical verses serve as texts for the treatise:

> This is the message we have heard from Him and proclaim to you, that God is light and in Him is no darkness at all. [1 John 1:5]

> And this is the judgment, that the light has come into the world, and men loved darkness rather than light, because their deeds were evil. [John 3:19]

MacDonald is orthodox enough in asserting that darkness, the absence of God's light, "is death" (*Sermons* 175). This follows the Augustinian concept of evil as the absence of good. Darkness as the absence of light, death as the absence of life are ordinary, even facile, formulations. In this sermon, people are "condemned for not coming out of the darkness, for not coming to the light" (175). MacDonald's opposition to those in darkness is strong: "he who refuses [to come to the light] must be punished and punished —punished through all the ages—punished until he gives way" (179). In preaching fervently against a darkness and a death that one could actually *love*, MacDonald implicitly amplifies the importance of the forces opposed to light and life. To posit a darkness that is no mere lacuna but an object of worship means to flirt with the heretical acknowledgment of a rival power in the universe. Manichaeism, according to St. Augustine (who knew the heresy well since he had been a youthful adherent of it), consists of the belief in "two principles, different from and opposed to each other, both eternal and coeternal." These two principles are supposedly responsible for the "two natures and substances, that is, one good and one evil" (Peters 33), constituting the created world. Manichaeism has traditionally been considered the heresy of heresies, for it manifests a primary denial of the Christian God's omnipotence. MacDonald's potential Manichaeism, born of setting the powers of darkness against the powers of light, in another context yields the polar symbolism of "The Day Boy and the Night Girl."

III

There is nothing facile about [MacDonald's] morality. He sees that the problem of evil really is a problem—MacNeice, Varieties of Parable

The polar scheme of "The Day Boy and the Night Girl" may well reflect the Calvinist heritage that MacDonald struggled with all his life, and above all his difficulty in locating the sources of evil or ways of dealing with it. The Scottish Presbyterian church of his childhood, founded by John Knox, followed closely Calvin's central doctrines—man's innately sinful condition, and God's predestination of some to salvation, others to eternal damnation. By contrast, MacDonald's intuition seems to have suggested an enveloping benevolence in the universe. He lost his pulpit in 1853, only three years after ordination in the Congregationalist church, for his speculations that animals might share in salvation and that the heathen might be given an opportunity to repent even after death (see Greville MacDonald 177–80), as well as for suspicions that "he was tainted with German Theology" (179). His early romance *Phantastes* (1858) reflects the forgiving disposition that might adopt these particular heresies. It closes with a Platonic conception of evil as mistaken good: "what we call evil, is the only and best shape, which, for the person and his condition at the time, could be assumed by the best good" (182).

The contrast between *Phantastes* (1858) and *Lilith* (1895) provides evidence of the growing gloom that settled over MacDonald's writing throughout his long career. The progression of mood is glimpsed on a smaller scale in the movement from *The Princess and the Goblin* (1872), a work mainly concerned with discovery of faith, and one which ends optimistically, to the troubling suggestions of ongoing conflict that close *The Princess and Curdie* (1882), which focuses throughout on attempts to overcome deception in a corrupt world. Apparently some sense of inborn human depravity, perhaps even of predestination, lurked in MacDonald's consciousness. A man who felt a particularly close relationship with his father (Greville MacDonald 31, 54, 129–32) might well experience anxiety in casting off his father's religion. Calvinism, moreover, positing a God responsible for everything that befalls a person—not only his salvation, but even his damnation—is a theology that radically resists being rejected, for it claims to be comprehensive. (Chesterton, interestingly, called the peculiar quality of MacDonald's writings "a sort of optimist Calvinism" [152].) Yet MacDonald did not always see God's universe as ultimately benevolent. Discussing "justice" in one of his "unspoken sermons" published in 1889, MacDonald writes that "for evil in the abstract, nothing can be done. It is eternally evil" (*Sermons* 124). More emphatically, Mr. Vane's spiritual teacher in *Lilith* says that "annihilation itself is no death to evil. Only good where evil was is evil dead" (328). *Lilith*'s conclusion strikes a definitely pessimistic note when the central character, who has supposedly progressed in spirtual knowledge, is inexplicably returned to his library at the moment of his approach to the "Ancient of Days."

Calvinism, as I have said, provides a systematic explanation of evil; the system's duality bears some resemblance to the polarization of good and evil in fairy tales. MacDonald's short fairy tales in general adopt a smug and somewhat condescending attitude toward evil. The heroine of "The Light Princess" takes revenge on her bewitching aunt by treading "pretty hard on her gouty toe," but the princess regrets even this mild action when the witch is buried next day in the collapsing ruins of her house *(Fairy Tales* 63). In "Little Daylight" we are told that "wicked fairies will not be bound by the laws which the good fairies obey, and this always seems to give the bad the advantage over the good, for they use means to gain their ends which the others will not. But it is all of no consequence, for what they do never succeeds; nay, in the end it brings about the very thing they are trying to prevent" *(Fairy Tales* 183). In *The Princess and the Goblin,* MacDonald kills or disperses most of the goblins by flood or by jumping on unshod feet; the remaining goblins become mildly mischievous creatures like Scottish brownies. In each of these works, evil is not only clearly identified but (eventually) easily defeated. The generic scheme of good fairies versus evil fairies (or witches) imposes itself. Even if MacDonald wished to show the inadequacy of such a contrast, the polar frame would remain an intrinsic part of the genre. In this context, his statement on the futility of fairies' evil becomes more significant. It recalls, to return to the religious arena, the Renaissance notion of the salvation of Satan: if God is to be "all in all," he must eventually encompass the entire creation in an ultimate defeat of Manichaeism. By analogy, MacDonald's fairy tales ordinarily emasculate evil, which is absorbed into the larger plan it tries futilely to combat.

"The Day Boy and the Night Girl" was written at the end of MacDonald's successful career as author of fairy stories. The collapsing polarization of symbolism underlying the characterization of Photogen and Nycteris suggests an author caught between the demands of rival symbolic universes, unable or unwilling to choose between allegiance to the darkness of Romanticism or the light of religious orthodoxy. The tale in part inverts religious symbolism, but it finally insists that merger or synthesis is required for wholeness. "Even the wicked themselves may be a link to join together the good" (288) observes Photogen's mother near the tale's conclusion. "The Day Boy and the Night Girl" entertains, in other

words, a necessary dialectic and synthesis quite different from
MacDonald's stated theology of a God who is all powerful, all
good, and all light. Its dialectic is also much more compelling in
its implications than the other tales' easy oppositions between
good and evil and the handy defeats granted the latter. In "The
Day Boy and the Night Girl" MacDonald separates light from
darkness, shows the value of each, and demonstrates their ultimate interdependence. Then, his self-censor at work, he destroys,
in the person of Watho, the part of himself that had invented
such a scheme.

IV

At this point I may seem to have placed MacDonald in the company of Barrie and Kingsley and other Victorians who relegated
private anxieties to a fictional world. But an allegorical reading of
"The Day Boy and the Night Girl" reveals another dimension to
the tale's symbolism, one which secures for it a place within orthodox religious tradition. At one level, the tale elaborates Augustine's commentary on the biblical creation narrative and offers its
own version of the Fall. In the first moments of creation, Augustine wrote, the angels looked at themselves; then some looked up
and beheld the light of their creator, while others sank into the
darkness of self-love.

The notion of *cognitio vesperanti* was reiterated by Aquinas and
echoed in *Paradise Lost*,[5] the only literary text which MacDonald
explicitly quotes in the tale. When Photogen first encounters the
darkness, he is described as "'How fallen, how changed'" (261)
from his daylight self. Satan's first words upon regaining
consciousness in hell are addressed to Beelzebub:

> If thou beest hee; But O how fall'n! how chang'd
> From him, who in the happy Realms of light
> Cloth'd with transcendent brightness didst outshine
> Myriads though bright. [Milton 1:84–87]

MacDonald's story in effect rewrites the Miltonic myth of the fall.
Watho (or MacDonald), in creating Photogen (Day) and Nycteris
(Night), plays the role of God in Genesis 1:5. Photogen, however,
enacts a Satan who is partially recovered from darkness, and Nycteris an Eve who falls into light. When Nycteris first glimpses Pho-

togen, "lying on the bank of the river," she thinks him "another girl like herself" (264). The scene recalls that of Milton's Eve who, first awakening to the created world, becomes enamored of her own reflected face and must be called away from her initial narcissism by the voice of God. MacDonald's myth of the fall is fundamentally Platonic, for it illustrates the difficulty of perceiving true forms in a fallen world. He points to the problematic nature of all creation, echoing Blake's view of creation (in "The Book of Urizen") as an ironic fall, a separation of the component parts of an originally harmonious whole. Blake, of course, is also associated with Manichaeism; "The Tyger" raises the question of a dark creator.[6]

The Augustinian tradition of *cognitio vesperanti* is theologically important because it offers an origin for darkness—and, by implication, for evil[7]—without positing a dark creator. Thus, it pulls the Genesis creation narrative back from the edges of Manichaeism by equating evil with self-love rather than with darkness. So too MacDonald's story posits day and night as parts of one primal whole, not products of two creators; and it offers a model for imaginative growth and creation. Until Nycteris recognizes and accepts Photogen's differences from herself, and until Photogen learns to sympathize with Nycteris and to give his strength to her, they suffer loneliness, emptiness, and guilt. Photogen especially is, in MacDonald's estimation, arrogant and full of pride until "taught by the other kind" (271). When Photogen and Nycteris are united, the forces of light and darkness are symbolically joined, and in reference to the *cognitio vesperanti*, self-love is conquered. The melding of forces is signaled by the recognition late in the story that the mothers of Photogen and Nycteris "had changed eyes in their children" (288). The Day Boy and the Night Girl have learned to see the world through one another's eyes.

According to Fletcher's theory of allegory, polarization such as that of "The Day Boy and the Night Girl" is related to the dualistic habit of mind that produces and embraces Manichaeism: "In attacking heresies, orthodox Christianity attacks all those beliefs that tend to split up the essentially unified notions of the single all-powerful, all-good deity. And orthodoxy requires an opposition, something to fight against. . . . All sorts of Manichaean thinking are at home in the daemonic universe, and allegory in general has a Manichaean appearance for that reason" (333–34).

MacDonald, forced from the pulpit for his heretical beliefs, had felt the sting of orthodoxy's self-protectiveness. His antipathy toward doctrine preceded the accusations of heresy, however. He wrote to his father in 1851, during the early days of his ministry, that "people have hitherto been a great deal too much taken up about doctrine and far too little about practice. . . . We are far too anxious to be definite and to have finished, well-polished, sharp-edged *systems*—forgetting that the more perfect a theory about the infinite, the surer it is to be wrong, the more impossible is it to be right" (Greville MacDonald 155). To a man of MacDonald's sensitivity, who saw "systems" as anathema, who rejected "darkness" in his God, the dreadful logic of a church inspired by Calvinism was bound to create spiritual problems.

His rejection of systems also returns us to the problem of allegory. MacDonald himself would perhaps have applauded Auden's directive against "symbol hunting" (Auden 85). Yet he praises St. Paul for the "practical" quality of his "poetic imagination," which can "embody things discovered, in forms and symbols heretofore unused, and so present to other minds the deeper truths to which these forms and symbols owe their being" (*Sermons* 42–43). And in the tales themselves, enigmatic remarks, secrets, and references to "meaning" call out for interpretation. A gnomic statement like "when we are following the light, even its extinction is a guide" (*Fairy Tales* 252) cannot be assimilated without some sort of symbolic system. Furthermore, while MacDonald insists, in the typical reflexive ploy of the allegorist, that readers must wrestle with problems of meaning, he complicates interpretation by juxtaposing Romantic and Christian symbolism.[8] Similarly, MacDonald's practice in a number of tales, including "The Golden Key" and "The Day Boy and the Night Girl," is to multiply a basic quest pattern so that the orientation becomes more complex and labyrinthine. If he starts from a familiar polarity, he often reverses it several times during the course of the story. In the case of both symbolism and quest, MacDonald uses system to undercut system.

"The Day Boy and the Night Girl" ends with the marriage of Photogen and Nycteris, a narrative event designed to reconcile symbolic polarities. But allegorical characters within a fiction must remain unreservedly themselves; they may change eyes, but they can neither exchange nor merge identities. The wedding therefore dictates the story's conclusion. The characters in MacDonald's allegory, although themselves the products of a compelling ambivalence, remain as luminously simple, as distinctive, as day and night. It was MacDonald's genius to connect, creatively, a child's initial experiences of opposition—good versus evil, light versus darkness—with his own struggles against orthodoxy and against the troubling systems of his religious heritage.

Notes

An earlier version of this paper was presented at the November 1985 meeting of the South Atlantic Modern Language Association.

1. *The Princess and Curdie*, published as a monograph in 1882, had been serialized in 1877 (Green 10).

2. MacDonald's description of *The Wise Woman* as a "double story" (222) may acknowledge the parable's double plot, or its double meaning, or both. In any case, Suleiman's comment that "the more a story 'speaks for itself,' without interpretation by its teller, the more it must rely on redundancies to make its point" (42) is relevant, both to *The Wise Woman* and to "The Day Boy and the Night Girl," whose plot is also double.

3. Mendelson describes a typical first response to *Lilith*: "amazement at the inventiveness of MacDonald's imagination and yet perhaps an uncertainty as to the signification of this dense fabric of highly charged imagery" (198).

4. For purposes of unity and emphasis, I have excluded consideration of the important role of gender in the story. However, the polarization of sex roles in this story and in MacDonald's work as a whole needs to be addressed.

5. Augustine, *De Genesi ad litteram*, IV.22; Aquinas, *Summa Theologiae*, la.63.6; Milton, *Paradise Lost*, 4:449−75.

6. Blake's poem "The Little Black Boy" resonates against this story, especially the hope that the souls of white and black children will learn "the heat to bear" and come to God. Photogen longs to help Nycteris "bear the heat of the sun" (287), perhaps for the same purpose. Blake's narrator understands heaven as release from polarities of white and black ("When I from black and he from white cloud free"). The poem's ending, however, is ironic: the little black boy longs to "be like him" (ambiguously "our father" or the "English boy") so "he will then love me." Greville MacDonald recalls four illustrations by Blake which hung in his father's study; one of them showed "an old man driven . . . into his tomb, to find himself reborn into the fulness of youth, with head uplifted to the risen sun" (Greville MacDonald 554). This device was used by MacDonald on his own bookplate.

7. In Genesis 1:4 God divides "the light from the darkness" on the first day of creation, and although he later pronounces "everything that he had made" to be "very good" (Gen. 1:32), he makes no such specific pronouncement about the darkness (as he does about the land, vegetation, heavenly bodies, etc.). To one frame of allegorical mind, for whom "evil and misery were deep and dark from the first" (Lewis, *Allegory* 44), the creation narrative could be interpreted as suggesting God's rejection, or casting away, of darkness.

8. Prickett, somewhat similarly, sees that juxtaposed viewpoints give life to MacDonald's work: "What Chesterton meant by 'optimistic Calvinism' was MacDonald's belief that mystical insight and religious experience was *potentially* open to all, and one day *would* be the possession of all, however rare it might be at the present,

just as Maurice's 'family' of the Church was for all. [Frederick Denison Maurice, a close friend of MacDonald, was an Anglican clergyman and proponent of Socialism.] Yet . . . MacDonald's Mauricean optimism is balanced by a no less thoroughgoing pessimism. It is this acute tension between two very different spiritual viewpoints that is the key to the best of his fantasy" (189).

Works Cited

Auden, W. H. Afterword to *The Golden Key*, by George MacDonald. Illus. Maurice Sendak. New York: Farrar, Straus, and Giroux-Ariel, 1967.

Avery, Gillian. *Nineteenth Century Children: Heroes and Heroines in English Children's Stories, 1780–1900*. London: Hodder and Stoughton, 1965.

Bettelheim, Bruno. *The Uses of Enchantment: The Meaning and Importance of Fairy Tales*. New York: Vintage, 1977.

Blake, William. *The Complete Writings of William Blake*. Ed. Geoffrey Keynes. London: Oxford UP, 1966.

Chesterton, G. K. *The Victorian Age in Literature*. New York: Henry Holt, 1913.

Fletcher, Angus. *Allegory: The Theory of a Symbolic Mode*. New York: Columbia UP, 1964.

Frye, Northrop. *The Anatomy of Criticism: Four Essays*. Princeton: Princeton UP, 1957.

Green, Roger Lancelyn. Introduction to *The Complete Fairy Tales of George MacDonald*. New York: Schocken, 1961.

Greenblatt, Stephen J., ed. *Allegory and Representation: Selected Papers from the English Institute, 1979–80*. Baltimore: Johns Hopkins UP, 1981.

Hein, Rolland. *The Harmony Within: The Spiritual Vision of George MacDonald*. Grand Rapids: Christian UP, 1982.

Lewis, C. S. *The Allegory of Love: A Study in Medieval Tradition*. 1936. London: Oxford UP, 1958.

———. *George MacDonald: An Anthology*. New York: Macmillan, 1947.

MacDonald, George. *At the Back of the North Wind*. New York: Airmont, 1966.

———. *The Complete Fairy Tales of George MacDonald*. Introd. Roger Lancelyn Green. New York: Schocken, 1961. All references to "The Day Boy and the Night Girl" are to this volume; the story is also reprinted in *Victorian Fairy Tales: The Revolt of the Fairies and Elves*, ed. Jack Zipes (Methuen, 1987).

———. *A Dish of Orts: Chiefly Papers on the Imagination and Shakespeare*. London: Edwin Dalton, 1908.

———. *Phantastes AND Lilith*. Grand Rapids: Eerdmans, 1964.

———. *Unspoken Sermons: Third Series*. London: Longmans, 1889.

———. *The Wise Woman: A Parable*. New York: Garland, 1977.

MacDonald, Greville. *George MacDonald and His Wife*. London: Allen & Unwin, 1924; rpt. New York: Johnson, 1971.

MacNeice, Louis. *Varieties of Parable*. New York: Cambridge UP, 1965.

Mendelson, Michael. "George MacDonald's *Lilith* and the Conventions of Ascent." *Studies in Scottish Literature* 20 (1985): 197–218.

Milton, John. *Complete Poems and Major Prose*. Ed. Merritt Y. Hughes. Indianapolis: Bobbs-Merrill, 1957.

Peters, Edward, ed. *Heresy and Authority in Medieval Europe: Documents in Translation*. Philadelphia: U of Pennsylvania P, 1980.

Prickett, Stephen. *Victorian Fantasy*. Bloomington: Indiana UP, 1979.

Reis, Richard H. *George MacDonald*. New York: Twayne, 1972.

Suleiman, Susan Rubin. *Authoritarian Fictions: The Ideological Novel as a Literary Genre.* New York: Columbia UP, 1983.

Tuve, Rosemond. *Allegorical Imagery: Some Medieval Books and Their Posterity.* Princeton: Princeton UP, 1966.

Wolff, Robert Lee. *The Golden Key: A Study of the Fiction of George MacDonald.* New Haven: Yale UP, 1961.

The See-Saw and the Bridge in Robert Cormier's After the First Death

Frank Myszor

In his novel *After the First Death*, Robert Cormier uses the metaphor of a see-saw to describe the feelings of Kate, one of the main characters: "Her emotions were on a see-saw now: up, down, up, down" (119). Elsewhere he has spoken of adolescence in general as "see-sawing between ecstasy and despair" (Hicks 1). But in *After the First Death* the metaphor not only describes the experiences of some of the main characters, it also provides a framework for the structure of the discourse and helps us to explain the reader's relationship to the text; thus the metaphor draws attention to features that make this an innovative adolescent novel. The bridge too is a central dramatic and symbolic device for Cormier. Much of the narrative takes place on a physical bridge, particularly the chapters concerning the captured schoolbus. Like the see-saw, the bridge suggests ambivalence, paradox, antithesis, and rites of passage, all of which, as Thompson has argued, are concepts important to the transition from childhood to adulthood. By inscribing these two critical metaphors in the narrative structure and symbolism of *After the First Death*, Cormier not only reproduced archetypal patterns but also broke new ground in the field of adolescent literature.

The concepts and terminology of Gérard Genette, the French structuralist critic, can help to explain Cormier's achievement. In distinguishing, as Genette does, between narrative (the discourse or narrative text itself) and the story (narrative content) that it recounts, it will be necessary to draw parallels between Cormier's narrative techniques and those used in cinema. However, we must begin with a brief analysis of the story and its underlying symbolism.

Cormier structures his novel around a violent political conflict: terrorists, led by Artkin and Miro, capture a schoolbus full of children, for whom Kate is responsible, and Miro eventually shoots her. At the thematic level, the novel can be seen as a series of binary oppositions between experience and innocence, adulthood

and childhood, power and powerlessness, patriotism and terror-
ism, male and female. At first glance, the characters also fall into
opposite camps. General Marchand, the patriot, has his opposite
in Artkin, the leader of the terrorist group; their sons Ben and
Miro (perhaps a foster son) are associated with the same hostile
factions as their fathers.[1] Miro and Kate in turn can be placed in
opposition because of their conflicting cultural backgrounds, their
roles as killer and victim, and of course their gender. But Cormier
also exposes the ambiguity of these oppositions. The general and
Artkin are equally guilty of sacrificing moral responsibility for a
political ideal. This is why the general says of Artkin, "We knew
each other across the chasm although we had never met" (153).
Similarly, Miro and Ben are both victims of their fathers' fanaticism, and even Kate and Miro share adolescent concerns such as
sex and identity.[2]

An explicitly political author, Cormier in *After the First Death*
makes a statement by first juxtaposing antagonistic factions and
then drawing parallels between them. Macleod, who links this political concern to the themes of innocence and hypocrisy, takes the
encounter between Miro and Kate in chapter 6 to be pivotal, for
Kate first realizes then the paradox of Miro's innocence (Macleod
79; see also Macafee). It is "monstrous" : "She'd always thought of
innocence as something good . . . but innocence, she saw now,
could also be evil" (105). Ambiguity is central not only to this
novel but to Cormier's distinctive contribution to the young-adult
novel, for he exposes an inherent danger in the romantic notion
of the purely innocent child by destroying the myth that for the
innocent everything comes out well in the end (Hamilton 32).

Chapter 6 also enhances other themes characteristic of the adolescent novel. Typically adolescent novels bring together young
males and females of contrasting backgrounds (Thompson 116;
Carlsen 60).[3] Carlsen identifies three stages associated with this
process: separation, initiation, incorporation. Kate is physically
and emotionally isolated by virtue of her captivity on the bus.
Miro is isolated from his homeland and from the security of his
brother, Aniel. Moreover, for him this mission is different from
the others, since it probably will lead to his full acceptance into the
terrorist fraternity. Thus it has the quality of an initiatory test,
Artkin being the judge of success or failure in Miro's eyes. According to Thompson, "Peers in Cormier's novel *The Chocolate*

War are a testing ground for individual conviction" (116). Kate's and Miro's conflicting ideologies lead Kate into a direct questioning of Miro's morality, and he is forced to justify himself to her as well.

Their initiation into adult responsibilities continues partly through learning to cope with the needs of the young children around them and partly through their quasi-sexual encounter. Through a kind of courtship ritual with Kate, Miro first begins to realize the fallibility of Artkin, thereby moving toward independence from adults. But the most important sequence occurs at the end of chapter 6, when Kate probes Miro, trying to find his weakness, a discussion that embarrasses both as it also sexualizes them. According to Campbell, Cormier originally intended the novel to be a love story [78–79].) Miro shrinks from such intimacy, yet his gun enters his mind as a phallic substitute: "The girl passed by, went out of his sight, and Miro resisted touching himself. He turned red-faced from the window and touched his gun in consolation" (24). Kate, fearing failure, turns to feminine flattery, evoking a flood of memories from Miro, who then regrets having revealed so much of himself. Each is trying to "win the other over," but neither realizes the other's intentions. That this primitive romantic encounter marks a stage of initiation is corroborated by Kate's insight into Miro's innocence, and by Miro's realization that he had mourned "not for Aniel but for himself" (106), insights that lead both toward adulthood. (Later both demonstrate attainment of adulthood, Miro symbolically by no longer needing to use his gun, and Kate by showing genuine concern for Miro's plight shortly before her death.

It can be seen, then, that chapter 6 is a key moment in the symbolic structure of the novel. To reinforce this key moment, Cormier emphasizes the chapter by setting it off temporally and spatially. Time loses definition at this point, when only adolescents are present and wakeful: "So began a time in mid-afternoon when the children came under the influence of the drugs" (78); "The afternoon was at a standstill" (82). Descriptive detail isolates Miro and Kate in a twilit world of their own: "The day had turned cloudy. The absence of sun and blocking out of light by the tape gave the interior of the bus an aspect of twilight. This false dusk softened the sharp edges of things. . . . the bus surrounded by silence" (82). These effects of time and light set off the scene and make it ambiguous, an ambiguity that reinforces the chapter's and the novel's central point: the paradox of innocence.

Physical signs also isolate and emphasize this crucial encounter. Most important, Miro and Kate are situated in the middle of a bridge between two precipices, high above a streambed. A more personal symbol, the conspicuous color orange, marks the bus and several other items in the scene. (*Orange*, in fact, was originally to be the title of the novel.) For Cormier the word *orange* is associated with isolation, because "it is one of the few words in the English language for which there is no rhyme" (Macafee 32−33). Psychologically, too, Cormier presents a no-man's-land. Kate is a captive, deprived of autonomy. Miro, who has never been a child, has not yet been accepted into adulthood; moreover, at this point he is on his own, since Artkin has left the bus. Finally, the children around them have been doped: "They ceased to have identities" (78).

To achieve these effects of ambiguity and balance, Cormier also exploits shifts in point of view. Important for the structure of the novel as a whole, these shifts also put chapter 6 into relief. This chapter lies in a gap between Ben's first-person narrative (chapters 1, 3, 5) and that of General Marchand (chapters 7, 9, 11), suggesting a bridge between the two halves of the novel and a transition from child to adult (see the accompanying figure). During this interval (translated into discourse time by chapter 6), Ben apparently commits suicide at Brimmler's Bridge, rejecting the adulthood embodied by his father, for whom, ironically, the bridge was a site of adolescent enjoyment. Thus chapter 6 is the turning point in the presentation of Ben's relationship to his father and of Ben's quest for adulthood. Silently, it marks his defeat. By combining the metaphors of the see-saw and the bridge, the chapter links the two narratives and points to itself as the central moment in the three-part pattern of separation−initiation−incorporation.

In broad outline, Cormier contrasts the first-person narratives of Ben and his father in the odd-numbered chapters to the third-person point of view in the "bus and bridge" episodes. In addition, the complex narrative strand concerning the bus juxtaposes opposing viewpoints, or more precisely, perspectives. Within the third-person narrative Cormier deliberately alternates between Miro and Kate as centers of consciousness.

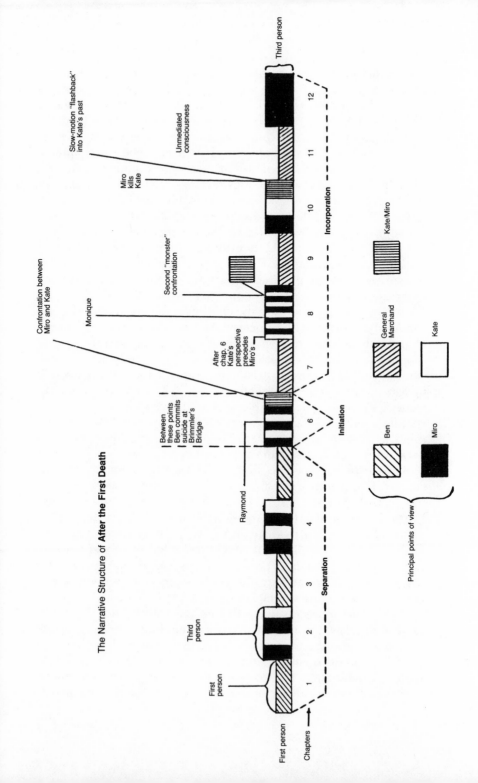

The Narrative Structure of **After the First Death**

First person

Third person

Third person

Slow-motion "flashback" into Kate's past

Unmediated consciousness

Miro kills Kate

Confrontation between Miro and Kate

Monique

Second "monster" confrontation

After chap. 6 Kate's perspective precedes Miro's

Between these points Ben commits suicide at Brimmler's Bridge

Raymond

Chapters   1   2   3   4   5   6   7   8   9   10   11   12

Separation   Initiation   Incorporation

Principal points of view

Ben

Miro

General Marchand

Kate

Kate/Miro

In principle, nothing is shown that is outside the experience of Kate or Miro, and we never see directly inside Artkin. Comments such as "did not disturb Artkin" (22) or "Artkin became conscious of Miro's study" (28) need not reflect omniscient knowledge of Artkin's mind but rather conclusions drawn from Miro's observations of Artkin. For example, the first three scenes of chapter 2 record Miro's visual observations and, more importantly, his thoughts, memories, and feelings. These statements thus explore within Miro and also look out from within him. Nothing is described that is outside his range of perception (or memory), and although there are two other characters involved, the reader is not permitted to see inside them unless the perception is focused through Miro's awareness. Comments on Artkin, for example, do not spring from the omniscient narrator's point of view but from observations based on Miro's past experience of Artkin's character: "Miro saw Artkin pondering the children. He looked doubtful, his forehead wrinkled with concern. Artkin seldom showed doubt. Had the drugs been too powerful? Or was Artkin merely deep in thought, selecting his possible victims: who would die and who would live?" (27). Miro's speculation about Artkin's thoughts tells us less about Artkin than about the youth's mental processes. In Genette's phrase, "the multiple nature of these hypotheses . . . accentuates their role as indicators of focalisation" (203); they remind us that we receive ostensibly objective, third-person information through a character's center of consciousness.

To be sure, Cormier occasionally violates this system of a dual center of consciousness established for the even chapters of the bus plot. During the second scene filtered by Kate, for example, Cormier interjects Miro's thoughts: "Miro thought fast" (37); "Miro found the words difficult to say, particularly to a girl and an American girl at that. But Artkin had told him to win her confidence" (38). Such interpolations (or speeded up alternations) suggest an omniscient narrator. Two other movements to incorporate another child's perspective, by their very rarity, mark significant structural transitions. But in general we find a framing, neutral third-person narrative position modified and given color by adherence to the perspectives of Kate and Miro. It is therefore most accurate to speak of "omniscience with partial restriction of field" (Genette 194). To apply another test of perspective, moreover, Cormier's third-person narrative is "personal," attached to particular characters, for it could be transferred to the first person "without any alteration of the discourse other than the change of grammatical pronouns" (Barthes, "Introduction" 283).

There are further restrictions of field. For the most part, we do not get the impression of an omniscient narrator who can move in and out of character at will. Once a particular perspective is adopted, it is usually maintained for several pages, in contrast to Barthes's observation that "the discourse of the traditional novel alternates the personal and the impersonal very rapidly, often in the same sentence" ("To Write" 140). The purely independent viewpoint never interprets intrusively or offers moral comments. It is merely descriptive—"The rain had stopped but the pavement was still wet" (182)—and never moves outside the range of the character through whose perceptions the action is focused at that moment.

Most of the even chapters present an alternation between extended blocks of experience, generally entering the perspective of Miro before that of Kate. In order to intensify the conflict and speed up the dramatic turning point of chapter 6, however, Cormier intercuts brief moments of perception by these two characters. During their important confrontation, Cormier rapidly switches from Kate's to Miro's perspective in the same way that a film director might use "cross-cutting," a technique in which scenes from two related pieces of action are juxtaposed in quick succession to heighten the tension of the action. The effect resembles the traditional omniscience of conventional discourse. As the thoughts of both are revealed, we see-saw from one to the other. First we are invited to sympathize with Kate: "My god, Kate thought, turning away, looking at the blank taped window. . . . She did not want to see him at this moment. He had seduced her with his pathetic tale." A few lines later, we are drawn into Miro: "Miro sat in anguish, empty of words now. Anguish because he could not understand this girl. And he also wondered why he tried to understand her" (105).

At the same time, antithetical ideas juxtaposed in quick succession achieve a parallel see-sawing effect at the semantic level. Many of these antitheses pertain to the emotions: truth/flattery, pain/pleasure, casualness/embarrassment, innocence/evil, speech/silence. Indirectly, through Miro's eyes, we observe Kate torn emotionally: "A strangeness in her eyes as if in a moment she

would either burst forth with laughter or dissolve in tears" (99).
Similarly, we see Miro filtered through Kate's perception: "He
had been so open one moment and then his face had closed her
out, his eyes dropping away" (99). Because each character filters
our view of the other, the narrator seems invisible; in both these
passages, omniscience is restricted and the theme of ambiguity, of
the difficulty of understanding others, is underscored.

If chapter 6 is demarcated as the symbolic climax of the novel
by intensified use of perspectival and semantic devices, it is also
set off by change of pace. From this point on, the novel reverts to
its former pattern of slow alternation, with one or two significant
exceptions. Chapter 8, briefly, and chapter 10, more extensively,
recapitulate the cinematic cross-cutting we have seen in the sixth
chapter, to very similar effect. Cormier accelerates the alternation
of focus in Chapter 8, when Kate once more tries to reach Miro
(137). During this minor sexual encounter, when Kate again reflects on Miro being a "monster," Cormier further juxtaposes antithetical ideas. Then, shortly before Kate's death (chapter 10,
173–74), the focus slips from Kate not only to Miro but also to
the impersonal narrator. At this important moment, Miro establishes his identity and begins his incorporation into the adult
world as he sees it. Here the gun is a phallic symbol (defining
manhood as violence) that enables Miro's symbolic loss of virginity
and, he hopes, secures his recognition by the adult world of Artkin. Its use also fulfills his original purpose, "to kill the driver,"
and thus gives him singleness of identity (17).

In another framing device, shortly before and shortly after the
central confrontation in chapter 6, Cormier disregards the limits
of his own narrative technique, entering into the background and
emotions of two children on the bus. He adopts the voice first of
Raymond, then of Monique, creating symmetry centered on chapter 6 and on the opposition of the two sexes.

Genette distinguishes between perspective and voice, between
"who sees" and "who speaks." That distinction tends to be elided
by Cormier, perhaps because of his cinematic conception of narrative. During an interview with Aidan Chambers in 1979, Cormier said, "When I write I see things cinematically. I don't think
of my books as chapters, I think of them as scenes" (132). His
changes in perspective are often (if not always) marked by
changes in aspects of the narrative voice. Thus which characters

are nameless depends on the perspective of the moment. When Miro first sees Kate, she is "the girl," but when a few pages later Kate's perspective is adopted, Miro and Artkin become "the boy" and "the man." The reader, already familiar with these two characters, is redistanced by such a shift. When the narrative passes through the focus of Raymond or Monique, it momentarily becomes childlike, although still in the third person.

But voice and perspective do not consistently act in unison. They are sometimes at odds with each other, the effect of which is to unsettle the reader and further undermine the authority of the narrator. For example, in chapter 2, when Miro and Artkin are waiting for the hijacking to begin, the scene is focused through Miro: "Miro looked away, towards the jukebox where someone was studying the selections" (19). An apparently neutral perspective follows: "The restaurant was small; barely a restaurant, more like a quick-lunch diner, a place for truck drivers, transients." The immediate sequel, "Like us, Artkin said," referring to a thought apparently framed by the omniscient narrator, extends to a *character* the relationship of knowledge normally between the narrator and *reader*, and thus blurs the distinction between authorial voice and character's voice.

This passage also points to a consistent feature of characterized perspective in the novel. Cormier frequently prefaces third-person description with sentences such as "Miro looked away" (19); "Miro studied the girl now" (26); "Miro saw Artkin pondering the children" (27); "Kate turned to look at the children" (36). These passages serve to define the perspective of the description to follow. Although some of those descriptions refer to other senses, they are predominantly visual, reminding us of Cormier's comment that he is cinematically oriented. March-Penny has spoken of *The Chocolate War* as opening with a series of inter-cuts (79); and Hamilton describes Cormier's novels as "taut cinematically written tales" (8). The importance of such indications of narrative angle of vision is to indicate the relativity in this novel of characters and action. There is no independent narrator telling us what really happened; we are simply shown events from various perspectives (including the characters' views of themselves). All in all there are seven voices: the two first-person narratives, and within the neutral narrator's voice four embedded voices. Since the "bus and bridge" plot figures in the narratives of Ben and his father, some of that action is narrated from four different perspectives.

Cinematic influences are also to be found in the first-person narratives. Most significantly, at the end of the first chapter, the reader is made to feel like a voyeur: "Who the hell are you anyway, out there looking over my shoulder as I write this?" (15). This has a twofold effect—first disorienting the reader in a postmodernist manner by bringing the fictional world and the reader's world onto the same plane; and second, naturalizing a presentation of events that would require no explanation in film (Lodge 98). Just as characterization is the result of the characters' observations of each other and of themselves, the reader becomes another onlooker who, like the characters in the novel, must construct a meaning rather than absorb one that has been ready-made by the author.

A similar effect is achieved through the novel's ambivalent and cinematic treatment of time. There are two independent time sequences, and although it is logical for the later one to embody "story now," a discursive present, the "bus and bridge" plot does not exist merely as a flashback dependent on the later sequence. It seems to occur concurrently, independently, and is indeed the "story now" we are left with at the end of the novel.

Within each narrative these devices of perspective and thematic polarity create ambivalence. The perspectives of Miro and Kate overlap temporally, but there is sufficient continuity in the story they perceive for a realistic effect to be achieved. The first-person sections make use of the privilege typically afforded by first-person narrative, namely that of moving frequently between past, present, and future, sometimes in consecutive sentences (Genette 67). At the same time in both Ben's and his father's narratives, what Genette calls "the narrating instance," the time at which the narration takes place, constantly shifts. Sometimes, as in the first chapter, Ben flashes back to the "bus and bridge" plot, which is not narrated until later; hence this flashback is an anticipation, as far as the reader is concerned. Sometimes Ben narrates a very recent past distanced only by the act of narration itself (interpolated narrative). And occasionally he is narrating the present within the present (simultaneous narrative): "Those asterisks denote the passage of time. From 8:15 A.M. when I began typing this to the present moment, 10:46 A.M. Don't ask what I was doing those two and a half (more or less) hours. But I'll tell you anyway" (12).

The contrasting demands of the novel are epitomized by General Marchand's narrative, the most difficult section of the novel. Chapters 7 and 9 are primarily flashbacks and interpolated narrative, whereas chapter 11 is what might be termed "unmediated consciousness." There are no spatial or temporal indicators. This has two functions: in story terms it marks the change from obsession with time, as in Ben's narrative, to an atemporality indicative of the general's mental instability; in terms of the discourse there has ceased to be any disparity between the story and the narrating. It is little wonder that critics such as Campbell (75–76) offer two or three readings of this chapter, without the evidence for any one appearing conclusive.

Ben's diary notes referring to his asterisks and the process of his own writing bear on the reflexive quality of the novel as a whole. Genette has observed that in interior monologue, "the simultaneous operates in favour of the discourse," that is, the act of narrating itself becomes foremost. Such reflexiveness can be seen in Ben's references to his own typing, his self-conscious qualification "more or less," and his address to the reader. Throughout Ben's narrative he tries to give the impression that he is in control of the hermeneutic code—the process of revealing information—and again he is self-conscious; he is aware that he has things to reveal and allows the reader to share this understanding. For example, he raises the relevant questions in the first few pages, "The first of many questions about my presence here" (1). Then he tries to answer them by narrating the appropriate episodes from his past. Ben's self-consciousness amounts to authorial comment, in contrast to its total absence in the rest of the novel. But because the narrator here is dramatized as a character in the novel and because of the nature of his character, the reader soon comes to question his reliability. So, once again, the reader is drawn toward the act of narrating itself.

It is important that this questioning of the narrator occurs at the beginning of the novel. The reader's conscious awareness of the act of narrating prepares the disparity between first- and third-person narratives. The reader is alienated in the Brechtian sense. Cormier breaks down realistic illusion by exposing the inner mechanisms of the novel; the discontinuities of the text, so charateristic of postmodernist writing, put into question not only the individual witnesses but the very ordering of event and perception into text. These discontinuities demand that the reader

reconstitute the text into a meaningful whole and become "a pro-
ducer and not merely a consumer of text" (Barthes, *S/Z* 2.[4] In
this reconstitution the reader must negotiate a labyrinth of myriad
interdependent perspectives, voices, and representations of time.
By "reading like a writer," as Smith puts it, the reader ultimately
provides authorial commentary on the action.

The effect of this novel, therefore, is to merge the functions of
reader and writer, and consequently to make acceptable a multiplicity of readings. This is the very antithesis of the didacticism
which Thompson says leads to "the closed message rather than the
open-ended proposition." While didacticism does not "help the
young person to construct his own autonomous value base"
(Thompson 122), Cormier does foster the autonomy of his readers. He achieves this moral goal by structuring the novel so as to
require an "interrogative" style of reading (Benton and Fox
17).[5] In developing a sympathetic view of the antihero, Miro,
and taking the reader "with" him from the bridge, Cormier invites
a balanced judgment on the action. For Miro is not just the ster-
eotypically presented personification of evil; his survival is a prov-
ocation that must be justified and understood as everyone's
responsibility.

After the First Death is therefore an adolescent novel that makes
moral, affective, and intellectual demands on its readership. Because of this, it meets the adolescent's need to enter into difficult
decisions at the threshold of a new life. Cormier gives *After the
First Death* its special status by discarding the linear temporality of
the traditional children's novel in favor of complexly intersecting
narrative lines. The apparently simple alternation between plots
in even and odd chapters masks more subtle oppositions, oscillations, and transformations. As the protagonists work through internally the conflicts that they dramatize externally, polarities become ambiguous. For all the centrality of the bridge metaphor to
the conflicts of this novel, the see-saw comes to seem an even
more appropriate metaphor for Cormier's vision of adolescence.

Notes

1. It is unclear whether or not Artkin is Miro's father, but what matters is that
Miro believes he is.

2. Kate's shame that she involuntarily urinates on several occasions reveals her fear of appearing childish or out of control and her awareness of her body image. Miro refers several times to the sexuality of American girls, and elsewhere he touches the gun, which acts as a substitute for his penis. The mask expresses Miro's concern over his identity: "Without the mask, he was Miro Shantas, the boy without even a real name to identify him to the world. With the mask, he was Miro Shantas, freedom fighter. He often wondered which person he really was" (36).

3. Carlsen relates this combination of extremes to a "pseudo-myth recounted by Aristophanes in Plato's *Symposium*": the original humans were like two people joined back to back, each half having opposite characteristics from the other and together forming a perfect whole. As punishment for attacking the gods they were cut in two and henceforth each half desires only to find his or her other self in order to reestablish a whole identity. "A number of adolescent love stories unconsciously use this theme in describing male-female pairing" (60).

4. Iskander has related types of realism to the creation of an active reader; see "Readers, Realism, and Robert Cormier."

5. In support of this line of argument, David Jackson comments on the role of books like Cormier's *I Am the Cheese*: "They can mark a shift in the child from being docile in front of print to the child wanting to see herself in the new role of constructive reader and thinker" (8). According to Benton and Fox, "Broadly speaking, a distinction may be made between the "interrogative" reader and the "acquiescent" reader. The former is one who tends constantly to question the text, to predict and speculate about events and outcomes" (17).

Works Cited

Barthes, Roland. "An Introduction to the Structural Analysis of Narrative." *A Barthes Reader*. Ed. Susan Sontag. London: Cape, 1982. 251−95.
———. *S/Z*. Trans. R. Miller. New York: Hill and Wang, 1974.
———. "To Write: An Intrasitive Verb?" *The Structuralist Controversy*. Ed. R. Macksey and E. Donato. Baltimore: Johns Hopkins UP, 1972. 134−56.
Benton, Michael, and Geoff Fox. *Teaching Literature, 9−14*. Oxford: Oxford UP, 1985.
Campbell, P. J. *Presenting Robert Cormier*. Boston: Twayne, 1985.
Carlsen, Robert. *Books and the Teenage Reader*. New York: Harper and Row, 1967.
Chambers, Aidan. "An Interview with Robert Cormier." *Signal* 30 (1979): 119−32.
Cormier, Robert. *After the First Death*. London: Gollancz, 1979.
———. *The Chocolate War*. London: Gollancz, 1975.
———. *I Am the Cheese*. London: Gollancz, 1977.
Genette, Gerard. *Narrative Discourse*. Oxford: Blackwell, 1980.
Hamilton, Alex. "Profile." *Guardian*, 22 July 1979.
Hicks, Belinda. *Robert Cormier Talks about Himself and His Work*. London: Gollancz, 1979.
Iskander, Sylvia Patterson. "Readers, Realism, and Robert Cormier." *Children's Literature* 15 (1987): 7−18.
Jackson, David. *Encounters with Books*. London: Methuen, 1983.
Janeczko, Paul. "An Interview with Robert Cormier." *English Journal* 66 (Sept. 1977): 10−11.
Lodge, David. *Working with Structuralism*. London: Routledge, 1981.
Macafee, Philippa. "Robert Cormier." *English Magazine* 4 (Summer 1980): 32−33.
Macleod, Anne Scott. "Robert Cormier and the Adolescent Novel." *Children's Literature in Education* 12 (1981): 74−81.

March-Penny, Robbie. "From Hardback to Paperback—*The Chocolate War.*" *Children's Literature in Education* 9 (1978): 78–83.
Smith, Frank. "Reading like a Writer." *Language Arts* 60 (1983): 558–67.
Thompson, Susan. "Images of Adolescence." *Signal* 34 (1981): 108–23.

Springs of Hope: Recovery of Primordial Time in "Mythic" Novels for Young Readers

M. Sarah Smedman

"Everyone can tell a child's book from one for adults, just as everyone knows hot water from cold. The difficulty lies in trying to define the essential nature of the difference" (Babbitt 155). Such attempted definitions are innumerable and usually unsatisfactory, descriptive rather than prescriptive. In the ongoing critical discussion, nonetheless, one trait repeatedly cited as defining a book for young audiences is "something which turns a story ultimately toward hope rather than resignation" (Babbitt 158), something "which plant[s] the stubborn seed of hope" (Paterson, *Gates* 38).

To say that a children's novel should end with hope may sound facile. For hope is prey to distortion, even—perhaps especially—to religious distortion. True hope is not a comforting illusion, an offering of "pie in the sky," nor, as Maurice Sendak would say, "a cutesy-darling place, a little Peterpanville' (44). Rather, hope is complex in its incentive and its object. Hope can be natural or supernatural, that is, it can derive from a belief in the basic goodness of nature (physical and human) or from faith in the infinite goodness of a supreme being whose mercies transcend natural imperfections and evil. Similarly, hope can aspire to a happy life in this temporal world, or it can aspire toward a blessed afterlife in an eternal, redeemed world. Finally, hope can be religious if it reflects devotion to a divine element, areligious if it does not. Because the constituents of hope can combine in a variety of ways, Mary Lennox in Frances Hodgson Burnett's *Secret Garden*, for example, can experience a natural, religious hope and Bridie McShane in Mollie Hunter's *Sound of Chariots*, a natural, areligious hope, for happiness during their mortal lives. Mei Lin and Wang Lee in Katherine Paterson's *Rebels of the Heavenly Kingdom* feel hope that is both natural and supernatural; they look for a just and peaceable kingdom in the next world, while they strive against odds to order their lives in this world. Hope is a vital dimension of a children's book, for it recognizes, at least implicitly,

91

that readers are at the beginning of life, in crucial areas still un-committed, even to their own personalities, and that for such readers growth and change are still to come. In a fictional world which purports to appropriate the world as we know it, the reso-lution must leave scope for such growth and change. But—particularly for children, whose aspirations and ideals have not yet adapted themselves to their own talents nor to the circum-stances of this world—hope must not be a bland optimism which never knows fear, poverty, injustice, or the pain of life. In his book *Christian Hope*, John Macquarrie posits that hope without fear is as meretricious as faith without doubt (6).

The history of the concept of eschatological hope in Western culture, as traced by Jurgen Moltmann, evolves from a tension between Greek philosophy and Biblical theology. In Greek antiq-uity hope proffered neutral expectations for an afterlife, "the content of which could be pleasant or unpleasant." In subsequent Greek thought hope was "increasingly interpreted in a positive way," despite negative "undertones of uncertainty and unrest" (71). In the Christian biblical tradition, hope anticipated a beatific afterlife dependent not so much upon the actions of finite beings as upon the providence of an infinitely good God. Thomas Aqu-inas developed a theology of hope and classified it, with faith and love, as a supernatural virtue. According to Aquinas, hope is at-tained with difficulty through the action of grace upon a consent-ing will; against the dire threat of death and hell hope affirms an eternal good life, achievable only through supernatural aid. For contemporary theologian Ernst Bloch hope, natural as well as su-pernatural, is the "driving force of all human initiative," the stim-ulus to a new social order in which "peace, justice and the con-quest of suffering and death" prevail (*Das Prinzip Hoffnung*; cited in Moltmann 271 and Kerstiens 652). Ferdinand Kerstiens believes that historical Christianity has overemphasized the de-pendence of hope upon the transcendent freedom of God and that, in actuality, hope "fixes its gaze" on the future made possible by the interplay of human "freedom, responsibility, decision, [and] possible failure" with the freedom of God (654).

Superficially, all hope seems to be directed toward that time we call future. Certainly it depends upon a world view which assumes that people have freedom to shape their futures, to set goals for themselves and to take action toward the accomplishment of those goals. Unlike the determinist, the person who uses the vocabulary of hope, Macquarrie believes, sees the world as "a project of man's existence and transcendence." True hope is, therefore, rooted in the hard facts of the past and the present, but it desires to transform—not to replace nor merely rearrange, but to transform—their undesirable patterns (9–13). Such transformation demands a space of time in which to occur—a time which may not be merely linear. Macquarrie believes a self or being exists "only at the level where one can transcend the instant so as to live in a 'span' of time possible only through anticipation of the future and retention of the past" (28). This transcendent "span of time" resonates with the same timbre as Mircea Eliade's sacred or reversible time. Primordial mythic time, Eliade explains, was preceded by no other time, coming into existence all at once (*Myths, Rites, Symbols* 1:43–50). This original time, to which John the Evangelist refers as "in the beginning," is sacred because it is contemporary with creation, sanctified by the actions of the gods. Cyclical and recoverable, this eternal present, *kairos*,[1] can be periodically integrated with chronological time, *chronos*, through rituals, rites, and festivals—that is, through human repetition of primordial acts.

In cultures which take myth seriously people believe that such rituals cut through the present, enabling them to live, momentarily, beyond chronological time in primordial, sacred time. Mythic peoples perceive the power of creation in every created being; *to be* means *to be sacred*. That they might relearn the lessons of their own sacredness, people wish to move closer to the power at the center of the world. Therefore, at certain special times in solemn ritual, they imitate paradigmatic models, those actions of myth supposedly performed by the gods in primordial time, for "through each imitation, man is projected into the mythical epoch in which archetypes were first revealed" (*Eternal Return* 35).

When ritual is not imitative, it may be parodic or carnivalesque. Sacred rituals may be blasphemed, as they were in the medieval feast of fools. In both imitative and parodic rites social structures are reversed in order to create a floating world in which social categories are blurred. For instance, in the Maundy Thursday rite the priest or religious superior becomes the servant, washing the feet of others who are, symbolically at least, the poor and the downtrodden. Such role reversals during festivals—ritualized times out of time—theoretically provide participants the opportunity to rethink social and cultural structures and regain hope for the possibility of a new order (Turner 166−68, 172−99). However likely it is that participants in such rites will lapse, comfortably or uncomfortably, into traditional structures once a festival is over, the very rituals keep alive the possibility of change. The excitement of blasphemy or reversal emphasizes the importance of the systems under attack, detaches them from a background of accceptance of the status quo so that there is hope for change of structure and for their regeneration from within. Whether ritual is imitative or parodic, extraordinary time suffuses ordinary time.

A return to the moment of creation is a return to the potential of unused time. The ritual break from chronological time enables adults to free themselves from the fetters of past choices and daily circumstances and in *kairos* recover hope: hope for change or hope for a deepened understanding that transforms unchangeable circumstance. In the child, still confronted with the potency of unused time, hope has less historical actuality to overcome; the soil which nurtures hope is simultaneously purer and shallower. In this respect, as we shall see later, some juvenile novels have effects similar to those of ritual.

Many children's books which inspire hope do so, at least partially, because they create a time-out-of-time, transcending the instant and making it possible for the child protagonist and reader to live, however briefly, in that " 'span' of time" which integrates past and future in the present. Because the stories I focus on are not fantasies but "realistic" novels, their characters live in clock time, but those stories also put readers in touch with sacred time, that decisive, ontological time when, as Madeleine L'Engle says, we will be known not by "some cybernetic salad at the bottom left-hand corner of a check, or [a] social security number or [a] passport number. In *kairos* [we] will be known by [our] name[s]" (245), that is, by our "isness," our essence.

Before we turn to specific novels for young people which evoke hope by tapping sacred time, it is appropriate to remember that response to any particular work is individual, personal; this response is not only inevitable but desirable. Norman Holland speaks directly to the necessity that any integral criticism take cognizance of the transaction between the reader and the text, frankly acknowledge, accept, and use the critic's role in her own experience as well as the literary text (334). In *Patterns of Grace: Human Experience as Word of God*, Tom Driver emphasizes that any story requires its hearer (reader) to locate that story with respect to herself at the time of the hearing. Because the story unfolds in an individual's imagination, that individual must recognize its gestalt——its structured, unified whole—its shape which arises from chaos. And she must judge now whether it is a true story for her or a lie, or whether it speciously attempts to dazzle her in order to distract her from making that judgment (Driver 129, 143). Consequently, no one may assume that the books which inspire her with hope and with a reverent joy will affect every reader similarly; even myths do not speak alike to all. However, one can argue that, because certain books recover primordial time for some readers, intrinsically they have a mythic dimension.

Eliade says, "myths describe the various and sometimes dramatic breakthrough of the sacred (or the 'supernatural') into the world. It is this sudden breakthrough of the sacred that really *establishes* the World and makes it what it is today" (*Myth and Reality* 6). When we consider the similar power of the creative imagination to establish worlds, we see that literary techniques allow for patterns of reality within those fictional worlds which "wrinkle" or transcend chronological time and space. Though it is structurally easier for fantasy than for realistic novels to embody the mythic, yet, like those rituals which are imitative rather than subversive, realistic novels can in some ways more credibly involve readers in their recreation of kairos and offer a tempered hope.

Within this context, I would like to look first at *The Secret Garden*, the first book which deeply affected me with joy, hope, and a sense of transcendence. As Madelon Gohlke pointed out when she wrote from the perspective of an adult critic of her profound experience as a child with *The Secret Garden*, "powerful response to a reading, even on the part of a child, acts as a sign of engagement, or what Iser would call the reader's 'entanglement' with a text" (901).[2] I too can affirm the power of the book on the imagination of my child self. The summer I was eight I discovered the book in my grandmother's basement and for several summers thereafter made a ritual of unpacking the book from storage, rereading it, and returning it to the basement at the end of my vacation. As an adult critic I too wished to know consciously why the book so impressed me. When many years later I reread *The*

Secret Garden, recalling few of its details but vividly remembering the aura of the enclosed garden, a secret and a saving place for two abandoned children, I was able to recognize it as a story of regeneration. Rereading *The Secret Garden* now with the same satisfaction, I see that the book does indeed incorporate a ritual of status reversal, does recover Eliade's mythic time and Macquarrie's span of time. Perhaps, indeed, it is *The Secret Garden*'s retrieval of primordial time which renders it timeless: an acknowledged children's classic in continuous publication; a perennial favorite among child readers, with the power to evoke a spark, even a blaze, of emotion among adult readers when they recollect their earlier "entanglement" with the book.

Mary Lennox finds a garden, the archetypal symbol of life and growth, which has been shut up for ten years; all but dead, it is described as a world of its own: "It was the sweetest, most mysterious-looking place anyone could imagine. The high walls . . . shut it in" (76); "it was different from any other place she had ever seen in her life" (77). "Everything was strange and silent and she seemed to be hundreds of miles away from any one, but somehow she did not feel lonely at all. All that troubled her was her wish that she knew whether all the roses were dead" (79). Mary's concern for the roses is significant, for the rose traditionally symbolizes the essence of completion, consummate achievement, perfection (Cirlot 275). Discovering that "even if the roses are dead, there are other things alive," Mary, in an act of reverent recreation, kneels down and, with a sharp stick, digs and weeds, making "nice little clear places around" the "green points pushing their way through the earth. 'Now they look as if they could breathe,' she said" (79).

As the garden, including the roses, blooms, so do Mary and her frail cousin, Colin, whom Mary has unlocked as she has the garden itself. One fresh morning when Mary had "unchained and unbolted and unlocked" the door and bounded into the greening, "uncurling" world, "she clasped her hands for pure joy and . . . felt as if she must flute and sing aloud herself and knew that thrushes and robins and skylarks could not possibly help it. She ran around the shrubs and paths toward the secret garden" (154). After Colin has been introduced to the garden, "he looked so strange and different because a pink flow of color had actually crept all over him—ivory face and neck and hands and all"; " 'I shall get well!' he cried out. . . . 'And I shall live forever and ever and ever' " (112).

Mary and Colin can know on an experiential level the sacredness of such moments of being, but, as children, they cannot articulate what they feel. Therefore, the author-narrator steps in to verbalize for them and us the continuity between chronos and kairos, between profane and sacred time, between time and eternity:

> One of the strange things about living in the world is that it is only now and then one is quite sure one is going to live forever and ever. One knows it sometimes when one gets up in the tender solemn dawn-time and goes out and stands alone and throws one's head far back and looks up and up and watches the pale sky slowly changing and flushing and marvelous unknown things happening until the East almost makes one cry out and one's heart stands still at the strange unchanging majesty of the rising of the sun. . . . Then sometimes the immense quiet of the dark blue at night with millions of stars waiting and watching makes one sure; and sometimes a sound of far-off music makes it true; and sometimes a look in someone's eyes. [213–14]

Before the story is complete, the characters name the power at the center of their cosmos. In mythic cultures, to recognize, to know, the sacred power is primary. Knowledge of the power is symbolized by the ability to name it. What one can name, one has power over, for naming indicates knowledge of the essence. Mary and Colin do not call the power God; perhaps because they recognize it as "Mystery" but yet inherent in nature, they call it "Magic," and Colin plans to grow up to analyze it scientifically, to have power over it in another way. By whatever name, however, the reader recognizes the power as life transcendent and creative: "Magic is always pushing and drawing and making things out of nothing" (239). Having named the creative power, the characters perform a ritual of praise. Joining in a circle, that symbol of wholeness and of eternity, they chant a virtual Te Deum: "The sun is shining. . . . The flowers are growing—the roots are stirring. That is the Magic. Being alive is the Magic—being strong is the Magic. The magic is in me. . . . It's in everyone of us. . . . Magic! Come and help!" (242).

The book ends with the return of Mr. Craven and the recreation of at least a partial family in which the children are parents to the man. Mary's, then Colin's, discernment of the regenerative force in physical and human nature has fostered an independence which will empower them to use their awareness of "Magic," the sacred immanent in the world, to change the stunted futures which seemed to lie ahead for themselves and Mr. Craven at the beginning of the book. Through the characters, readers, too, are put in touch with kairos and recognize in themselves, no matter how weak or contrary, the potential for moving into a mode of living where they also can shape their futures toward their dreams. For the reader, as for Mary and Colin, kairos, with the changing seasons, subsumes chronos in hope.

But Mary and Colin are privileged children. The fictional world of *The Secret Garden*, unquestionably class-bound, is pastoral, portraying poverty like that of the Sowerbys as picturesque, nurturing, and compensated by common sense and love for nature, physical and human. The seemingly stable world of the book is threatened only by disease and accidental death; personal griefs are eventually overcome by discoveries within the setting of home, discoveries that generate rebirth, growth, and reunification of the family. However, contemporary novelists, haunted by the cosmic terrors of war, genocide, and the increasing prevalence of homelessness, starvation, and threat of nuclear devastation, face a real challenge in finding protected settings for the operation of sacred time in the lives of their child characters and rituals that are communal rather than exclusionary. The difficulty of that challenge may account in part for the proliferation of both fantasy—which can create new worlds that include magic midnight gardens—and works of gritty realism which end in near despair or simplistic wish fulfillment. The best of today's writers for children cannot retreat into privilege; they must deal directly with the selfishness, the squalor, the suffering, and the sorrow of the unmediated human condition. Poverty is not picturesque; war is not glamorous; death is real and not restricted to the past or to far-off lands.

Two contemporary novels which confront the horrors of modern life yet still proffer hope are Mollie Hunter's *Sound of Chariots* and Katherine Paterson's *Rebels of the Heavenly Kingdom*. Unlike *The Secret Garden*, *A Sound of Chariots* ends with the physical separation of the protagonist from her family, and *Rebels* portrays the complete destruction of the protagonists' pasts and their reclamation of the land only as a new family. Yet these books evoke in my reading self (as far as possible to be distinguished from my critical self), joy, hope, and a sense of transcendence that call forth from memory my "entanglement" with *The Secret Garden.* Consequently, my own experience as reader has been a decisive factor in the choice of Hunter's and Paterson's books as the focus of my discussion of contemporary novels which offer hope through the recovery of mythic time and through actions which have meaning as personal, if not public, ritual.

A Sound of Chariots looks frankly, almost brutally, at human vulnerability and fear, particularly the fear of one's own mortality. Bridie McShane's story, like that of Mary Lennox, is one of regeneration; but here rebirth occurs through reenactment, not of the archetype of creation, but of the archetype of sacrifice. Bridie's sacrifice incorporates the death of her father and the paradoxical separation from her mother through a grief which ought to have brought them together.

Bridie is nine years old when she loses her father, the father who had taught her by word and deed that Christ was a revolutionary and with whom she had been one in spirit from the day she was born. When Bridie comes to understand what physical death is—"eyes blind, ears stopped up, senses all swallowed up in coldness and blackness, everything ending in cold black nothing" —and the fact that she too will die, the glory of heaven, which her mother had taught her is but one short death-step away from life, grows impossibly remote to her imagination. What does become clear to her is that she is *now* alive.

> All the time that she walked she could hear a refrain beating in her mind, "*I am alive! I am alive!*" and knew without having to reason out why it should be so . . . that there was no going back now to the moment before she understood what death was and that it would happen to her. Nor did she wish to go back, for, in spite of the painful fear of death that had projected it, the miraculous sharpening of her perceptions had swung her up to a peak of exaltation beyond anything she had ever reached before. [135]

Like any of us, Bridie cannot hold on to her moment of exaltation: "Time, like a visible specter, loomed up over her then and fought on equal terms with her exaltation so that she felt her brain would burst with the pressure of the battle going on inside it" (136). Bridie becomes again an ordinary, scared little girl; she rushes home to the comforting arms of her mother but finds grief has closed them against her. "Finding her last refuge had failed her, Bridie broke down and wept too" (136). What the child has realized, what she can never unlearn, is that death sets a limit to finite life and that, "like music, life derives its meaning and beauty by working out its material in a finite, temporal pattern" (Macquarrie 19). Bridie's new awareness comprehends hope for a rewarding temporal life but has no apparent reference to a life after death; and, despite the presence of Christian allusions and motifs in her story, Bridie's own hope seems areligious and natural.

Continuously aware of "a great and terrible *something* surrounding them all" (149), Bridie is furious, not only at her father's death but at her mother's grief that "lurked in the center of all the dark and interlocking mazes that trapped her" (161). One spring day when Bridie goes to gather some early-blooming violets as a special surprise for her mother's birthday, she jumps the fence onto the flowering bank, as she has before. This time she lands in a viscous mass of lambs' tails, trimmed that morning by the shepherd. In an ensuing symbolic ritual, the child is washed in the blood of the lamb:

> She landed face down on something soft and wet and slippery that sent a pungent smell shooting up her nostrils. Her hands slithered over the wet softness as she levered herself up, opening her eyes as she did so. She was lying across a mound of something dirty-white and red. White of wool and red of blood—lambs' tails! . . . There was blood on her hands, her dress—gluey, sticky blood. Blood was stinking in her nostrils. Her face was smeared with blood.
>
> She gasped, then screamed aloud with the horror of it. . . . She writhed forward, her face slithering over the bloody tails and the gasps of revulsion choking back into her throat as she closed her lips tightly against the soft disgusting feel of them. [155]

Several psychological, pastoral, and religious motifs come together in this scene. The time is April, the season of new beginnings; through the horror, Bridie asserts life, even cruelly, by refusing any longer to be pulled down into the destructiveness of her mother's grief. The violets (whose name derives from the same Greek word as *iodine,* a tincture used for healing wounds) are never picked, and Bridie gives her mother nothing for her birthday. To consummate Bridie's bloody redemption from her mother's darkness and from her own horrific nightmares of the maimed and dying, she partakes of a symbolic eucharist: the shepherd's wife cleans her up and gives her "a bit scone" and elderberry wine, which "tasted hot and sweet with an after-bitterness" and spread a "warm glow in her chest" (159).

Never able to contemplate nor hope for eternity as Mary Lennox does, Bridie does recover times of self-transcendence in the daily world, for example, in the early morning, as she delivers newspapers:

> There was no one . . . to come between herself and the live, springing freshness of their gardens at this hour. She could stand in any one of them and stare at a leaf, a petal, a silvered snail track, the pattern of a tree against the sky, until the impression of its color and shape was so vividly imprinted on her mind that it became an integral part of her; until sometimes, by some deep magic of transference, the process was reversed and some part of herself was totally absorbed into the high point of glory on which the light and color of the morning seemed momentarily to tremble.
>
> Almost, at these moments, it seemed that Time stood still for her and she was painfully, breathlessly, on the point of escaping from the closed circle of life and death in which she knew she was caught. But the feeling of identification with something outwith and beyond her normal consciousness was too fragile in concept to be sustained by the stumbling process of her thoughts. It touched her mind only lightly, and even as she struggled to understand, it would dissolve in her grasp and leave her with only a nameless yearning for something— she could not quite remember what it had been. [169–70]

Before the end of the novel, Bridie has closed her palm gently around a luscious, sun-warmed peach and held in her hand— summer, the time of joy, ripeness, the pride of life (174–75).

The end of *A Sound of Chariots* is much less conclusive than that of *The Secret Garden*. Fourteen-year-old Bridie leaves school and home for Grannie's and her first job in Edinburgh. Dr. McIntyre, her English teacher, has helped her to understand that all people "are afraid of the passage of Time carrying them to Death," but that she, Bridie, is one of the very few in each generation who have both the "awareness of each passing moment as a fragment of the totality of Life itself" and "the talent to express their awareness in some creative form" (237). That awareness of kairos within chronos, granted to Bridie at the time of her father's death, is not an end for her; rather it is "a beginning, and in time . . . [she] will learn, [she] *must* learn, to build consciously, creatively outward from it!" For only in such creation can Bridie hope to find "the compensation for [her] loneliness of understanding" (238).

The reader last sees Bridie alone on an Edinburgh tram, traveling hopefully into her future: "No one in the street, no one in the world but Bridie McShane gripping the golden rail that steadied her at the helm of her galleon plunging through perilous seas. And in her head a poem was moving, a poem that held the sudden ghosts of roses in the grape-bloom darkness of an empty room" (242). If the prose seems a bit purple here, it is not because Hunter cannot rise above clichés but because fourteen-year-old Bridie is only just on her way toward becoming a poet and her complete, mature self. The author has taken us further than Burnett into the specific means by which Bridie will continually recover kairos in the world of chronos. All she needs: "A little light. A little time"—the words with which the novel closes. And thus, as Andrew Marvell says in the poem which inspires the title of the book, "though [she] cannot make our sun / Stand still, yet [she] will make him run."

Katherine Paterson has said that she "will not write a book that closes in despair" (*Gates* 38), for she wants young people to know that "despite all the evidence the world seeks to crush them with, there is room for hope" (*Gates* 52). Though she is distinguished by the clarity with which she confronts the evidence leading modern children to despair, each of her novels succeeds in powerfully reminding readers that indeed there is room for hope. Although we may not read them consciously alert to the interrelationships of characters' actions, archetypal models, and rituals which signify the recovery of primordial time as a wellspring of that hope, evidence comes immediately to mind: Takiko's marriage to Goro in

Of Nightingales That Weep; Kinshi's sacrifice of his hand to save Jiro's mother, Isako, in *The Master Puppeteer*; Gilly's surrender of the illusions of her mother's love and the immediate pleasure of living with Trotter; Louise Bradshaw's decision in *Jacob Have I Loved* to minister to the Appalachian ill and poor rather than to nurse an implacable self-pity. In this context, I would like to look more closely at *Rebels of the Heavenly Kingdom*, which under the guise of a story about a mid-nineteenth-century Chinese war raises such contemporary issues as religious fanaticism, poverty, racism and the breakdown of government under autocratic rulers.

On first reading, the hope offered by *Rebels'* ending seems tenuous, at best a hope against hope, though the protagonists Mei Lin and Wang Lee imitate numerous archetypal acts: rebirth through baptism, breaking of bread (here, the sharing of rice), fratricide, ritual cleansing, marriage, procreation. Wang Lee is baptized a reluctant recruit in the army of the God-worshipping Society that is fighting to overthrow the Manchu demon-rulers in order to establish a Heavenly Kingdom of Great Peace. He overcomes his repugnance to killing through repeated practice, betrays a friend who questions the morality of war, and suppresses his love for Mei Lin, as she rejects awareness of hers for him. Veritable pawns in the conduct of war, their souls have little time to catch up with their bodies. When they do, each realizes that the advocates of the Heavenly Kingdom have, in their zealotry, betrayed a fundamental principle of that kingdom: "You should not kill one innocent person or do one unrighteous act, even though it be to acquire an empire" (2). After a bloody battle in which a virtually crazed Wang Lee has senselessly murdered an infant and the mother who protected her, he retches, then, carefully removing his gun and clothing, walks into the river and stoops down: "For a while he stayed there, kneeling neck deep, clouding the water with grime and blood from his body, waiting until the current carried the defilement away. Then he put his face in. . . . He opened his eyes and looked at the shimmering stones—like the pavement of some celestial city. How easy it would be for him never to raise his face" (140). He does crawl out, to collapse, drained and reborn, on the shore. When Mei Lin rescues him, Wang Lee is almost overcome by the recognition of his love and desire for her. Conjugal love, however, is treasonous during the war; and after the war Mei Lin will be chosen to be the king's bride.

Before the love between Wang Lee and Mei Lin is consummated, minor characters, too, recapitulate primordial acts, complicating the story and becoming individuals about whom readers care deeply. Shen, the philosopher friend whom Wang Lee betrays, is a scapegoat, executed because he boldly questions the discrepancy that Mei Lin and Wang Lee have silently recognized between the precepts of the Heavenly Kingdom and the practices of its fanatic followers. In a bitterly ironic scene, reminiscent of Christ weeping over wicked Jerusalem, the warrior-goddess General San-niang, who has fought for truth, not political preferment, and so discerns the evil of war, views the destruction and numberless dead of Nanking. "And it was said that when [she] saw all that had been done for the glory of Heaven, she sat down upon the broken stones of the city wall and wept for joy" (206).

Through deceit San-niang, in reparation for her part in the war and out of love for her friend, substitutes herself in mortal sacrifice for Mei Lin and enables her to run away with Wang Lee. Then, "he gave himself to her, and it was as though they had plunged into the Son of the Ocean and washed away all the shame and suffering and death of the former days" (219). Married, they return together to Wang Lee's ancestral farm, whose fields have stood bare since the opening of the novel, "a great angry wound upon the flesh of the earth" (4). Although his parents have disappeared without a trace, the seed rice his father had hidden behind the fifth brick in the northeast wall of the family's hut is still there, a promise of future healing. The epilogue of *Rebels* tells us, with the taut, emotionally charged restraint characteristic of the novel, that in the ensuing ten years, the couple have two daughters and two sons and await their fifth child; they do not bind their daughters' feet; they teach the girls, as well as their sons, to read. They cultivate the fields, having begun with the seed rice, in its stead sealing behind the fifth brick San-niang's parting gift to Mei Lin, a crucifix of the Jesus People. The family lives quietly, but the Heavenly Kingdom of Great Peace endures "only as a promise sealed in a wall. Someday, perhaps, we shall take root in the earth" (227).

Paterson has interwoven fiction and historical fact in a story which recreates the past, applies to the present, and has implications for the future. The ending of *Rebels* alleviates little of the pain of the book's previous pages, for although the story takes place in nineteenth-century China, it is a graphic portrayal of frightening aspects of our contemporary world; its penultimate sentence is as true today as then—as it is at almost any period in history: "We knew the Heavenly Precepts, but we chose a different path; so the Mandate of Heaven was taken from us" (227). Despite the characters' mythic actions, they cannot prevail over the chaos wrought by religious and political zealots: their only victory is survival and the remembrance of a kairos mediated to them through experience of human love and human sacrifice. However, in their corner of the world, they have through deliberate, responsible choices achieved a time of new beginnings, created a place of fruition and social well-being, and retained, albeit buried, a promise for the future. In this novel Paterson faces sadly but squarely the selfishness, the greed, the hypocrisy of human kind; she depicts neither a heaven on earth nor a redemption of chronos through artistic creation. She does, in the face of heavy odds, cling to belief in the power of the humble, loving few to recover sacred time in the events of their lives and to the slim but strong hope that through cooperation with a supernatural though hidden power, those few may begin afresh, co-creating a world of justice, equality, and peace. Through the interplay of natural and supernatural hope, her characters, and those readers disposed to comprehend it, discover "the strength to hold out even in the profoundest darkness, without despairing or giving up" (Kerstiens 654).

Perhaps only those willing to accept a religious perspective will interpret the books discussed here—and such others as Esther Forbes's *Johnny Tremain*, Sue Ellen Bridgers's *Home before Dark*, Madeleine L'Engle's *Ring of Endless Light*, and Cynthia Voigt's *Dicey's Song*—as hopeful because they successfully reintegrate chronological with sacred time. For as Eliade points out, the repetition of ritual acts emptied of religious content necessarily leads to pessimism: "When it is no longer a vehicle for reintegrating a primordial situation, and hence for recovering the mysterious presence of Gods, that is, when it is desacralized, cyclic time becomes terrifying; it is seen as a circle forever turning on itself, repeating itself to infinity" (*Myths, Rites, Symbols* 1:35).

Stories are not rituals, but they do provide the foundation from which rituals arise; as acts of naming experience, stories express in a different mode the truths that actual rituals attempt to express dynamically. As festival days give way to mundane routine, adumbrations of kairos in a novel must vanish into chronological time at the conclusion, for the novel's very existence is based upon linear reading time. The momentary vision of kairos cannot be forced or prolonged at the expense of daily life, nor must it be abandoned in bitterness; like the readers entangled with the text, the characters by implication get on with living, affected by their insights but circumscribed by the limitations of human beings and the probabilities of their respective worlds.

Those select children's books which may contextually be called "mythic" novels provide occasion for a reintegration of body, mind, and spirit that rekindles hope for personal and societal transcendence. If children weep when they read these books which strengthen hope, "the advocate of the immense openness of the promised future amid the reality of . . . history" (Kerstiens 654), their tears are for the joy of hope as well as sorrow for its fragility.

Notes

1. The Greeks have two words for time: *chronos* for measured clock time and *kairos* for that decisive, ontological time, "primordial" time. The Greek dictionary also tells us that *kairos* may be construed as "a long space of time"; thus, it is frequently translated as "eternity." In his discussion of the relationship between hope and time, Macquarrie argues that *eternity* does not connote "sheer timelessness": "it admits a before and after, but not a no-longer or a not-yet." He cites as support Boethius's definition of *eternity*: "the whole, simultaneous and complete fruition of life without bounds" (Macquarrie 23–24).

2. Gohlke ascribes the intensity of her engagement with *The Secret Garden* to the sudden death of her father and her own protracted bout with rheumatic fever. Since I was a healthy child and did not lose to death even a grandparent until I was seventeen, my experience with Burnett's novel, if not emotionally distinct from Gohlke's response, certainly derived from different aspects of the book. This essay explains, in Gohlke's terms, the recovery of my younger self.

Works Cited

Babbitt, Natalie. "Happy Endings? Of Course, and Also Joy." *Children and Literature: Views and Reviews*. Ed. Virginia Haviland. Glenview: Scott, 1973. 155–59.
Bridgers, Sue Ellen. *Home before Dark*. New York: Knopf, 1976.
Burnett, Frances Hodgson. *The Secret Garden*. 1911. New York: Dell, 1981.
Cirlot, J. E. *A Dictionary of Symbols*. 2d ed. Trans. Jack Sage. New York: Philosophical Library, 1971.
Driver, Tom. *Patterns of Grace: Human Experience as Word of God*. New York: Harper, 1977.

Eliade, Mircea. *Myth and Reality*. Trans. Willard R. Trask. World Perspectives 31. New York: Harper, 1963.

———. *The Myth of the Eternal Return*. Trans. Willard R. Trask. Bollingen Series 46. Princeton: Princeton UP, 1965.

———. *Myths, Rites, Symbols: A Mircea Eliade Reader*. Ed. Wendell C. Beane and William G. Doty. 2 vols. New York: Harper, 1975.

Forbes, Esther. *Johnny Tremain*. Boston: Houghton, 1943.

Gohlke, Madelon. "Re-reading *The Secret Garden*." *College English* 41 (1980): 894–902.

Holland, Norman. "Transactive Criticism: Recreation through Identity." *Criticism* 18 (1976): 334–52.

Hunter, Mollie. *A Sound of Chariots*. New York: Harper, 1972.

Kerstiens, Ferdinand. "Hope." *Encyclopedia of Theology: The Concise Sacramentum Mundi*. Ed. Karl Rahner. New York: Crossroads, 1984. 650–55.

L'Engle, Madeleine. *A Circle of Quiet*. The Crosswicks Journal 1. New York: Seabury, 1979.

———. *A Ring of Endless Light*. New York: Farrar, 1980.

Macquarrie, John. *Christian Hope*. New York: Seabury, 1978.

Moltmann, Jurgen. "Hope." *Westminster Dictionary of Christian Theology*. Ed. Alan Richardson and John Bowden. Philadelphia: Westminster Press, 1983. 270–72.

Paterson, Katherine. *Gates of Excellence*. New York: Elsevier/Nelson, 1981.

———. *The Great Gilly Hopkins*. New York: Crowell, 1978.

———. *Jacob Have I Loved*. New York: Crowell, 1980.

———. *The Master Puppeteer*. New York: Crowell, 1975.

———. *Of Nightingales That Weep*. New York: Crowell, 1974.

———. *Rebels of the Heavenly Kingdom*. New York: Dutton, 1983.

Sendak, Maurice, with Virginia Haviland. "Questions to an Artist Who Is Also an Author." *The Openhearted Audience*. Ed. Virginia Haviland. Washington: Library of Congress, 1980.

Thomas Aquinas. *The Summa Theologica*. Tr. Fathers of the English Dominican Province. 18 vols. London: Burns Oates & Washbourne, 1916. Vol. 2, part 2, questions 17–22.

Turner, Victor. *The Ritual Process: Structure and Anti-Structure*. Ithaca: Cornell UP, 1977.

Voigt, Cynthia. *Dicey's Song*. New York: Atheneum, 1983.

Happy Families Are All Invented: Randall Jarrell's Fiction for Children

Richard Flynn

Introducing Christina Stead's novel *The Man Who Loved Children* (1965), Randall Jarrell indirectly reveals the familial theme that links his children's books to his other late work.[1] He formulates there the tragic consequences of individual development for the original childhood experience of the family as a "composite entity." Furthermore, he links the pattern to a theory of language, in which "baby talk" is the primal—largely lost—language uniting all people and all tongues:

> A man on a park bench has a lonely final look as if to say: "Reduce humanity to its ultimate particles and you end here: beyond this single separate being you cannot go." But if you look back at his life you cannot help seeing that he is separated off, not separate—is a later, singular stage of an earlier plural being. All the tongues of men were baby talk to begin with: go back far enough and which of us knew where he ended and Mother and Father and Brother and Sister began? The singular subject in its objective universe has evolved from that original composite entity—half subjective, half objective, having its own ways and laws, its own life and death— the family. [*Third Book of Criticism* 3]

Childhood, this idealist passage argues, permits us as members of a pre-Oedipal family to experience "plural being," an organic unity that, according to Jarrell, breaks up in the process of individual development.

Undoubtedly Jarrell's view of childhood was informed by extensive reading in psychology and psychoanalysis. A psychology major at Vanderbilt, he considered Freud one of his heroes, as Mary Jarrell states in her 1971 introduction to *Jerome*. Freud's theory in "Family Romances" that the child imagines a family was, as we shall see, central for Jarrell. In addition, Mrs. Jarrell has noted that he was interested in Piaget, whose theory of an infantile perception of unity between subject and object is reflected in Jarrell's

109

introduction to Stead's novel. She adds that Jarrell's interest in actual children seemed almost "clinical" (personal interview, 12 June 1984).

Jarrell's view of childhood was influenced also by his own experience, first as a child who lost his father and lived with his mother and younger brother, Charles, with whom he did not get along, then as an adult who never had a child of his own. Jarrell himself insisted on the importance of his childhood in a broken family. Writing to Amy Breyer de Blasio, his first love, he thought their different childhoods might explain their estrangement: "It's all true about growing up—you'd lived at home, in one place, in the middle of the Biggest Family in the World, and never been alone at all. I've lived all over, and always been separated from at least half of a very small family, and been alone as children ever are" (*Letters* 60). Mary Jarrell says she "never got the impression that Jarrell's childhood was miserable" but adds that when they first met Randall said to her, "Oh, my family's a disaster" (interview). Jarrell wished he had belonged to a big happy family. He often expressed a wish to be adopted, but the closest he came in his own childhood to having a family with which he could be satisfied was the period he spent with his paternal grandparents and great-grandmother, a period that became the subject of "The Lost World." This extraordinary, elderly family must have fostered his acute sensitivity to aging and death. Paradoxically, writing for children served to reinforce this apprehensiveness about aging. In 1962 he wrote to Robert Lowell, "I feel pretty young myself but I admit there're two houses near whose children call, 'Santa Claus! Hi Santa Claus!' " (*Letters* 457).[2]

Jarrell himself was childless and seems to have experienced difficulty adjusting to the fully formed family he joined in 1952 when he married his second wife, Mary, who already had two daughters, Alleyne and Beatrice. Mrs. Jarrell stated, "Randall was more of a playmate than a father to my daughters" (interview). Suzanne Ferguson speculates that he was disappointed that "there was no little boy, no second self" (letter to Richard Flynn, 12 February 1986). Indeed, Jarrell's preoccupation with the relationship between the child and a natural or created family became an obsession in his later work, and nowhere is this obsession more pronounced than in his writing for children, begun in 1961 when he was forty-seven years old.

In the past, critics of Jarrell's children's books have tended to stress the theme of the child's estrangement from and nostalgia for the family. Maurice Sendak, for example, has observed: "I know how desperately Randall needed a family. That's the whole message of everything he wrote—this incredible need for a family" (quoted by Griswold, forthcoming). The topic is most fully developed in Jerome Griswold's interpretation of the children's books in light of "separation anxiety." In Griswold's view, the master plot of these stories is the male child's quest to regain his mother's affection, an Oedipal quest.[3] Among the other critics who touch briefly on this topic, Leo Zanderer traces in three Jarrell books the child as "explorer or seeker," whose heroic journey helps the reader overcome "the image of man fatally anchored to his role in society" (78). And John Updike, who lists Jarrell's "habitual themes of individual lostness, of estrangement within a family, of the magic of language, of the wild beauty beyond our habitations," notes briefly but tellingly, "Jarrell's vision of bliss [is] adoption by members of another species" (59).

As against the regressive movement Griswold observes, Updike's comments suggest a creative, outward-bound quest for family. Yet that substitute family is not the adult, sexual relationship one might expect. As Roger Sale points out in *Fairy Tales and After*, Jarrell wishes to write about a mythical family in which familial affection is separate from sexual affection (88). This essay will develop the insights of Updike and Sale in order to explain not only the narrative structures of these stories but also the telltale points at which Jarrell's obsession created aesthetic difficulties for him.

One reason that the theme of family acquired such resonance in Jarrell's oeuvre is that he fused his theory of child development with a theory of poetic development. His preoccupation with childhood found significant expression not only in his decision to experiment with children as an audience but in his theory of poetic voice. Significantly, his theory of the audience and of the poet stresses a "composite entity" of the adult and the child. The ideal audience for children's books, Jarrell was to say many times in interviews and letters, was not exclusively an audience of children. Rather, he liked to think of his stories as "half for children, half for grown-ups" (Mary Jarrell, Liner notes).

Similarly, Jarrell perceived the poet as someone who is a "once a child," in the phrase from his translation of "The Grown-Up" by

Rilke (*Complete Poems* 239). The child, Jarrell believed, has already the spirit of a poet, though he cannot articulate this spirit in poetry. For Jarrell, as for Wordsworth in *The Prelude*,[4] the success of the adult poet is contingent on his or her ability to retain or recapture the poetic spirit of childhood and to articulate it. Without recourse to that spirit, the poet is unable to create poetry as distinguished from mere "verse." Echoing the Scriptures, Jarrell says in *A Sad Heart at the Supermarket*, "unless ye be converted and become as little children, ye shall not enter into the kingdom of art" (95). To be sure, Jarrell insists not that one should become a child, but rather that one should become "as a child," retaining contact with the childhood that was "once." Like Wordsworth, Jarrell sees poetry as a dialogue between the primary, nature-connected spirit of childhood and the mature, expressive powers of man. Though the "lost world" of childhood and the world of maturity conflict, the aim of the poet is not to escape from the adult world into the "lost world," like Peter Pan, but to transform the world of maturity imaginatively.

Jarrell rebels against the Edwardian cult of the child as innocent. His vision of childhood includes Wordsworthian "fear" and the violence of the Brothers Grimm and Rilke: children's lives are "full of sorcerers and ogres" (*Complete Poems* 106), images of darkness that equal those of adult fantasy. His training in psychology led him to observe the darker aspects of a child's animism in a 1935 letter to Robert Penn Warren:

> I've had to interrupt this letter for an hour to play with a three year old boy that visited us. He was very interesting telling about the dark man, and the rain man, and the thunder man. They live above the clouds, in the sky, with God; God makes them do what they do. The dark man is all covered with dark, the thunderman with thunder. The dark man doesn't live in the sun, but along with the rest of them. He got me to draw him a picture of the dark man. The dark man looks exactly the same as he does, except he is grown up. At night after he goes to sleep he thinks about the dark man; he doesn't play in his dreams or do anything except think about the dark man. [*Letters* 3]

The natural world is not innocent but "charged" by the child's dreams of his hidden self. Similarly, the family is not only a natural but also an imaginative construct, perhaps the first instance of the child's poetic activity.

Jarrell found his way to the full expression of these themes gradually, at first adopting other writers' plots as they seemed to fit his needs, then elaborating his own. The plot of *The Gingerbread Rabbit* (1964), Jarrell's first original book for children, followed his translations of the tales of Grimm and Ludwig Bechstein, and it is a curious amalgam of the plots of the traditional tale "The Gingerbread Man" and Margery Williams's *Velveteen Rabbit*; even Garth Williams's illustrations for Jarrell's book recall those of William Nicholson in *The Velveteen Rabbit*. The sentimental theme of Jarrell's story is the same as that of *The Velveteen Rabbit*: a man-made rabbit escapes destruction by an adult and, by being loved, becomes "real." In *The Gingerbread Rabbit*, a mother makes a gingerbread rabbit for her daughter to replace a real rabbit that has run away into the forest. In the midst of her baking, she is distracted by a vegetable man, and the gingerbread rabbit comes to life, runs away, is deceived and nearly eaten by a fox, but escapes with a real rabbit who takes him home to his wife and adopts him.

Jarrell's own unstable family may be reflected in the human family of *The Gingerbread Rabbit*, which consists of a mother and her only child, Mary, who live in lonely isolation on the edge of the forest. Though Mary's father is mentioned, he is conspicuously absent from the story, just as Jarrell's father was absent in his youth. The mother in the story seems a "near relation" of the speaker of "Next Day" (*Complete Poems* 279–80). She is nervous, harried, and lonely—a characterization reinforced by Garth Williams's illustrations. This mother is always having to make the best of bad situations; she is forced to accept substitutes as a matter of course, and the rabbit himself is a substitute for the real rabbit that will not be there when her daughter gets home from school. From our adult perspective the mother seems above all distracted. Indeed, it is when she is distracted by the vegetable man that the gingerbread protagonist comes to life. From the gingerbread rabbit's perspective we see the mother's latent violence: in a comical conversation with a paring knife, a mixing bowl, and a rolling pin, he discovers that his fate is to be cooked and eaten. He has no sympathy for his sad creator, whom he sees as a pursuing giant.

The gingerbread rabbit is a true innocent, and as such he is much less interesting than the later protagonists; he seems to possess the child's ignorance and gullibility without any serious indication of the child's potential. The real loss experienced by the child Mary finds no expression. Furthermore, the evocation of family values in the rabbit warren after the gingerbread rabbit has been adopted by a pair of real rabbits seems reductively materialistic; the warren offers "carrots and watercress" and "this nice rushy bed" (42–43). Emotional ties and needs remain undeveloped, as do the risks of pain involved in human relationships. In contrast with later created families, the rabbit family into which the gingerbread rabbit stumbles seems not only fictional but unbelievable.

And yet adoption is the heart of the matter for Jarrell.[5] Commenting to Michael di Capua, Jarrell expresses his pleasure with the illustrations by Garth Williams: "The old rabbit in the colored sketch makes me want to be adopted by him" (*Letters* 464). As one of the notes in the manuscript of *The Gingerbread Rabbit* stresses: "FAMILY ROMANCE / parents not real parents." In the gingerbread rabbit's quest for freedom we may see an embodiment of that Freudian "family romance" whose expression Jarrell so admired in Kipling (*Sad Heart* 137). Significantly, Freud theorizes that the child comes to terms with the apparent hostility of the parents by splitting them into good and evil pairs, a pattern we see here in the opposed human and animal families of Jarrell's gingerbread child. Even more important, according to Freud the child copes with evident signs of parental weakness by fantasies about "true" parents. In fantasy, the child invents a story of adoption; he seeks "the replacement of both parents or of the father alone by grander people . . . equipped with attributes that are derived entirely from real recollections of the actual and humble ones" (240). In a remark that must have been seminal for Jarrell, Freud observes that this "romancing," normal among children, may continue for certain adults: "a quite peculiarly marked imaginative activity is one of the essential characteristics of neurotics and also of all comparatively gifted people" (240). Jarrell will take this point further, metaphorically tying the adoption fantasies of the child to the imaginative activity of the artist. Families are works of art just as poems are, and because they are works of art, they can be successfully created only by someone who retains the Rilkean sense of being "once a child"—the mature artist drawing on the poetic spirit of childhood and articulating it.

If *The Gingerbread Rabbit* through its inherited narrative structure lays its main stress on flight from the threatening parent (since the rabbit family is discovered only by accident), *Fly by Night* (1976)[6] stresses the quest, the lonely child's turn to fantasy to invent a family. These two books represent two poles in Jarrell's central theme, as outlined in "An Unread Book" (*Third Book of Criticism* 3−5). On the one hand, the child attempts to define himself or herself as an individual—"a single, separate being"; on the other, he or she seeks to become a member of a community or "plural being," a family.

The protagonist of *Fly by Night*, David, seems very close to the speaker of Jarrell's best poems about lonely children, such as "A Sick Child," "A Story," or "The Elementary Scene." David also resembles the Jarrell of "The Lost World" when he grieves to leave his tree house for reality: "He sits in it so much that the sparrows are used to him, and light just out of reach in the branches" (*Fly by Night* 4). Also like Jarrell, his playmates are animals—"there aren't any children for him to play with" (4). He has an occasional conversation with the mailman, reminiscent of "A Sick Child," but for the most part his daytime existence is mundane and very lonely. But "at night David can fly" (4).

David's flight takes him through the house, where he sees his parents' dreams without really understanding them, and through the night, where he sees the disturbing dreams of his pets, who dream of their prey.[7] As he continues his journey, different animals such as sheep and ponies elude him, until at last an owl invites him to become "An owl till morning" (18). David watches the owl feed her owlets in a scene reminiscent of the cardinal scene in *The Bat-Poet*, and he finally hears her tell them "The Owl's Bedtime Story." "The Owl's Bedtime Story" (written in terza rima like "The Lost World") both reassures David about the value of familial affection and reminds him of what he lacks—the company of other children.

As always, Jarrell's fictional world is populated with only children and incomplete families. At the end of the bedtime story, the mother owl and both her children nestle together, but the children have no father. David sees how affectionate they are despite their father's absence, and it helps him come to terms with his own family, without siblings and distanced from his father. David's subconscious both removes his father, who has removed himself from David's lonely daytime world, and gives him the siblings he longs to have.

Ultimately, *Fly by Night* may disconcert by its apparent pessimism, for it does not resolve David's daytime problems. David wakes up and as usual he forgets his dream; he is able only to fly by night. The dream world is ambiguous. Is it a retreat? Or as the site of dream-work, does it represent the function of imaginative retelling and the child's own quest to realize new values?

As *Fly by Night* suggests, there is a nocturnal side to the child's quest, the darker aspect of the romance Jarrell noticed in Freud, in the Märchen, and in Kipling: "The world [is] a dark forest full of families: so that when your father and mother leave you in the forest to die, the wolves that come to eat you are always Father Wolf and Mother Wolf, your real father and real mother, and you are—as not even the little wolves ever quite are—their real son" (*Sad Heart* 137). Kipling's identification of the adoptive family with wild animals clearly touched Jarrell's imagination. Autonomy and abandonment, adoption and devouring envelopment define the quandary of the child.

A family cannot become a true one until it is affirmed by choice—the sense Jarrell's boy protagonists must gain is not only that they are wanted but that their own choices matter too. Both poets and children, these boys want to have it both ways—they want to be original and highly individual while at the same time they want to be accepted by society. But their quest for acceptance by society in real life is doomed; as Jarrell notes in "Poets, Critics and Readers," "The public has an unusual relationship to the poet; it doesn't even know he is there" (*Sad Heart* 90).

It is this difficult task of creating a chosen relationship, of establishing a poetic family, that shapes the narrative of *The Bat-Poet* (1964) and *The Animal Family* (1965). The Bat-Poet is an extraordinarily talented prodigy—one of the "Children who are different" (manuscript, Jarrell's translation of Rilke's "Childhood," University of North Carolina at Greensboro). His quest is both a child's quest and Jarrell's quest, in that it combines a need for an understanding family with the need for an audience. The end of the story hints at success but remains ambiguous, for the public says to the unique lyrics of the poet what the bats say to the Bat-Poet: "When you say things like that, we don't know what you mean."

The Bat-Poet differs from the other bats: "a little bright brown bat, the color of coffee with cream in it" (1). Because he is a poet, he is estranged from a society he longs desperately to be a part of; he wants above all to say his poems to the other bats, but they are unwilling to listen to him. Like Jarrell, the Bat-Poet sees that society has "taken away his audience," and he seeks out the audiences of poets of other species (The Mockingbird) and of naïfs (the Chipmunk); but in truth the only audience that the bat cares deeply about is the audience of his fellow bats. When he finds an attentive audience in the chipmunk, the bat mimics the mockingbird by saying, "It's a pleasure to say a poem to—to such a responsive audience" (17−18), yet he mimics not only the mockingbird's words but his insincerity as well. For the bat wants more than a superficially "responsive" audience; he wants an audience that will be truly appreciative of his poems—in short, a community or family. Poetry, to the bat, is an exchange like the purest kind of chosen familial affection.

In *The Bat-Poet*, the development of the poet echoes the development of a child. When the other bats move into the barn, away from the comfortable home of the porch rafters, he wants them to come back but somehow feels that he cannot join them in the barn. Like a child growing up, he has a sense of being separate from the family and a sense that he is powerless to remedy this; able to become an artist only because he is an outcast, he still has a profound desire to be a part of the group if he can do it without sacrificing his autonomy. So he begins to be a poet by adopting a mentor and by imitation. The transformation from imitator to creator involves a crisis of self-recognition similar to those described in Rilke's "The Grown-Up" and "Childhood."

The uneasiness that the bat feels when he tries to write about the cardinal might well be attributed to the repressed memories of his own childhood. He notices that the cardinal feeds his children even though they are old enough to feed themselves.[8] The bat is not fully conscious of the loss of his own family, but it disturbs him so much that he cannot write about the cardinal. This intimation of his need for family combined with his growing dissatisfaction with imitation keeps the bat from writing another vivid but

superficial "portrait in verse" like "The Chipmunk's Day."[9] Instead, the bat needs to escape the influence of his mentor, the
mockingbird.

In "The Mockingbird," the bat recognizes that the mockingbird's song, though it is a convincing imitation of life, is not life
itself. The bat admires the mockingbird, who is unquestionably a
real poet and a mentor, as Tate and Ransom were to Jarrell, but
he comes to see that his art is mostly artifice, and his criticism
pedantic. The mockingbird imitates what he drives away: he is
more interested in imitation than in life. He may be able to imitate
the world so well that one cannot tell "Which one's the mockingbird? Which one's the world?" but it is only "for a moment, in the
moonlight." Rather than imitate a world he drives away, the Bat-
Poet wants to make poems that will reconcile him with the world,
particularly with the world of the other bats who will reconstitute
his family.

By becoming a poet, the Bat overcomes his wish to remain a
child at all costs, but he does not forget his childhood; rather he
taps its poetic resources and through the mature, articulate means
of the adult artist, transforms them into poetry. With the creation
of his last and best poem he finally becomes a "once a child"—an
adult who is able to use successfully the promise of childhood, not
with a false nostalgia but with an ability to remember its true nature. The poem "Bats" when it comes, comes easily: "all he had to
do was remember what it had been like and every once in a while
put in a rhyme" (35). First he is able to write a poem that the
other bats will be able to understand, and then he finds his own
style as a poet. The poem marks his emergence from his
apprenticeship.

By remembering "what it is like to be a child" without reverting
to infancy, the Bat-Poet is able to rejoin the others, to snuggle
closer to them as the mother "folds her wings about her sleeping
child." By becoming a "once a child," the Bat-Poet successfully
becomes both a poet and an adult. He can leave his childhood
home, confront the loss of his mother and father, and join his
new family. It is significant that Jarrell concludes *The Bat-Poet* ambiguously. The Bat-Poet does not get to say his poem to the other
bats, an ending which may indicate the vanishing and fragile nature of the fictional family; it is important that the Bat-Poet adopt

the family of bats on faith, a faith that transforms a vanishing fiction into a sustaining one.

Like *The Bat-Poet, The Animal Family* is about making a family as a poet makes a poem. But the major difference between *The Animal Family* and Jarrell's other children's fiction is that it does not have a child or childlike protagonist. Furthermore, *The Animal Family* transcends its precursor text, as the weaker books do not. Roger Sale has pointed out that Jarrell's family romance is influenced by Hans Christian Andersen's "Little Mermaid," and Jarrell's familiarity with Andersen's story is clear from the poem "A Soul":

> It is evening. One bat dances
> Alone, where there were swallows.
> The waterlilies are shadowed
> With cattails, the cattails with willows.
>
> The moon sets; after a little
> The reeds sigh from the shore.
> Then silence. There is a whisper,
> "Thou art here once more."
>
> In the castle someone is singing.
> "Thou art warm and dry as the sun."
> You whisper, and laugh with joy.
> "Yes, here is one,
>
> "Here is the other .... *Legs* ...
> And they move so?"
> I stroke the scales of your breast, and answer:
> "Yes, as you know."
>
> But you murmur, "How many years
> Thou hast wandered there above!
> Many times I had thought thee lost
> Forever, my poor love.
>
> "How many years, how many years
> Thou hast wandered in air, thin air!
> Many times I had thought thee lost,
> My poor soul, forever." [*Complete Poems* 73]

In *The Animal Family*, the hunter shares the Bat-Poet's feeling that "the trouble isn't making poems, the trouble's finding somebody that will listen to them." The hunter is in harmony with nature, but he is also alone with nature. His land is a magical and beautiful one, but he has no one with whom to share it:

> In spring the meadow that ran down from the cliff to the beach was all foam-white and sea-blue with flowers; the hunter looked at it and it was beautiful. But when he came home there was no one to tell what he had seen—and if he picked the flowers and brought them home in his hands, there was no one to give them to. And when at evening, past the dark blue shape of a far-off island, the sun sank under the edge of the sea like a red world vanishing, the hunter saw it all, but there was no one to tell what he had seen. [8]

It is apparent from the beginning that the hunter lacks more than an audience. His loneliness is profound; what he misses is a family—not just a mother, as has been suggested, but a complete family consisting of father and mother and child. In his dreams, the hunter remembers his lost family. He lies in his bed listening "to the great soft sound the waves made over and over. It seemed to him that it was like his mother singing. And before he could remember that his father and mother were dead and that he lived there all alone, he had drifted off to sleep—and in his sleep his mother sat by the bed singing, and his father sat at the fireplace waxing his bowstring or mending his long white arrows." (7–8). One senses, reading this passage, the same nostalgia Jarrell evokes in "Children's Arms"; the hunter's father reminds one of "Pop" who helps the young Jarrell fashion "The bow that only Odysseus can wield." The hunter longs for an end to his isolation, for companionship, and for the security of domestic routine—the "ways that habit itself makes holy"—but, of course, his parents are dead, the past is only a dream. Drawn by the sound of the sea that reminds him of his mother, he courts and wins a mermaid who, unable to accept the sea-people's dictum that "all good comes from the sea," is attracted to the land because "the land is new." If the land is new to the mermaid, the mermaid is new to the hunter, and together they begin to invent a family.

Like Jarrell, the hunter has an intense need for a family. After he and the mermaid have "lived together a long time" this need pervades his dreams. His earlier, wistful dream of domestic security is transformed into a nightmare of a broken, incomplete family, a shadow of a family because it is childless. The hunter has lost his childhood because he has lost his parents, and, because he is not a parent himself, the loss of childhood amounts to a loss of self:

> "My father was standing by the fire and he was double, like a man and his shadow—I was his shadow. And my mother sat there singing, and she was double too, like a woman and her shadow; and when I looked at it you were her shadow. But when I looked over to where I used to lie on the floor by the fire, there was nothing, not even a shadow; the place was empty. And the empty place got dark, and the fire went out, and I woke." [59−60]

" 'It's a bad dream,' " the mermaid says, though she knows it is a dream the hunter cannot help dreaming, and she proceeds to interpret the dream as the hunter's wish for a child.

But, since there are "no human beings from whom they could beg or borrow or steal a child" they experiment, like the Bat-Poet, and adopt animal children. First they take in a bear whose mother the hunter has killed and then a lynx the hunter steals from his mother. Though they are quite fond of their animal children, the hunter and the mermaid quickly recognize that the bear and the lynx are not really "boys": the lynx grows to be unmanageable and is unavoidably feline, and having a bear who sleeps all winter is like having "Sleeping Beauty for a pet" (85). Finally a boy, the only child who is not ill-gotten, is washed ashore in the arms of his dead mother. In fact, the hunter is not the agent of the boy's joining the family at all; the boy is discovered by the lynx and brought back by the lynx and the bear. But it is clear from the moment of the boy's arrival that he is much more than a pet. He is a real child:

> The mermaid said: "I never knew what it was like when you lived here with your mother and father, I never had seen a little one. He's half like a little man and half—oh, *different!* His arms and legs are so short and white and his head's different—look how soft his hair and skin are! He looks all helpless and not finished yet. He's so new!" [142−43]

After he finds out that the boy's mother is dead, the hunter realizes that with the addition of this real child his family is complete: "He smoothed the boy's hair with his big hand and left; when he came home, hours after, his face looked absent and remembering, as if he were back with his own mother and father" (144).

With the boy's arrival, the hunter and the mermaid finally have a family they can believe in: "In a little while they forgot that they had ever lived without the boy." If they are ever reminded about their real and sometimes painful pasts, they need only look at the boy to remind themselves of their sustaining fiction of family. The hunter helps his son to make his own "children's arms," and the mermaid teaches him to tell stories in a voice that sounds "like one of the sea people" (155). The boy accepts his new family as a child too young to remember does: "Except for one or two confused, uneasy dreams, all the boy's memories were memories of the mermaid and the hunter; he *knew* that the hunter was his father and the mermaid his mother and had always been" (156–57). The fictional family that the hunter and the mermaid have created for him is one which he does not question (162). The hunter and mermaid, however, can remember having been unhappy, and they are reminded from time to time of their lonely lives before they created their family. The mermaid is fully aware of the costs involved in belonging to a family, and she articulates them in a very moving passage: "They don't know how to be bored or miserable. One day is one wave, and the next day the next, for the sea people—and whether they're glad or whether they're sorry, the sea washes it away. When my sister died, the next day I'd forgotten and was happy. But if you died, if he died, my heart would break" (170).

With this assertion, the mermaid becomes the clear heroine of *The Animal Family*, because she chooses the land in all its heartbreaking difference from the sea. Like the Bat-Poet, she is able, through poetry, to create the supreme fiction of family. With her family complete, she begins "to talk, and to talk, and to talk as she had never talked before" (165). To the boy, she becomes the highest sort of poet, the storyteller whose fictions are essential to the boy's existence—"there was nothing he liked better than the mermaid's stories" (174). The animal family itself is the mermaid's fiction, a saving one.

The land is better for the mermaid because she is able to have a family, able to experience the possibility of heartbreak. And there appear to be hints that separation looms in the future; the boy is beginning to yearn for the sea just as the mermaid once yearned for the land. Though the hunter and the mermaid tell him that the lynx found him, he "knows" that it's not true. He thinks that the story is part of an amusing game, and soon the hunter and the mermaid come to believe it's a game too. At the end of the book, the roles of parent and child are curiously reversed: the boy tells the truth, "The lynx found me," believing it to be a lie, and the hunter and mermaid tell a lie, "We've had you always," believing it to be the truth.

Randall Jarrell's children's fictions, especially *The Animal Family*, help the reader to understand his relationship to that "original composite entity," the family. Although they are "family romances," they transcend simple wish fulfillment in that they emphasize the making or invention of that family on the part of its members. We have no choice about the family we are born into, and yet we are not mere victims of circumstance. We must participate actively in making and defining a place for ourselves in that entity by understanding its peculiar jurisprudence and by understanding that it is a fragile but vital fiction, if we are not to be "separated off." *The Animal Family* and *The Bat-Poet* provide arguments for the usefulness of fiction in helping us make our place both in our particular family "with its own ways and laws" and in the larger community of men, women, and children. Even as we acknowledge that belonging to a family or community is difficult and involves compromise, we see the value of faith in a controlling, supreme fiction. The wish embodied in the epigraph to *The Animal Family*, "Say what you like, but such things do happen—not often but they happen," is a wish but not "a blind wish . . . / What the wish wants to see, it sees" (*Complete Poems* 335). While he acknowledges the value of wishes in his children's fiction, Jarrell also argues that mere wishes are not enough; we must make something out of our wishes, as a child makes a family, as a poet makes a poem.

Notes

I would like to thank Emilie Mills and the staff of Special Collections, Walter Clinton Jackson Library, The University of North Carolina at Greensboro, for their assistance. In addition, I would like to thank Mary Jarrell, Judith Plotz, Suzanne

Ferguson, and Jerry Griswold for reading the manuscript of this article at various stages.

1. "An Unread Book," reprinted in *Third Book of Criticism* 3–5. For an exploration of the theme of family in the later poetry, see my article "Randall Jarrell's Lost World of Childhood," forthcoming from the Institute for Southern Studies, and my dissertation, "Randall Jarrell and the Lost World of Childhood," George Washington University (1987).

2. Writing for children also lent a new vitality to all of Jarrell's work. From 1962 to 1964 he wrote with manic intensity, assembling an anthology of modern poetry, finishing his translations of *The Three Sisters* and *Faust, Part I*, writing most of the poems for *The Lost World*, and the four children's books. Manuscripts of *The Gingerbread Rabbit* and *The Animal Family* held by the Berg Collection in the New York Public Library contain drafts of poems that were later to appear in *The Lost World* and explicit statements about the importance of happy families being adoptive ones.

3. Griswold's study is particularly good in describing the conversation between the texts and the illustrations.

4. Jarrell quotes the infant babe passage of *The Prelude*, ironically, in "A Sad Heart at the Supermarket" (*Sad Heart* 67). Mary Jarrell has also said that Jarrell spoke of writing a long piece on *The Prelude* before his death (personal interview, 12 June 1984).

5. In Jarrell's only novel for adults, *Pictures from an Institution*, the adoption motif also figures prominently in the improbable, invented family of the Rosenbaums and Constance. I have explored this theme at length in my dissertation (see note 1).

6. Though not published until 1976, *Fly by Night* is Jarrell's penultimate children's book, not his last. The reason for the long delay may be partially explained by Sendak's difficulty in illustrating the book. Griswold gives an excellent account of this difficulty.

7. David's dog is named Reddy, which was the name of Jarrell's pet rabbit whose death the child fears in "The Lost World." Curiously, Jarrell here gives the name to a dog and has him dream that he has killed a rabbit. The image of a loved one killing animals is prevalent in the poetry. One reason for its recurrence in Jarrell's work, perhaps, is that his grandmother did have his rabbit killed, a fact of which Jarrell was aware as his mother later told him about it (interview with Mary Jarrell, 12 June 1984).

8. It seems to me significant that the cardinal is a father. One may convincingly speculate that the bat is disturbed by seeing a nurturing father, something he seems not to have had himself.

9. "The Chipmunk's Day" is the only poem from *The Bat-Poet* that Jarrell chose to exclude from *The Lost World*, and it is clearly the least interesting of the bat's poems.

Works Cited

Freud, Sigmund. "Family Romances." *Standard Edition of the Complete Psychological Works of Sigmund Freud.* Trans. James Strachey. Vol. 9. London: Hogarth, 1959. 237–41.

Grisworld, Jerome Joseph. *The Children's Books of Randall Jarrell.* Athens: U Georgia P, 1988.

Jarrell, Mary. Introduction to *Jerome: The Biography of a Poem*, by Randall Jarrell. New York: Grossman, 1971.

————. Liner notes to *The Bat-Poet: Read by the Author,* by Randall Jarrell. New York: Caedmon Cassette CDL 51364, 1972.

Jarrell, Randall. *The Animal Family.* Illus. Maurice Sendak. New York: Pantheon, 1965

————. *The Bat-Poet.* Illus. Maurice Sendak. New York: Macmillan, 1964.

————. *The Complete Poems.* New York: Farrar, 1969.

————. *Fly by Night.* Illus. Maurice Sendak. New York Farrar, 1976.

————. *The Gingerbread Rabbit.* Illus. Garth Williams. New York: Macmillan, 1964.

————. *The Golden Bird and Other Fairy Tales from the Brothers Grimm.* New York: Macmillan, 1962.

————. *Kipling, Auden & Co.* New York: Farrar, 1981.

————. *Letters: An Autobiographical and Literary Selection.* Ed. Mary Jarrell. Boston: Houghton, 1985.

————. *The Lost World.* New York: Macmillan, 1965.

————. *Pictures from an Institution.* New York: Knopf, 1954.

————. *Poetry and the Age.* New York: Knopf, 1953.

————. *The Rabbit Catcher and Other Tales of Ludwig Bechstein.* New York: Macmillan, 1962.

————. *A Sad Heart at the Supermarket.* New York: Atheneum, 1962.

————. *The Third Book of Criticism.* New York: Farrar, 1969.

Sale, Roger. *Fairy Tales and After: From Snow White to E. B. White.* Cambridge: Harvard UP, 1978.

Updike, John, Review of *Fly by Night,* by Randall Jarrell, *New York Times Book Review,* 14 Nov. 1976. Reprinted in *Critical Essays on Randall Jarrell.* Ed. Suzanne Ferguson. Boston: G.K. Hall, 1983. 57–60.

Williams, Margery. *The Velveteen Rabbit.* Illus. William Nicholson. Garden City: Doubleday, n.d.

Zanderer, Leo. "Randall Jarrell: About and For Children." *The Lion and the Unicorn* 2 (Spring 1978): 73–93.

The Wind in the Willows *and the Plotting of Contrast*

Michael Mendelson

All readers or listeners know that there are really two stories in *The Wind in the Willows*: that of the madcap, adventurous Toad the Gaol-breaker; and that of friendship, home life, and the simple joys of "messing about in boats," the story of Mole, Rat, and Badger. The story of Toad-of-the-Highways is centrifugal, an outgoing, Odyssean song of the open road; the other is centripetal, a riverbank idyll of domestic, pastoral pleasure. And because the values of the dusty road and the riverbank seem so opposed, readers naturally tend to align themselves with one of these stories at the expense of the other.

Roger Sale, for example, has a distinct predilection for the homely adventures of the River Bank; for him, the book as a whole is " 'about' coziness," while Toad belongs "over to one side" (174, 185). William W. Robson also finds the finest insights in the friendship of Rat and Mole, with the Toad chapters playing "a scherzo in the symphony" of quiet domestic life (98). And Humphrey Carpenter, though he grants that Toad "has a certain energy," maintains that the idiom of adventure was not the author's forte and that Toad lies outside the "heart of Grahame's Arcadian dream" (*Gardens* 154, 161). Such priorities were not, of course, shared by the work's first audience, Alistair Grahame, who responded enthusiastically to his father's original stories in which "Toad played the principal part" (Carpenter and Prichard, *Oxford Companion* 573).[1] Most other child readers remain devoted to the Toad, as we may deduce from adaptations of Grahame's story: A. A. Milne's unifocal dramatization of the story in "Toad of Toad Hall"; the 1949 Disney film, which claims that for children Toad is "the most fabulous character in English literature"; and more recently, the Nederlander Theater's production, promoted with buttons that read "I Toad You So."[2]

This split between child and adult sensibility, between what Geraldine Poss calls the mock-heroic and arcadian impulses within the text, has itself been the focus of considerable criticism.[3]

Peter Green was perhaps the first to refer to the "double theme" of the book (*Grahame* 202), while Carpenter asserts that "there are really two separate books" (*Gardens* 229n). Peter Hunt has taken this position to its logical end, arguing that "if there are two texts in *The Wind in the Willows*," they are structurally autonomous: "Mole's serious story once resolved, we can go on to Toad's more farcical one" (116).[4] Criticism, then, has tended to separate the two stories, as if the contrasting impulses that motivate the narrative action operated independently. I will argue, however, that the clash between two such natural instincts as domesticity and romantic enthusiasm generates the special richness of the text as a whole. Instead of separating the two stories and devaluing one, I examine how Grahame not only juxtaposes but interlaces his two different plots and values.

The question of narrative structure becomes all the more provocative when we remember that the oscillation between the two stories resulted from careful engineering. Peter Green has argued plausibly that Grahame composed the Toad sequence first, the episodes of the River Bank and the Wild Wood second, and the two set pieces, "The Piper at the Gates of Dawn" and "Wayfarers All," last (*Beyond the Wild Wood*, chap. 11). In the final 1908 copy, however, Grahame steadily alternated between the stories of the open road and those of the woodlands, an alternation that I will argue functions as a narrative dialectic between the "contrary states" of individualistic hedonism and communal affection.[5] As the plot progresses, Grahame advances ever more subtle variations of this dialectical argument. It is my intention, then, to explore Grahame's dialectic by paying close attention to the plotting of the work (the narrative order in which the simple chronology of the two stories is rearranged) and especially to the relation between adjoining chapters and groups of chapters.[6] This method should clarify embedded contrasts and parallels that require the reader to activate their meaning by filling in lines of connection only suggested by the text. Ultimately, this formal, comparative effort will clarify the structural subtlety and interdependence of the two contrasting stories and states.

The first two chapters of the book can be read as companion pieces that illustrate Grahame's comparative method of plotting. In both we find what myth critics refer to as "the call to adventure" (Campbell 49−58). In the first chapter, Mole is busy with spring cleaning at Mole End, deep in the earth, when the call of "something up above" overpowers his commitment to routine and regularity and draws him up into a pastoral world filled with "the joy of living and the delight of spring without cleaning" (2). In this mock-heroic episode of rebirth or "emancipation," the humble hero, "bewitched" by the "imperious" call of nature, happily subordinates mundane responsibility to the pleasure principle.[7] The Mole, then, is the first character to express the romantic, centrifugal pole of Grahame's dialectic. Once emancipated, however, Mole is quickly "absorbed" by the aimless, epicurean life of the River Bank, enjoying the domestic bounty of the Water Rat's picnic. But the idyll is threatened by the sense of intoxication that such pleasure engenders. On his way back from the picnic with Ratty, Mole impetuously grabs the oars and overturns the little scull, almost losing the beautiful picnic basket in the bargain. This scene echoes an earlier incident in which the Rat, waxing rhapsodic, steers the boat into a bank, causing "the joyous oarsman" to flip onto his back in the bottom of the boat, "his heels in the air" (5). By such repetitions and parallels Grahame stresses the nature of his contrary states.[8]

Along the River Bank, however, a sense of moderation and community tempers the excesses of individual adventure, so that the Mole quickly recognizes his mistake and apologizes for his "foolishness and ungrateful conduct" (15). In this world, passion is no excuse for incivility. The threat posed by excess finds additional, emblematic expression in a small vignette characteristic of Grahame's technique. Just after the narrator has introduced the Toad as a rower "splashing badly, and rolling a good deal," we glimpse "an errant May-fly [swerving] unsteadily athwart the current in the intoxicated fashion affected by the young bloods of May-flies seeing life" (12). In the next sentence, the fly is eaten and disappears without comment by the narrator, and we are left to contemplate the relation between this event and the activities of our other intoxicated adventurers. The same technique on the macroscopic level juxtaposes chapters and blocks of chapters to dramatize contraries. Once the initial sense of "divine discontent and longing" in chapter 1 is reinforced by the related impulse toward the open road in chapter 2, the note of concern sounded in the mayfly incident will become considerably more significant.

In "The Open Road," Toad expresses the same longing for adventure, for "travel, change, interest, excitement!" (22), that animated Mole in the first chapter. But the impulse that is controllable in the Mole is excessive in the Toad, as indicated by a change in the means of adventure and emancipation. Mole gives himself up to the spirit of the season and "the joy of running water" (16), both of which bring him into closer contact with nature. But for Toad, boating has become a "silly, boyish amusement" (22), the river "dull" and "fusty" (23). His boats hung up in a deserted boathouse, he now longs for "the dusty highway" and the chance to see "camps, villages, towns, cities!" (22). The desire for adventure may be the same, but the path that desire takes in Mole and Toad is perilously different. As Mole and Rat arrive at Toad Hall, their host easily convinces them to join him in a gypsy caravan in pursuit of the "Life Adventurous" (24). The trio soon meets disaster "fleet and unforeseen . . . disaster momentous" (27); once again, impetuosity capsizes its victims. In chapter 1, when Mole grabs the oars of the scull, Rat cries, "Stop it, you silly ass . . . You'll have us over" (14), and the damp, repentant Mole quickly acknowledges, "Indeed I have been a complete ass, and I know it" (15). By contrast, when the Toad sits overturned in the road, "spellbound," it is the Mole who says, "O stop being an ass, Toad" (29). The "crazed" Toad can only dream of renewed risks "on my reckless way" (30). By changing the initial order of composition and placing Mole's springtime adventure of emancipation first, Grahame establishes a dominant mood of temperate indulgence alongside of which the overheated, midsummer's extravagance of the Toad, while charming, seems nonetheless an aberrant response to the call.

Kenneth Burke writes of the "categorical expectations" with which we approach literary form, and which lead us to expect, for example, Pope's couplets to rhyme and epics to begin with an invocation (126–27; see also Philip Stevick). In extended narrative, our expectations are in part chronological; we ask "What happens next?" And when, in a work as lovingly devoted to natural processes as *The Wind in the Willows*, we skip in chapter 3 from midsummer to the depth of winter, we reasonably ask why. The answer, of course, is that while nature may be sequential, art is patterned and thematic. We skip seasons here in order to develop through the Mole the temperate chord of natural instinct rather than the discord of extravagant impulse. The break in our chronological expectations draws our attention to contrast and helps us distinguish between the Toad's summertime intoxication and the Mole's natural desire to explore. Even more important, the shift from summer to winter announces a transition to the text's second movement, a block of three chapters (3−5) that introduces the other pole of Grahame's dialectic, the homing instinct. Devoting an extended sequence to the River Bank friends at this early point in the action effectively links the reader's angle of vision to the Mole's-eye-view and to the powerful claims of home and community. Toad's subsequent adventures may be diverting, even enthralling, but to the reader alert to the thematic resonance that formal juxtaposition can create, they will also seem exorbitant, even "crazed," the escapades of a charming but "silly ass."

This second movement begins with a shift in attention from the gregarious, exhibitionistic Toad to the reserved yet hospitable Mr. Badger. It also begins with repetitions of formal motifs from the two previous chapters: as in chapter 1, the Mole is seized by the impulse to explore, and as in chapter 2, he is excited by the desire "to make the acquaintance of" a new friend (cf. 18, 33). Unlike his springtime excursion, however, Mole's adventure here is not seasonal; for in winter the dominant animal activities are sleep and story-telling. That Mole breaks this natural pattern may explain his eventual difficulties. In the barren winter landscape, Mole initially believes that "he had never seen so far and so intimately into the heart of things" (35). Here is the crystallizing vision of the romantic adventurer, or so we briefly think; but just as Toad's lark on the open road led to unforeseen danger, Mole's excursion soon leads him to "the Terror of the Wild Wood" (38). And just as he and Rat had to rescue the crazed Toad in chapter 2, the Rat must rescue Mole here. This third parallel narrative reinforces a pattern of impulse/adventure/calamity/rescue. Cumulatively such repetitions force our recognition of what we might call the wages of adventure: its tendency toward calamity and the absolute dependence of the impulsive upon the aid of their friends. The Mole's excursion into the Wild Wood is distinct in that it is solitary and thus more intense than its predecessors. A winter's tale in darkening tones, it makes the contrary state, the snug hospitality of the Badger's den, all the more satisfying and meaningful. At this moment, when the two storm-driven friends find safe anchorage with Badger, Grahame's dialectical narrative swings decisively from the call of adventure to the lure of home.

At the Badger's (and later at Mole End), the movement "up and outward" reverses to a centripetal drive: the lure of the burrow.[9] The seasonal changes of the River Bank and the dust of the highway yield to the permanence and warmth of the underground haven. Generically, ironic romance turns to low-mimetic comedy. In a counterpoint to the adventurous values of the first two chapters, Mr. Badger's home offers the very security and tranquility that adventure undermines—a place "to eat and talk and smoke in comfort and contentment" (51). In a characteristic parallel, Grahame introduces two young hedgehogs who, like Rat and Mole, have also been lost in the snow and who also happen across Mr. Badger's back door. The repetition emphasizes the never-ending need for domestic security, and the enduring shelter of home.

For the Mole, the "domestic architecture" of the Badger's home has special psychological significance. Like Badger, "an underground animal by birth and breeding" (55), the Mole immediately responds to the Badger's domain: "once you're underground, you know exactly where you are. . . . You're entirely your own master" (60). The self-containment and domestic virtues glorified here look forward to the pleasures of the Hobbit-hole; for just as the quiet stability of domestic life nourishes the mild heroism of Tolkien's epic, so does the insulated, centered existence in the burrows of the Wild Wood allow Mole and Badger, like Bilbo and Frodo, to develop the reserves necessary to redeem their world from threat.[10] Returning home, the Mole clearly recognizes that he is by nature an animal of confined spaces: "For others the asperities, the stubborn endurance, or the clash of actual conflict. . . . He must be wise, must keep to the pleasant places in which his lines were laid and which held adventure enough, in their way, to last for a lifetime" (65). In light of the battle for Toad Hall, this is not, of course, the last word on Mole's abilities; but we realize the appropriateness of Mole's recognition at this point because the new ethic has been juxtaposed so dramatically against its counterpart.

Whereas the relation between preceding chapters has been one of contrast, the winter journey of chapter 5 intensifies the ideas of chapters 3 and 4. Although there is a temporal break between

"Mr. Badger" and "Dulce Domum," the same animals reenact a snowbound journey that again climaxes with the unexpected discovery of safety. In this parallel narrative, Grahame corroborates the power of the homing instinct and the satisfactions of the "magic circle." Moreover, since the journey is one of return, not departure (as in "The Wild Wood"), and since the place the travelers return to is not just a friendly haven (like the Badger's) but Mole's own home, the instincts on display are all the stronger. The chapter begins with the two friends, Rat and Mole, coming across a village. Unlike the Toad, Rat and Mole "did not hold with villages, and their own highways . . . took an independent course" (81). Still, they happen to pass a cottage, and in a well-known vignette, Grahame shows us the two looking in on "the little curtained world" of a bird cage from which "the sense of home" pulsates (69). This episode forms a counterpoint to Ratty's earlier rescue of an overturned bird cage and "its hysterical occupant" from the demolished caravan (30). Through this reference to an earlier image, Grahame fills out the differences between the homing instinct and its opposite. However, repetition rather than contrast is the dominant note here, as once again the Mole stumbles across a safe haven; once inside all is warmth, dryness, full larders, and merry friendship; instead of hedgehogs, there is a choir of field mice; and instead of Badger, the Rat now plays the gracious "general" (84). The effect of this parallelism is to enhance the potency of the countertheme, a theme repeated because the lure of home is less dramatic than the call of the Life Adventurous. Through such formal emphases, Grahame shifts the weight of his argument from "fresh and captivating experiences" (72) toward "that small inquiring something which all animals carry inside them" and which inevitably leads home (68). Formal arrangement thereby continues to orient our allegiances.

T. S. Eliot writes that "home is where one starts from," and with "Dulce Domum" we return to Mole's home, the starting point of these adventures and the close of the narrative's second movement. To recapitulate the progress so far: the first movement shows the up-and-down curve of the Life Adventurous (chaps. 1 and 2). The outward drive of these chapters is natural, but it can also be unpredictable and even disastrous. When the drive recurs in chapter 3, a new theme is added: beyond the calamity and exhaustion of adventure lies the contrasting attraction of home.

Chapter 3, therefore, functions as a narrative link between the two sets of chapters (1 and 2, 3 through 5) as it begins with adventure but ends with the exhausted friends on the doorstep of "the contrary state." Instead of the up-and-down swing of the first movement, the second set of chapters moves out and back, as the Mole sets out from one home, rests at another, and returns in the end to his own. The initial sense of adventure is decisively offset by a repeated emphasis on the appeal of home (70). Having introduced the theme and countertheme in these first two movements, Grahame next refines and expands that dialectic through a series of ever more distinct juxtapositions. In the next four chapters, from "Mr. Toad" through "Wayfarers All," he explores the conflict that the romantic impulse to explore and the instinctual need for the magic circle can create within his characters, most of whom quite naturally long for both. Here again, the formal juxtaposition of individual chapters articulates a complex debate. By alternating allegiances Grahame allows his contrary states to interact and reverberate without destroying either the gentle humor of his book or the balance of his argument.

We return to Grahame's formal strategy of contrast in the adventure of "Mr. Toad" (chap. 6), which deals not with the discovery but with the escape from home. It is summer again (the season of the Toad), and Badger arrives to take Toad "in hand." Mole chimes in that "we'll teach him to be a sensible Toad" (88), indicating that as a result of his own experience, Mole is a thorough convert to common sense and domestic practicality. Badger's position is that "independence is all very well, but we animals never allow our friends to make fools of themselves beyond a certain limit" (91), a limit the Toad has reached. However well-intentioned, this point of view is restrictive, even despotic; it casts Toad in the role of the recalcitrant adolescent and invites us to contemplate the potential tyranny of parental, communal strictures. The Mole goes so far as to assert that his friend will be "the most converted Toad that ever was before we're done with him" (88). As a result, we are partly in sympathy with the Toad's resistance when the friends set themselves up as a tribunal to defend the norm in opposition to individual expression. Ignoring his friends' concern, escaping by a rope of knotted sheets, and "marching off light-heartedly" (98), Toad is at this point the champion of freedom and the willingness to venture forth.

Within moments, however, the narrator establishes the dangers of Toad's rebelliousness. Unlike Mole in "Dulce Domum," who struggles to subordinate his own longing for home to his loyalty to Rat, when Toad sees the motorcar, he immediately surrenders to "the old passion." As a result, he is transformed into "Toad the terror, the traffic queller, the lord of the lone trail, before whom all must give way or be smitten into nothingness and everlasting night" (101). The hedonistic egocentrism of this role represents the dialectical extreme of adventurism: Toad is "fulfilling his instincts, living his hour, reckless of what may come" (101), which turns out to be a sentence of twenty years in jail. Our recognition of Grahame's indictment of the Toad's excess is in part obscured by all the fun along the way and by the inevitability of his escape. Yet as the entire chapter swings back and forth between exuberance and despair, we realize that Toad's irrepressibility has become a form of enslavement, not an expression of freedom.

The transition from chapter 6 to "The Piper" could hardly be more jarring: we go directly from Toad's confinement in the "grimmest dungeon" in the "innermost keep" of the "stoutest castle" in England (104) to the Mole languorously stretched out on the riverbank in the "blessed coolness" of midsummer's eve (105). Even more important, we shift from the Toad's isolation to an all-encompassing network of mutual aid.[11] Such implicit contrasts require the reader as intermediary to bring the two stories into meaningful interplay.[12] "The Piper" also provides the first significant indication that the domestic and romantic impulses can be resolved.[13] This act of accommodation begins as Rat and Mole go out in search of Portly, the son of Otter, who is always getting lost because "he's so adventurous" (107). Again a desertion from the magic circle leads to a rescue. In the process, however, an ordinary event becomes an extraordinary one: the two rescuers become entranced and transported, emotions that chapters 1 and 2 connected with the excitement of adventure. Yet adventure here is of a different kind, for Pan, the source of their excitement, has revealed himself to them "in their helping" (116).

The desire to help may not seem a spectacular virtue, but for Grahame its power resides in its ability to harmonize the contraries: to put adventure (the willingness to " 'do' something," as the Mole has it [108]) at the service of friends and family. This blend of opposite instincts produces what Ratty calls "this new divine thing" (111), powerful yet affectionate, ordinary yet awesome. Indeed the whole chapter provides supporting analogies to this fusion of contraries: the epiphany takes place on a small island, which mingles the important images of river and earth; it happens in the "imminent dawn," which brings together night and day; it is presided over by Pan, the satyr, who is both man and beast; it engenders a state between dreaming and intense wakefulness; and the experience itself, says Ratty, is "something very exciting . . . yet nothing in particular has happened" (118). Only when individual power and friendly helping coincide does such fusion take place; and yet, as we now begin to realize, such moments occupy central positions in this narrative, as when the well-armed Rat rescues Mole from the snowdrift or when the friends join together for the siege of Toad Hall. This episode, when the Rat and Mole are vouchsafed their vision of " 'power at the helping hour' " (119), marks the essential moment in Grahame's narrative argument when friendship, home, and helping take on some of the allure of romantic individualism, and when we as readers become alert to the middle ground in Grahame's dialectic.

When we turn from Pan to "Toad's Adventures," we again switch "stories" and move back from the pastoral idyll to the sirens' song of adventure. Grahame, however, continues to explore the middle ground; for if in "The Piper" helping becomes heroic, in chapter 8 heroism needs and elicits a good deal of friendly help. Throughout these adventures, the Toad entertains by his machinations, but he is not quite the Toad of "surpassing cleverness" (133) he takes himself to be. By contrast with the reverence of "The Piper," the playful irony deflates and amuses. Most thoroughly deflated is the "handsome, popular, successful Toad," who on closer inspection betrays the "horrid, proud, ungrateful animal" (126) the gaoler's daughter accuses him of being. Yet Toad, despite his mock-heroic escapades, is constantly in need of help—first from the gaoler's daughter, then from the washerwoman, and finally from the train engineer, who says to Toad, "you are evidently in sore trouble and distress, so I will not desert you" (135). In this narrative world, adventure most often leads to "trouble and distress" and adventurers like Toad or Portly invariably depend on the quiet, domestic types to rescue them. This chapter, then, is an ironic complement to its predecessor, and it expands our notion of "helping" as a bridge between the contraries.

And yet, in the dialectical progress of Grahame's argument, no synthesis is permanent. Our emotions and instincts are seasonal, subject to "the other call" (144) that in its own time is as "imperious" as the community of friends. No chapter expresses this emotional mutability more poignantly than "Wayfarers All." Once again, a total break shifts the action from the Toad alone, cold, and hungry to the Rat strolling through "late-summer's pomp" (139) among his many friends preparing to migrate. Though he protests that he cannot understand how the swallows can leave "your friends who will miss you and your snug homes that you have just settled into" (142), he too begins to feel "that chord hitherto dormant and unsuspected . . . this wild new sensation" (143). He is musing on "the wondrous world . . . and the fortunes and adventures . . . out there beyond" (145) when he encounters his cousin, the seafaring rat. This jaunty mariner praises the domestic bliss of the woodland life; but, like Tennyson's Ulysses, he is now leaving it because he has had his own call, heard his own "wind in the willows" and is heading out on the road to "his heart's desire" (147). His stories make the Water Rat feel the "somewhat narrow and circumscribed" (148) nature of the riverbank; they ask us to reconsider our estimation of "the best life" (147). Despite all the trouble upon the open road, the call to adventure still intoxicates. Like the Mole before him, Rat can feel that impulse so contradictory to his essential nature, and he almost capitulates—until, that is, Mole wrestles him to the ground, talks to him of the "hearty joys" of home life, and the spell is broken. Our comparative method suggests that this episode is especially significant because it happens to the Rat. For shortly before, the Rat heard most clearly the "glad pipings" of Pan and concluded that this melody and its inscrutable message was "the real, the unmistakable thing" (119). On this later day and in this different season, Rat decides that, like his friends the swallows, his own blood now dances to different music (144). Pan's gift of forgetfulness may explain the Rat's present temptation; nonetheless, after the break of only a single chapter, we find the Rat not only "restless" (139) but actually distressed with the boundaries of his own life. This polarity of supreme satisfaction on the one hand and querulous discontent on the other suggests that despite the hint of accommodation in chapter 7, the contraries continue to make their antithetical claims on our allegiance. And indeed, Grahame argues through the dialectical structure of his plot that both calls must be recognized in their "due season" (144).

Ratty's temptation and the migration of the swallows appear just at a time when the Toad's profligacy might incline us to see the call to adventure as vain and injurious; their instincts lead us to recognize just how imperious that call can be. Similar impulses call the Mole, lure the baby otter, and claim the helpless Toad. Repetition again deepens and universalizes our understanding. Nevertheless, the allure of this drive is affected substantially by the fact that its most attractive presentation (in "Wayfarers All") is bracketed by the excesses of Toad's own adventures. This compromise results from a deliberate artistic choice on Grahame's part: not only is "Wayfarers All" interjected into the chronological order of Toad's adventures, but its late-summer setting, as opposed to the early-summer date of Toad's travels (162), also breaks the seasonal rhythm and specifically directs our attention to the shift in narrative focus. We are led once again by form to reflect upon the synchronic relationships of the plot as opposed to the linearity of the simple story; we are led, that is, to recognize the interplay between the "two stories" and the need for compromise.

The return to Toad's adventures in chapter 10 marks a transition to the fourth and last cycle of the tale, which focuses primarily on the Toad, making this section (chaps. 10–12) the companion piece to the earlier focus on the Mole (chaps. 3–5). In spite of the title "Further Adventures," the narrative motive here is no longer the expansive, explorative impulse of Toad's earlier forays; instead, the centripetal motive to return home dominates. Narrative juxtaposition suggests a comparison between Rat's spell, which is severe but temporary and which he effectively sublimates, and the manic oscillations of the Toad, who exhibits a hysterical instability totally alien to the seasonal, temperate impulses that affect the swallows, the Sea Rat, and the Mole. One moment Toad is fearless, confident, Odyssean in his resourcefulness; the next he is "sinking down in a shabby, miserable heap" (177). This careening back and forth between vanity ("the cleverest animal in the world" [175]) and self-deprecation ("what a conceited ass I am! What a conceited, heedless ass!" [181]) exhibits more than just the comic fluctuations of a flimflammer on the loose. Unlike Rat's response to the universality of the call to adventure, which is essentially in tune with the seasonal change around him, Toad's mercurial oscillations show the romantic iconoclast reaping the harvest of his lack of orientation. The vehicles of adventure in chapter 10 (a boat, a caravan, and a motorcar) repeat those of chapters 1 and 2, a parallel suggesting that Toad is still caught up in the same round of excesses (224). The schizophrenic adventurer can only hope that (like Mole, or Portly, or Rat before him) he will be rescued from himself. It is Grahame's ultimate irony (and insight) that this rescue and the Toad's redemption are the heroic work of those who have chosen to remain at home.

With Toad's rescue by Rat (at the opening of chapter 11) the two stories finally dovetail. Indeed, Grahame connects the stories of Toad and Mole through an explicit repetition of wording: when Mole meets Ratty in chapter 1, he notices first "a dark hole" with a "twinkle" in its depths, then a "brown little face," "grave" and "round," with "neat ears and thick silky hair"; "it was the Water Rat!" (4). Toad's rescue by Rat in chapter 11 recapitulates every detail of the original scene, in the original order and almost in the original language (183). Grahame in this way insists upon the parallel: Toad is welcomed back into the family of friends in the same way that Mole was introduced to the "splendid spaces" of the River Bank by the Rat; only Mole was coming out, while the Toad is going back. After this introductory allusion to the text's own opening, the two stories continue to coalesce, as the reunited friends resolve to retake Toad Hall from the weasels and stoats, a consolidating motive that will call up heroic adventurism in the service of the pastoral home.

But before this final, unifying siege, a polite though significant skirmish between Rat and Toad contrasts the two world views they represent. In authority throughout the beginning of "Summer Tempests," the Rat adheres to his position with much greater constancy than he did in chapter 2, when Toad proposed the adventure of the gypsy cart. The returning Toad repeatedly tries to inflate himself by narrating his exploits, while Rat answers him first with "gravity and firmness" and then with a detailed indictment of his foolishness. In response, Toad continues to wax and wane between the extremes of "puffing and swelling" and disin-

genuous apology. Still unable to control his impetuosity, he runs
off to see Toad Hall for himself and narrowly misses being shot.
Moments later, in another ill-conceived plan, he succeeds in sinking Ratty's favorite boat. This time the Rat strictly censures him,
most specifically for the anticommunal sin of ingratitude. This episode finally brings the two contrary states into direct and
extended debate; what before had been presented as a series of
alternations between chapters and subtle variations in the dialectical presentation of the contrary states is now a gentlemanly but
direct confrontation. Toad's utter inability to recognize his own
behavior as disastrous suggests that for Grahame romance and
impetuosity make an unending series of claims on common sense,
and that impulse always whispers "mutinously" in one's inner ear
(188). The chapter resolves the debate by making Toad the subordinate member of the cast of heroes, a role that indicates the ultimate place of volatile impulse in Grahame's scheme of values.

Toad's contribution to this scheme should not, however, be totally dismissed. For when the ever-sympathetic Mole finally allows
Toad to boast of his adventures and relate much that belonged
"more properly to the category of what-might-have-happened,"
the narrator adds, "and why should [such stories] not be truly
ours, as much as the somewhat inadequate things that really come
off" (206). As a purely imaginative mode, the longing for adventure and the vision of what-might-be can be both compensatory
(as is the case with Rat the poet and, we suspect, with Grahame
the banker) and inspiring.[14] Certainly Toad's adventures have
their effect on the Mole; for this most domestic of animals proves
capable now of the highly imaginative scheme of dressing himself
in the washerwoman's outfit and reconnoitering among the stoats
on sentry at Toad Hall. Whereas Toad chafed in egotistical shame
at having to wear such a costume, Mole assumes the disguise effectively because his motives are not self-serving. Naturally, the
success of Mole's exploit drives the Toad "wild with jealousy"
(205); but we may plausibly assume that Toad is the model for
Mole's adventure. Imagination and derring-do in fact have a place
in the life of the River Bank as long as they do not threaten the
communal order of things. Once again, then, in the dialectical
interplay of the contrary states there are really no absolutes; Toad
can be "the best of animals" (19) and the Rat possessed by wan-
derlust. The fact, however, that the Mole could prove both clever

and courageous goes an especially long way toward correcting our conventional view of the domestic, pastoral life by suggesting that there is more at home than we might have guessed, and less to be gained on the open road alone.

It has been argued that the final episode—"The Return of Ulysses"—is not much more than an adventurous tag, a grand finale that forgets the more subtle themes of the River and the Woodland chapters.[15] Close attention to the dialectics of the text, however, would indicate that the climactic episode enlists the adventurous impulse in the recapture of the magic circle and so provides an appropriate knitting together of the novel's contrary states. Certainly, the problem that the friends face is intimately connected with the homing instinct, for the Wild Wooders have usurped the Toad's ancestral home and extended his own bad habits to the point of profligacy.[16] But the problem is not simply Toad's exile from home but also whether or not the magic circle is to be cut off from all approach. For "in their helping," Mole and Badger, those quintessential homebodies, have moved into Toad Hall, been evicted, and are now being forced "to camp out in the open . . . living very rough by day and lying very hard by night" (194). The critical question, then, is whether the Wild Wooders, who are prone "to break out sometimes" (8) and who represent that impulse antithetical to the spirit of "dulce domum," should inherit Toad Hall. It is a question that Grahame shared with contemporaries like John Galsworthy, Arnold Bennett, and E. M. Forster. Grahame responds, however, in the manner of Robert Louis Stevenson.[17] For in the midst of this "civil war" (225), the day is won by a desperate display of heroism and valor: "the mighty Badger" brandishes a great cudgel, Mole terrifies his enemies with "an awful war-cry," Rat brings an entire arsenal to bear upon his foes, and Toad, "swollen to twice his ordinary size" by excitement, takes out after the Chief Weasel (211). All this is very comic and is over in a page; nonetheless, in taking back the home ground, the domestic corps exhibits the courage and power we conventionally associate with romantic, adventurous heroes who— like Ulysses—spend most of their time on the open road. In the siege of Toad Hall, we are invited again to reject as extreme the view that the love of one's home and the capacity for heroic achievement are irreconcilable, and to contemplate the successful accommodation of contrary states of feeling.

The distinction between these events and the epiphany of "The Piper" is important. In their rescue of Little Portly, Rat and Mole were essentially witnesses to the " 'power at the helping hour' " and were overwhelmed by it. In the retaking of Toad Hall, the friends become warriors rather than bystanders, exemplars of that special power. Such a heroic victory does not, of course, belie the fact that theirs is essentially a triumph for domesticity, for good food, clean sheets, and hand-written dinner invitations; nor does the victory mean that Toad is now a convert and that the seasonal impulse to break out has been tamed. Once again, the Toad must be taken into "the small smoking room" (cf. 91 and 220) and talked to, and once again he protests. And yet, in what may be his own middling reversal, Toad begins to see how modesty, not bombast, can make him "the subject of absorbing interest" (223).[18] What is clear is that our original view of this snugly domestic world has been corrected and that by the close of Grahame's narrative argument "messing about in boats" and feeling the call of "home" do not seem quite so pedestrian. For we are shown something heroic in defending one's own ground, in fighting for domestic values, and in achieving the balance and consistency that only come by recognizing the omnipresence of temptation and the siren call of adventure. In the end, it is the "bijou riverside residence" (4) that breeds the heroes of legend (225), and the life this side of the "well-metalled road" that "holds adventure enough."

Notes

This paper was born during an NEH Summer Seminar at Princeton under the tutelage of U. C. Knoepflmacher. It is dedicated to him. My thanks also to Rebecca Selden, Kitty Steele, and Susan Carlson for their careful reading of the manuscript.

1. For Alistair's response, see also Patrick R. Chalmers, 121 ff.

2. Milne was, however, a bit equivocal in defense of his Toad-centered adaptation, saying "I have left out the best parts of the book; and for that, if he has any knowledge of the theatre, Mr. Grahame will thank me"; cited in Peter Green, *Grahame*, 348. For a discussion of a River-Bank-oriented drama, see Richard L. Schneider, 64–68. In addition, two other Toad-oriented dramas were staged in London in January 1987, one at the Mermaid, the other at the Bloomsbury; for brief review see *City Limits* (London) 1–8 Jan. 1987, 61.

3. Carlee Lippman also analyzes the split between "cloistered comfort and the hunger for the new, the strange, the adventurous" (418). See also Christopher Clausen, who writes interestingly about the dichotomy between attempts at adventure and attempts to get home.

4. Hunt's view of the form of the book is in direct opposition to my own, but his essay is packed with stimulating hints on reader response and the application of narrative theory to children's literature in general.

5. For a rich application of this Blakean concept to Victorian children's fantasy, see U. C. Knoepflmacher, "The Balancing of Child and Adult."

6. For a brief discussion of the distinction between "plot" and "story" and its origin in Russian Formalism, see Robert Scholes, *Structuralism in Literature*.

7. For a discussion of the "imperious" call, see Sale, 186.

8. Cf. Sale, 181.

9. For a particularly helpful discussion of the concept of "felicitous space," see Lois R. Kuznets's essay on Grahame and topophilia, "Toad Hall Revisited."

10. On the similarity between Grahame's world and Tolkien's, see Clausen.

11. See Geraldine Poss (84) on the theme of protection in this chapter.

12. For a discussion of the reader's role in connecting disparate narrative events, see Wolfgang Iser, 29−56.

13. Poss discusses this same accommodation of contrary feelings, though in connection with Toad (87).

14. See Kuznets's comment on Grahame's own "imaginative sublimation of wayward impulses" (127*n*). For a discussion of the place of imagination in general in the text, see Carpenter, *Gardens*, 160−166.

15. See, for example, Sale: "The book must end lamely since a chastened Toad is of no interest; and the unchastened Toad has too many tales told of him already" (185). And Robson: "We feel that the author could have thought of other adventures for Toad. They provide a plot and an exciting climax to the book, but that is all" (98). On the other hand, Carpenter believes that in the end "poetry has been restored to its rightful place in the order of things" (*Gardens* 160). For Clausen, it is the return home in the end that makes this, not *Huck Finn*, the children's classic (142).

16. The Wild Wooders have taken Toad's own excesses, like sleeping late, singing songs, and "carrying on generally" (124), to the point of "lying in bed half the day," "singing vulgar songs," and general riotousness (190). In a sense, Toad Hall has fallen to its own excesses.

17. Galsworthy's *Forsyte Saga* (1906−21) and Bennett's *Old Wives' Tale* (1908) are generally concerned with the problem of inheritance, while Forster's *Howard's End* (1910) is a symbolic struggle for England's destiny built around the inheritance of a house. Stevenson's *Master of Ballantrae* (1889) and *Kidnapped* (1893) also involve struggles for family supremacy.

18. I am not claiming any dramatic peripeteia for the Toad, only the possibility of "anagnorisis."

Works Cited

Burke, Kenneth. *Counter-Statement*. Los Altos, Calif.: Hermes, 1953.

Campbell, Joseph. *The Hero with a Thousand Faces*. Princeton: Princeton UP,1949.

Carpenter, Humphrey. *Secret Gardens*. London: Allen and Unwin, 1985.

Carpenter, Humphrey, and Mari Prichard. *The Oxford Companion to Children's Literature*. Oxford: Oxford UP, 1984.

Chalmers, Patrick R. *Kenneth Grahame: Life, Letters, and Unpublished Work*. Port Washington, N.Y.: Kennikat, 1972.

Clausen, Christopher. "Home and Away in Children's Fiction." *Children's Literature* 10 (1982): 141−52.

Grahame, Kenneth. *The Wind in the Willows*. 1908. New York: Bantam, 1982.

Green, Peter. *Beyond the Wild Wood: The World of Kenneth Grahame.* New York: Facts on File, 1982

——. *Kenneth Grahame: A Biography.* Cleveland: World Publishing, 1969.

Hunt, Peter. "Necessary Misreadings: Directions in Narrative Theory for Children's Literature." *Studies in the Literary Imagination* 18 (Fall 1985): 107–21.

Iser, Wolfgang. *The Implied Reader.* Baltimore: Johns Hopkins UP, 1974.

Knoepflmacher, U. C. "The Balancing of Child and Adult: An Approach to Victorian Fantasies for Children." *Nineteenth Century Fiction* 37 (1983): 497–530.

Kuznets, Lois R. "Toad Hall Revisited." *Children's Literature* 7 (1978): 114–28.

Lippman, Carlee. "All the Comforts of Home." *Antioch Review* 41 (1983): 409–20.

Poss, Geraldine D. "An Epic in Arcadia: The Pastoral World of *The Wind in the Willows.*" *Children's Literature* 4 (1975): 80–90.

Robson, William W. "*The Wind in the Willows.*" *Hebrew University Studies in Literature* 9 (1981): 76–106.

Sale, Roger. *Fairy Tales and After: From Snow White to E. B. White.* Cambridge: Harvard UP, 1978.

Schneider, Richard L. "*The Wind in the Willows*: Lyric Prose into Music." *Literature in Performance* 2 (April 1982): 64–68.

Scholes, Robert. *Structuralism in Literature.* New Haven: Yale UP, 1974.

Steig, Michael. "At the Back of *The Wind in the Willows.*" *Victorian Studies* 24 (1981): 303–23.

Stevick, Philip. "The Theory of Fictional Chapters." *The Theory of the Novel.* Ed. Philip Stevick. New York: Free Press, 1967. 171–84.

The Undoing of Idyll in The Wind in the Willows

Sarah Gilead

It is commonly assumed that children's literature properly simplifies moral, social, psychological complexities so as to suit the limited intellects of children. In this view, authorial comprehension of and control over the literary product is complete, and the author's sense of the reader is unambiguous. Both these assumptions are highly debatable. The first implies that literary meanings directly reflect the author's intentions and are manifest in the primary text; the second implies that the literature that academic tradition or publishers' promotions designate as "children's" is indeed for children, and that there is unanimity between the author's and community's sense of audience. Such simple identities constitute a theoretical utopia, a closed system like a *hortus conclusus* that most critics would recognize as unrealistic. Several decades of scrutiny have led us to regard authorial intent and manifest meanings as extremely difficult to determine, for they are undermined by such factors as unconscious intentionality and the multivalence of signifiers. We may even say such claims are ontologically uncertain, because of the tendency of literary texts to deconstruct their overt patterns of meaning.

Equally problematic are issues concerning the reader in children's literature. Because the postulated reader is a child, dominant themes in children's literature have centered on the idyll of childhood as a prelapsarian kingdom free from the anxiety, social pressures, and self-division we identify with adulthood. Yet, as Zohar Shavit has argued, children's literature is not only written, published, distributed, and purchased by adults, but at each of these stages it is read by adults. Some literary works now enjoyed by children were not originally intended for them; conversely, works intended for children may prove more popular among adults. The very concept of the child, which should unify our understanding of both reader and theme in children's literature, is ambiguous. We define childhood by opposition to the adult, and we tend to overlook the socioeconomic and psychological realities

that produce children's literature and that inevitably if covertly
inhabit its texts. In fact, the concepts "child" and "childhood" are
insubstantial and secondary reflections of adults' wishes, memories, and fantasies rather than ontologically independent concepts
or direct representations of external reality.

The generic norms of the idyll, regression and simplicity, appear to guide the production of children's literature. But the
prevalence in children's literature of oblique symbolism, imagery,
and allusions suggests that it is a peculiarly subversive literature,
full of absent presences and present absences. However successfully evoked, the projected child's experiences, mentality, or feelings reflect an adult's need for escape from necessity, conflict, or
compromise. Determined cheerfulness or confident morality
mask a guilty poignancy. An ostensibly unambiguous realm, the
idyll is filtered by adult intellectuality, by an awareness of irony,
sexuality, conflicts, and social power arrangements. Child-
oriented characters and themes are inevitably (though sometimes
quite subtly) accompanied by the shadowy presence of adult emotions, knowledge, and interests. And conversely, the implied goal
of most children's literature—to facilitate the socialization and
maturation of the child—is undercut by the latent critique of
adult mental habits, behavioral codes, and institutions, a critique
that is embedded in the ideal of childhood. In short, the concept
of the "child" alone cannot unify the genre. These conceptual
contradictions lead to generic contradictions that explain both the
lowly status and the fascination of this literary field.

As in the more narrowly defined idyllic mode of adult fiction,
the utopian simplifications and conventions of closure that commonly delimit children's literature have multiple, contradictory
functions. Literary works for children attempt to translate adult
interests into pedagogical effects on child readers; some of the
most common, overt purposes are to offer moral or religious instruction; to inculcate social values; to encourage a greater understanding and control of fears and anxieties; and to broaden
awareness of the complexities and problems of adult life. Yet if
these concerns generally look forward to the transformation of
child into adult, others invert the process. Purporting to amuse
the child, the author satisfies adult needs. One concealed, less frequently acknowledged adult purpose that haunts and sometimes

dominates texts for children is to escape into a fantasy world where the self is powerful, protected, or extraordinary; where moral issues are consolingly simple; where conflict is resolved by the providential entrance of benevolent magical forces; where in sum, one is offered a pleasurable alternative to the responsibilities, problems, and obligations of ordinary life. As in many utopias, we find regressive fantasies of return to the idealized, protected world of childhood or the womb. Or the fantasy realm may allow free, guiltless expression of aggression, whether punitive rage directed outward against society and family (both parents and sibling rivals) or inward against the self. These dreams of self-transformation and empowerment suffuse concealed themes or plots that coexist with, undermine, or overwhelm more manifest plots.[1]

Such dynamic tension "undoes" the idyllic closure to which many theorists of children's literature still cling as they project an ideal of organic unity onto the works they canonize. But precisely the canonical works of children's literature manifest this subversive dynamic. Indeed, it may be from just such contradictions that the great works of children's literature derive their power. Thus the Alice books of Lewis Carroll ostensibly celebrate the innocently playful, protected world of childhood and offer entertainment in the form of "nonsense"; but their fantasies contain potent symbolic journeys into the womb, Kafkaesque nightmares of guilt and punishment, bizarre figurations of violence and rage, and absurdities that defamiliarize all aspects of reality—cosmic, social, familial, and philosophical.[2] Hans Christian Andersen's "Little Mermaid" concludes with a conventionally Christian moral lesson extolling self-sacrifice and sharpening the child reader's sensitivity to guilt, but the ending consorts oddly with the preceding puberty psychodrama and its violent images of self-mutilation, defloration, self-hatred, and impulses to murder. Similarly, C. S. Lewis's Narnia series exhorts readers to manly Christian courage through the narrative form of heroic quest adventures, but it seduces its readers to regression with escapist fantasies of return to an idealized medieval past, where starkly contrasting and unambiguous moral distinctions prevail, where the aggrandized self is endowed with magical skills and protected by immortal and divine guardians. In summary, one could say that children's literature almost by definition generates conflicting or uneasily coexisting sets of meanings and derives strength from clashing purposes. Typically, it is a form of literature that works against itself.

In most cases the structural split may be invisible, even inaccessible to the author, subliminally worked out through images that betray internal strife. Other classics operate through an explicitly binary system that readily inverts itself (as Blake held Milton's Satan to be the true hero of the epic). Thus Christina Rossetti's "Goblin Market" may be read in conventional moral terms or as a covertly feminist rendition of the social oppression of women, female heroism, and sorority. It is at once a monitory child's version of the fall of man, within a more literal and prosaic context of warning against greed, and a seductive dramatization of unnamed, taboo sexual behaviors such as masturbation, incest, and lesbianism. Subversively, the richly imaged poetry of the goblin-speakers celebrates precisely those oral or sexual delights forbidden in the overt moralism of the text. In such instances, the artistic success of the antagonist may undercut the authority of the protagonist, the error become more attractive than the lesson.

A striking example of the fully elaborated plot and counterplot is Kenneth Grahame's *Wind in the Willows*, which is constructed on two interlocked narratives, the stories of Mole and Toad. At first glance, these hardly seem to oppose each other or to generate significant internal tensions. Both narratives feature comic adventures and accidents in which real danger or unhappiness is either averted or short-lived; good fellowship rules over personal interaction, so that loyalty, tolerance, mutual aid, and sympathy predominate; necessity, work, mortality, family life, and illness hardly exist; there is abundance of food and leisure; and evil can be conquered by luck, by the protection of stronger and wiser fellows, or by a good fight whose happy outcome is providentially ordained. Though Toad repeatedly threatens to violate the pastoral order, each time he is brought back to it.

And yet, the pattern of alternation between the two plots does imply a certain rivalry. The first, the Mole/Rat narrative (chapters 1, 3–5, 7, 9), is a version of pastoral idyll. The second, Toad's adventures (chapters 2, 6, 8, 10–12), takes place in a more socialized narrative landscape where class differences, money, modern technology, social criticism through satire, political allegory, overt moral dramas and didacticism, all come into play. Such elements are virtually excluded from the Mole/Rat narrative. If the stress through chapter 5 is on Mole, the middle section alternates the two plots, and after chapter 9 the balance shifts in favor of Toad. Gradually, one plot displaces the other.

The comic spirit rules both the opening and the conclusion of Grahame's novel. Chapter 1, which initiates the Mole/Rat plot, celebrates individual freedom, conviviality, leisure, and innocence; the final chapter, which concludes the Toad plot, as its title indicates, is a comic parody of "The Return of Ulysses." While the opening invitation to release and hedonism establishes a light-hearted, brilliantly escapist comic mode, the more conservative final chapter develops into conservative social comedy. There fellowship based on play, echoed in the reunion of Toad with Badger, Mole, and Rat, is transmuted into communal solidarity against a common class enemy, the lower-class weasels and stoats. The "squire" is restored to his hereditary rights and learns to restrict his egotistic boasting to the secrecy of his chambers; in short, the social (class) as well as the psychological bases of civilization have been preserved.[3] As an uninhibited comic impulse yields to a much soberer one, the protagonists of the first drama become the authors of the second, who restrain its protagonist, Toad.[4] Their dual role represents the primary pleasures of the idealized child-realm as compatible with socialization.

Though the work generates a number of tragic possibilities, tragedy as such is repeatedly averted by luck or providence. In the world of nature, Mole is lost in the Wild Wood and there encounters "the Terror" of predatory animals, cold, exhaustion, and hunger, but he is soon rescued. A baby otter is lost and feared dead but is protected by Pan, the Helper of animals. In the social world, a speeding automobile wrecks Toad's cart but no one is physically injured. Toad is arrested, tried, and imprisoned, but he escapes and returns home.

At the turning point of the novel, however, in chapter 9, a subtle yet highly consequential tragedy does take place. Rat, by rejecting the Sea Rat, abandons the realm (indeed the possibility) of comic pastoral that he had not only inhabited but embodied in the first chapter. Mole, inexplicably, is revealed as already alien to that realm; and the work as a whole abandons the rich and persuasive fantasy kingdom that initiates it. This change of mood and underlying values undoubtedly accounts for the shift from iconoclastic and individualistic comedy to conservative, communal comedy. Conservative values (domesticity, security) appear early in the work, but until the ninth chapter they seem to blend with the iconoclastic spirit of the opening. The incompatibility between the two perspectives is thus denied until chapter nine, where it finally becomes manifest as a sociocultural absolute similar to the antagonism that Freud postulated between the pleasure principle and the reality principle. Called to footloose adventure and the enjoyment of Edenic pleasures, Rat unsuccessfully struggles to preserve his free, one might say childlike, self. But Mole as superego triumphs and that child self is repressed by Rat's adult self. Similarly, the pastoral plot of the idyll yields to the social-moralistic plot of Toad.

As the following reading will demonstrate, chapter 9 replays, but with reversed significance, the themes, images, and tonalities of the opening chapter, and thus it functions as a regretful but firm repudiation of the premises of the initial narrative of Mole and Rat. When Toad's story continues, Rat and Mole will be merely secondary figures. The narrative strand with which Grahame will close rejects the fantasy of a childhood kingdom where pleasure principle and reality principle do not clash. In the first narrative strand, food and warmth, safe enclosures, comfort and fellowship effortlessly coexist with or follow adventure, novelty, and risk. Maturation can take place by learning new skills and coping with new experiences. In the second strand, however, Grahame lets us glimpse the adult realities of dullness, necessity, inner conflict, and hard choices. It is these that intrude, tragically, into the plot of Mole and Rat in chapter 9.

In the first chapter, Mole's escape from spring housecleaning partakes of a pagan holiness: spring penetrates Mole's house and indeed his consciousness "with its spirit of divine discontent. Something above was calling him imperiously" (11). Mole's desire for pleasure and his wish to flee the predictable routines of ordinary adult life are conflated with animals' instinctive responses to seasonal change. We celebrate a protagonist who bowls over "an elderly rabbit" demanding sixpence " 'for the privilege of passing by the private road!' " (12) (the alliteration alone reveals the contemptible unimaginativeness of rule-bound reality). Mole rejects and symbolically transcends by his upward trajectory the adult world of "busy citizens" devoted to onerous labor, duty, and responsibility. Once out in the open, he heads for the river, described as an objective correlative of Mole's impulse to play and his desire for a less structured existence. Like Mole and Rat, the river is both animal and symbolic child: "this sleek, sensuous, full-bodied animal" plays a raucous game of hide and seek, flinging "itself on fresh playmates that shook themselves free, and were caught and held again" (14). The water thus images the meaning of Mole's narrative and indeed seems prophetically to recite that narrative, as both storyteller and story. The stories the river tells are, like the opening chapter as a whole, promises of future delight. Mole, like the reader, is "bewitched, entranced, fascinated" by the untold tales to come. "By the side of the river he trotted as one trots, when very small, by the side of a man, who holds one spellbound by exciting stories" (14).

The sacredness of Mole's play impulse is magnified in and confirmed by the river's dazzling beauty and power and by its secret knowledge, which Rat hints at: " 'What it hasn't got is not worth having, and what it doesn't know is not worth knowing' " (18). The river provides an emblem of the idealized and inviolably comedic child-kingdom that Rat and Mole, briefly, inhabit. Idyllically limited by its banks, which offer safe dwelling to the Rat, and encircling the island of Pan, the river is an entire universe of pleasant experience that the narrative will unfold to both Mole and the reader.

Rat magically emerges from the river like its own emanating spirit; if the river objectifies Mole's freshly liberated fantasy child-self, then Rat personifies that self. He appears first as a twinkle in the heart of the river, becoming an eye, then a face, then a body— materializing like a wish come true. Indeed, when Mole follows Rat into his boat he is merely following his own impulses made more concrete and embodied in Rat, who is stronger, more experienced, and competent, but still a pleasure-seeking child living in a protected environment, and without an adult's earnestness, anxiety, or oppressive sense of duty.[5] Rat reveals to Mole and to the reader the possibility of a timeless and egalitarian realm of fellowship where events take place in an ever-unfolding dream present free of sexuality, mortality, and temporality.[6] Rat as Mole's hierophant articulates the credo of the river: he lives " 'By it and with it and on it and in it' " (18), imaging a life dedicated to the immediacy of experience. In this world, basic social institutions become unnecessary. " 'It's brother and sister to me, and aunts, and company, and food and drink . . . . It's my world, and I don't want any other.' " Rat teaches Mole the consoling lesson, corollary to the river credo, that the " 'Wide World,' " that is, adult reality, " 'doesn't matter, either to you or me. . . . Don't ever refer to it again, please.' "

The Toad plot, introduced in chapter 2, adopts but subtly alters the themes and images of chapter 1 and thus begins a process that, in chapter 9, will culminate in their reversal. To be sure, we retain Mole's point of view and the "golden afternoon" lyricism of the opening chapter. But in the Toad plot, the story also implies an adult critical perspective of satire and realism that attributes primary importance to social responsibilities and limitations on behavior. At first Toad seems to offer Mole and Rat (as Rat had earlier offered Mole) the delights of fellowship: food, variety of experience, open-ended travel, escape from familiar routine. But Toad's offer seems risky and selfish, and his pleasure-seeking, unlike Mole's, is not sanctified by instinct and the natural order, nor does it express the religious awe and even mysticism to which Rat's boating eventually leads. From the perspective of social reality (as Rat's reactions suggest), Toad's obsessions with play seem neurotic and antisocial.[7]

Thus, Rat, who had assisted Mole in gratifying his wishes, in the Toad narrative context represents self-denial, domestic order, and familiarity; he has perceptibly moved away from the realm of adventure and new experience. Grahame in effect transfers much of the iconoclasm, adventurousness, contempt for routine, and pleasure-seeking from the Mole/Rat plot to the Toad plot. In the first plot line, such qualities are defined as nature's divine gift to her creatures; in the second, they are linked to perverse and selfish human neuroticism and even moral corruption, both of which eventually threaten society. The Toad plot thus, in absorbing many of the elements (characters, incidents, psychic impulses, and states of mind) from the Mole/Rat plot, screens them through a conservative and adult perspective.

The Toad plot functions in two contrary ways. It indicates the latent problems of the pastoral idyll of Rat and Mole; progressively, it links the self-gratification and escapism of the idyll to antithetical criminality and competitiveness. At the same time, the Toad plot enables the idyll, by draining off its antisocial implications. In chapter 9, the separation fails; the two plots merge, but the result effectively disables the Mole/Rat narrative domain. What remains is Toadian social satire, merely decorated with features of romantic idyll.

This attenuation of the Ardenic, green world comedy of Mole's story can already be noted in chapter 3, "The Wild Wood." Pursued by predatory animals in the harsh winter weather of the Wood Mole is still adventurous and curious but also foolish and ignorant; in contrast to the first chapter, his folly here has no divinity about it. In chapter 3 Rat is at best an elder brother who tries to rescue his sibling but needs a much stronger and wiser adult, Badger, to rescue them both. Badger offers them the delights of fellowship—cosiness, warmth, food, stories—but the preceding adventure in the Wild Wood, unlike the boat trip of chapter 1, has value mainly as a moral lesson. This essential plot, denigrating adventure in favor of prudence, is repeated in chapter 7 with the story of the lost otter child who is ultimately saved by Pan; in both cases specific dangers outweigh rewards. For the vision of Pan remains with the otter child only as a sense of loss; and the terror of the vision for Rat and Mole is so great that it must be erased from their minds.

Chapter 9 completes the Mole/Rat plot by rewriting it. The plot, in a double sense, turns upon itself. Now it is Rat, like Mole of chapter 1, who is restless and bored and who responds to seasonal change (here, the autumnal excitement of migrating animals and birds). The River Bank is no longer all the society he knows and needs. Mole had initially been encouraged by Rat to view pleasure-seeking as a feasible way of life. Rat's craving for change similarly generates an encounter with a mentor, the enabling figure of the Sea Rat—image of a potential freer, bolder self—who recounts adventure, travel, a rich variety of pleasurable experiences. Just as Rat had initiated Mole, the Sea Rat is willing to initiate his double into a larger, more exciting world once again symbolized by boat travel (so much more "fluid" with possibilities than travel by land). But in sharp contrast to Mole, who in chapter 1 learns that his new desires are sanctioned by a divine nature, Rat immediately feels guilty of betrayal. Daring "to dream a moment in full abandonment" (168) of a different life in the fabled South, "his loyal heart seemed to cry out on his weaker self for its treachery" (169). Mole's bold contempt for the busy and unimaginative citizens is shown in Rat to be mere moral laxity and selfishness. The Rat episode of chapter 9 realizes the psychomachia that was potential but suppressed in Mole's story: conflict between a socialized adult self and a projected, freer child self, between agonistic narrative and static, idyllic description. Rat's consciousness of a desire to seek new experiences immediately becomes self-conscious and self-critical. He perceives such desire as an affront to received social morality, now virtually cognate with the idyll ethos. Rat reliving Mole's tale finds himself instead inhabiting Toad's.[8]

Although Rat's "call," like that of Mole, is derived from animals' instinctual responses to seasonal change, in chapter 9 responses to nature's urgings are sanctioned only when they are regular acts such as migration and hibernation. No longer permitted are individualistic, idiosyncratic gestures like Mole's springtime flight from home and work. Mole appears justified in grappling with Rat, as Badger, Mole, and Rat will be in imprisoning Toad in his own house. Renouncing his escape, Rat sits "collapsed and shrunken" into himself (182). For Rat as eventually for Toad, fellowship comes to mean repression of individual desire.

The opening chapter's paean to the river's beauty and unrestrained energy is echoed, even intensified, in the Rat's ninth-chapter dream of the sea and then again in the seafaring rat's tempting and dreamlike descriptions of the sea life. Rat's desire to extend his horizons inspires his dream of the "unseen"—"what seas lay beyond, green, leaping, and crested! What sun-bathed coasts. . . . What quiet harbours, thronged with gallant shipping bound for purple islands of wine and spice, islands set low in languorous waters!" (169–70). Recalling the evocative though brief description of the river as all "glints and gleams and sparkles" is Venice's Grand Canal: "the air is full of music and the sky full of stars, the lights flash and shimmer" (175).

In another parallel, the two rats have a picnic, as did Mole and Rat, in what seems again to be a festal ceremony initiating fellowship and future adventures. Sea Rat enchants Rat with stories and ballads of sailors and storms, sunsets and fishermen, winds and sails—"the fights, the escapes, the rallies, the comradeships, the gallant undertakings" (179)—and triumphant returns to port. The stories expand the promissory tales told Mole in chapter 1 by Rat and indeed by the river itself. But if the river was a magical child-kingdom, briefly realized in the initial Mole/Rat story, the sea is that same kingdom and story denied, defined now as unrealizable and self-indulgent wishfulness.[9] What the river presented, the sea makes impossibly remote. For all the luxuriant sensuousness of imagery, the sea's descriptions lack the natural and supernatural allusions present in the descriptions of the river. The river was itself a pagan deity; that is why chapter 7, where Pan appears, seems redundant. The river has already demonstrated Grahame's mythopoeia, so that when he introduces a ready-made mythic figure, albeit with some original characteristics, he seems to gild the lily. In the sea life, sensual pleasure alone has intrinsic aesthetic value; the god at its heart is missing.

Rat heeds the call to adventure, just as Mole did in chapter 1, but ironically, it is Mole (a very different Mole) who prevents him from acting on his desire: "Grappling with him strongly he dragged him inside, threw him down, and held him" until the fit had passed away and "left him sane again" (182–83). Rat had embodied Mole's desire to seek pleasure; here Mole embodies Rat's self-repressing conscience. The child reader may be reassured by the rejection of risk and enforcement of security; the adult reader may recognize in Rat's grief the pain of sublimation and suspect an unhealthy fear of new experience.

In chapter 1 storytelling is imaged as a spontaneous welling up and affirmation of the desire for pleasure; in chapter 9, literature (Rat's poetry) is a safety valve for impermissible wishes and thus a means of social control. Incapable of acting on his fantasies, Rat is helped by Mole to learn to live within the feasible, the respectable, the routine. The original relationship between Rat and Mole as initiator and initiate has been transformed into one of violator and suppressor.

Grahame too has reversed himself and recanted his joyous opening vision, now reconceiving it as morally and socially perilous. Biographical bases for this altered perspective have been adduced by Robson (104) and Green (254–55), but it is perhaps more useful to consider chapter 9 of *The Wind in the Willows* as a reflexive gesture. For Grahame here not only comments obliquely on the work's initial themes and moods but symbolically acknowledges the dual and often contradictory premises and purposes of most children's literature. The opposed elements in this chapter both envision an idealized childhood as antirealm to an oppres-

sive, limited, and joyless adult reality and at the same time pro-
mote the reader's acceptance (whether child or adult) of necessity,
self-denial, and moral responsibility.

The ninth chapter adds to the work the new dimensions of self-
conscious literariness[10] and self-referentiality. With the intrusion
of such literary moods and events the work attains, briefly, a modernist sophistication. But the cost of such modernity is high, sophistication and self-consciousness being anathema to the idyllic
kingdom of Rat and Mole, a kingdom where coherence of meaning, mood, and narrative purpose reign. In this first comedic
realm of singleness of meaning, essential oppositional categories
of culture and psyche are elided. In the Eden of Mole and Rat, as
in Blake's song of innocence "The Lamb," the distinctions
between child, animal, and adult soften and nearly disappear.
The female is virtually absent or subsumed; play and work merge
into a happy if indistinct busyness; class differences and antagonisms do not exist; the family with its oedipal and sibling rivalries,
its intergenerational cultural conflicts, is rarely mentioned.

Chapter 9 reveals that the coherence of the comic idyll is maintained only at the price of violent repression, both social and psychic. In the modes of satire, farce, and parody (*Lavengro* and *The
Odyssey*), the final three chapters likewise maintain the comic order
by stringent exclusions that enable Toad to suppress his antisocial
impulses. The weasels and stoats who have taken over Toad Hall
are metaphors for Toad's libidinal aggressive/erotic drives. To
rout the unsocialized creatures, Toad must traverse an underground passage (his own dark self) and do battle wielding "enor-
mous cudgels" (235) in the company of his friends (the power
needed to subdue the self comes from society and its demands
upon the individual). The banquet marks a ritual initiation of the
subdued Toad into society, at a dinner "run on strictly conventional lines." Even the Wild Wood is "successfully tamed" (249).

The Wind in the Willows in its tragic subtext reinvents and rein-
states precisely those constraining structures (psychological as well
as sociocultural) that Mole and Rat apparently had so effortlessly
escaped. Much children's literature similarly dramatizes conflict
between a child-realm and an adult realm, without being able to
settle conceptually in either one. "Childhood" may be lost in the
past and retrievable only through distorting adult fantasy, wish,
or memory; "adulthood" may be intolerably weighted with frus-

tration and loss. But it is rare to find these issues dramatized in the interaction between two rival plot lines and in their alternate narrative perspectives. In Grahame's novel, we find the narrative structure itself made metaphor for the psychocultural conflicts within the characters, the work as a whole, and perhaps the literary genre which that work exemplifies.

Notes

1. Using *The Wind in the Willows* as a main example, Peter Hunt asserts that, of all texts, "children's literature is the most "self-deconstructing, because its adult structures and assumptions declare themselves as part of the proposed education of their audience into adult (that is *text*) ways of thinking." (121).

2. The cover story reassures us that reality, unlike Wonderland, is meaningful and safe; the covert story tells us that Wonderland is reality itself, revealing the motiveless hostility and hunger for power of adult authority figures.

3. Peter Green analyzes social symbolism in the Toad plot and discusses Grahame's ambivalence toward the conservative social morality he consciously adhered to; see *Kenneth Grahame* 242–50.

4. Different ways of dividing the narrative in two have been proposed by readers of Grahame. Roger Sale, for example, sees two alternating strands, while Peter Hunt sees two successive stories. See also Michael Mendelson's essay in this issue.

5. William Robson notes the following as a source of tension in *The Wind in the Willows*: "The characters belong to the timeless ideal world of children, freed from adult care and responsibilities. Yet they have the independence of adults" (83).

6. Sale characterizes the idyllic quality of the work until chapter 7: "The abolition of worry about the future . . . encloses Grahame's animals in a secure present where all time is rhythmic time" (176).

7. Sale also argues that Toad is dangerous because he has no "natural instinct to guide him" (183). Toad, he holds, is subject to passion, which for Grahame is "the great enemy, because its dangers lie within us" and exclude us from living fully in the present and from being open to others and to experience. I wish to stress that in chapter 9 Rat's vision of immediacy and openness to experience is presented as dangerous to social norms and therefore impermissible, like Toad's obsessiveness and egotism. The distinction previously maintained between sanctioned and unsanctioned impulsive and self-gratifying behaviors disappears.

8. Robson also points out that in chapter 9 Rat's likeness to Toad emerges and that in Rat's poetry therapy Grahame "was tacitly recognizing that his River Bank could never be anything more than a country of the heart" (102–3).

9. Robson (104) and Green (251 and 254–55) discuss the characters of the work as projected aspects of Grahame's personality.

10. See Richard Gillin's essay in this issue on Romantic allusions in *Wind in the Willows*.

Works Cited

Freud, Sigmund. *Civilization and Its Discontents*. Trans. James Strachey. 1961. New York: Norton, 1962.

Grahame, Kenneth. *The Wind in the Willows*. 1908. London: Oxford UP, 1982.

Green, Peter. *Kenneth Grahame, 1859–1932: A Study of His Life, Work, and Times*. London: John Murray, 1959.

Hunt, Peter. "Necessary Misreadings: Directions in Narrative Theory for Children's Literature." *Studies in the Literary Imagination* 18 (Fall 1985): 107–21.

Robson, William. "On *The Wind in the Willows*." *Hebrew University Studies in Literature* 9 (1975): 76–106.

Sale, Roger. *Fairy Tales and After: From Snow White to E. B. White*. Cambridge: Harvard UP, 1978.

Shavit, Zohar. *The Poetics of Children's Literature*. Augusta: U of Georgia P, 1986.

Dialogue and Dialectic: Language and Class in The Wind in the Willows

Peter Hunt

> *The Toad, having finished his breakfast, picked up a*
> *stout stick and swung it vigorously, belabouring imagi-*
> *nary animals. "I'll learn 'em to steal my house!" he*
> *cried. "I'll learn 'em!"*
>
> *"Don't say 'learn 'em', Toad," said the Rat, greatly*
> *shocked. "It's not good English".*
>
> *"What are you always nagging at Toad for?" in-*
> *quired the Badger rather peevishly. "What's the mat-*
> *ter with his English? It's the same what I use myself,*
> *and if it's good enough for me, it ought to be good*
> *enough for you!"*
>
> *"I'm very sorry," said the Rat humbly. "Only I think*
> *it ought to be 'teach 'em', not 'learn 'em'."*
>
> *"But we don't want to teach 'em," replied the Badger.*
> *"We want to learn 'em . . . and . . . we're going to do it, too!"*

The Wind in the Willows, as Neil Philip points out, is "a densely layered text fairly cluttered with second meanings" (104), and, for the British reader at least, one of the main subtexts is that of class dialectic. This is not simply a tension or conflict between the sense of settled social harmony of the River Bankers and the subversive working-classes of the Wild Wood; rather, class is identified with power, and there are symbolic or actual conflicts between adults of different classes, between adults of the *same* class, between adults and children—and even between animals, each living "by instinct . . . according to his nature" (Elspeth Grahame 28). Just as the sizes of the animals constantly change, so the power/class perspectives constantly shift. But how are we aware of them? Are they implicitly or explicitly stated?

Kenneth Grahame was a great stylist, who saw himself in a direct line from Sir Thomas Browne, and we might therefore expect his prose to be sensitive to the class-conscious undercurrents of the text—especially when members of the various classes actu-

159

ally speak. The remarkable "blindness" of the dialogue to this major motivating feature is partly due to Grahame's habit of parody
and pastiche; it certainly provides a fascinating sociolinguistic
commentary on the structural essences of the text.

Grahame's tendency to avoid or disguise the voices of "the people" can be illustrated by the police sergeant, who speaks in a mer-
ciless parody of William Harrison Ainsworth and his ilk: "'Odds-
bodikins . . . Rouse thee, old loon, and take over from us this
vile Toad, a criminal of deepest guilt and matchless artfulness and
resource. Watch and ward him with all thy skill; and mark thee
well, grey-beard, should aught untoward befall, thy old head
shall answer for his—and a murrain on both of them!'" (125).
This "instability" of the text, with characters vacillating between
parody, normal or "authentic" speech, and authorially mediated
speech, allows the text to evade very potent linguistic class distinction and to evade the confrontations latent in a book which deals
obliquely with so many societal issues. For example, Toad, the
gentleman in distress, confesses all to a working-class worthy, the
engine-driver who helps him to escape: "The engine-driver
looked very grave and said, 'I fear that you have been indeed a
wicked toad, and by rights I ought to give you up to offended
justice. But you are evidently in sore trouble and distress, so I will
not desert you. I don't hold with motor-cars, for one thing; and I
don't hold with being ordered about by policemen when I'm on
my own engine, for another . . . . So cheer up, Toad! I'll do my
best, and we may beat them yet!'" (160). Elizabeth Cripps saw in
this passage "the literary man seeking applause in the self-
conscious phrasing and overall polish" (22), but the fact that the
linguistic artificiality diffuses (or defuses) a serious sociological
point about both cross-cultural alliances and individualism suggests a more subtle reading. Is this a point which Grahame *had* to
evade?

It is instructive to compare Grahame's technique with that of his
contemporary, E. Nesbit. Describing a similar encounter with
working-class independence in *The Railway Children* (published
two years before *The Wind in the Willows*), Nesbit makes a clear
linguistic distinction between her characters. When Peter and his
sisters collect birthday presents from the villagers for Mr. Perks,
the porter, he is grossly offended. Peter's upper-middle-class
argot and Perks's nonstandard usages (both italicized in the following extract) are quite clear.

"We'll take the things away if you're unhappy about them," said Peter; "but I think everybody'll be *most awfully* disappointed as well as us."

"I'm not unhappy about them," said Perks. . . . *I don't know as ever I was better pleased.* Not so much with the presents—though they're *an A1 collection*—but the kind respect of our neighbours. That's worth having, eh, Nell?"

"I think it's all worth having," said Mrs Perks, "and you've made a most ridiculous fuss about nothing, Bert, if you ask me."

"No, *I ain't,*" said Perks, firmly; "if a man *didn't respect hisself, no one wouldn't do it for him." [161]*

Nesbit, who "was a Fabian Socialist and [who] took a keen if erratic interest in all the forward movements of her day" (Crouch 12) here uses the language of class naturally, even though the book is not centrally *about* class. In contrast, Grahame's "nagging terror of the mob" (Green 247) leads him to discuss class warfare both at specific points and in the major metaphorical plot sequences. Why, then, does he avoid class dialect? He was, at least on the surface, writing comedy, and this makes it even more surprising that he does not make use of class differences—things which were, after all, the stock-in-trade of many of his contemporaries, such as Jerome K. Jerome and George and Weedon Grossmith.

A brief examination of the way in which Grahame treats inter- and intraclass exchanges may well throw some light on specific evasions and absences as well as on the underlying structures of the text.

The most obvious class distinction (and perhaps the least interesting) is that between Rat and Badger and their compatriots who, in Fred Inglis's words "do no work, but . . . rule the river quite naturally" (119), and the "canaille" who are threatening the collapse of the rural squirearchy (Green 242). This has been brilliantly brought out in Jan Needle's deconstructive antireading, *Wild Wood*, where the story is retold from the point of view of the "working-class" stoats, weasels, and ferrets. These characters (who are named, with a finely calculated appeal to nostalgia, after small independent breweries which produce "real ale") all speak some form of nonstandard English, the better to make Needle's political point.

The dialects and the viewpoints may be fruitfully compared by reading the "same" episode in each book. For example, in *The Wind in the Willows*, when Badger, Rat, and Mole decide to take Toad in hand, a new car has just been delivered to Toad Hall: "The Badger . . . turned to the chauffeur in charge of the new motor-car. 'I'm afraid you won't be wanted today,' he said. 'Mr Toad has changed his mind. He will not require the car. Please understand that this is final. You needn't wait.' Then he followed the others inside and shut the door" (111). The chauffeur, thus peremptorily dismissed (and interestingly enough, excluded from E. H. Shepard's illustration of the scene [110]) is, in Jan Needle's parallel text, Baxter Ferret, the narrator of much of *Wild Wood*. The actual circumstances of his employment are as irrelevant to Grahame as they are to Badger, possibly an example of what Grahame called "character economy" (Green 234) disguising a political statement. (The servants employed by Badger, Rat, and Toad are "invisible," just as most of the child population is ignored in other contemporary texts [Leeson 103–05]). Needle makes him Toad's employee—and this is the second time that Toad has, directly or indirectly, caused him to lose his job. Boddington Stoat, the revolutionary agitator, points this out:

> "You was employed by Toad, and you done your work well, all right? No one had no right to dismiss you. Even Toad—"
> "But Toad didn't dismiss me!" I screeched. "It wasn't Toad that done it! It was his ruddy friends!"
> The stoat clenched his fists beside his two ears.
> "Yes yes yes yes!" he shouted back. "His friends! That's it! If Toad didn't have no right to sack you, what right could *they* possibly have? Sheer vicious arrogance is what! What do they care? What do they care about your job? About your Ma and your sisters and brothers?" [109–10]

Just as in *The Wind in the Willows* we rarely hear the working classes speak for themselves, so in *Wild Wood* we rarely hear the "river bankers." However, on one notable occasion when Toad, terror of the highway, has smashed up the lorry that the unfortunate Baxter Ferret is driving (causing him to be sacked for the first time), we actually hear Toad speak. Baxter's response faces us with just the unpalatable truth that Grahame never gives us.

> "We've come for the waggon. 'Tis the gaffer's." . . .
> "Good men, good men [said Toad]. Tow the old warhorse back to rest, eh? Just the fellows I wanted to meet. Give me the . . . er . . . gaffer's name if you'd be so kind so that I can get in touch and settle the account with him."
> I saw a glimmer of hope through my misery. Took my courage in both hands. Spoke to the gentleman.
> "Would you be saying . . . ? I mean, does that allow you . . .?"
> . . . It was no use. I was in a new world, a different world. I didn't even know how to speak the same language. [63]

In *The Wind in the Willows*, most of the class interactions are either unmarked linguistically (for example, Toad and the gaoler's daughter, Rat and the Sea Rat) or seen in terms of the adult-child relationship. There is little doubt that class and age are closely associated in the book (perhaps naturally enough in a paternalistic society), and it operates as much with Rat as with the more obvious father-figure of Badger. Thus, in "Wayfarers All," when Rat comes across the field mice getting ready for winter, we see the upper class talking to the lower class, and, probably because *rural* poor were not such a threat to Grahame, it emerges as an adult addressing the children: " 'What games are you up to?' said the Water Rat, severely" (165). Similarly, there are the hedgehogs at Badger's house, both children and children of the poor: " 'I understand,' said the Rat. . . . 'And what's the weather like outside? You needn't "sir" me quite so much,' he added. 'O, terrible bad, sir, terrible deep the snow is,' said the hedgehog. 'No getting out for the likes of you gentlemen today' " (73).

Where the interactions between classes *are* linguistically marked, they are almost always linked to or in the context of money. The famous encounter between Toad and the bargewoman, perhaps the most spectacular example of Grahame's dexterity in changing the sizes of his animals and dancing an intricate quadrille around questions of class, is resolved finally by Toad's "long pocket": "Under severe compulsion from the Badger, even the bargewoman was, with some trouble, sought out and the value of her horse discreetly made good to her, though Toad kicked terribly at this, holding himself to be an instrument of fate, sent to punish fat women with mottled arms who couldn't tell a real gentleman when they saw one" (255). Toad's experience at the railway ticket office and his thoughts about the engine-driver are all linked to cash, and the phlegmatic gypsy, of course, the most classless character in the book, is most centered upon it: "The gypsy looked the horse over, and then he looked Toad over with equal care, and looked at the horse again. 'Shillin' a leg,' he said briefly" (199). Money is very significant; it symbolizes exclusiveness but does not address the essence of class. As Green points out, the society of the River Bank (itself, perhaps, a mild pun) has more in common with the rich bourgeoisie than the aristocracy, and it may be that Grahame's self-consciousness about not really belonging to the class that he admired is "one of the underlying emotional driving forces" of the book (249). It is only in the secure final triumph that we actually hear the wild-wooders speak (at least in the corporate voice of the mother weasels) and here the dialect of class comes through directly, only this time in the context of power: " 'Look, baby! There goes the great Mr Toad! And that's the gallant Water Rat, a terrible fighter, walking along o' him!' " (256).

A. A. Milne, an altogether more secure character, took a necessarily more circumspect view in his adaptation *Toad of Toad Hall*: "There is a horrid realism about the theatre, from which, however hard we try, we can never quite escape. Once we put Mole and his friends on the boards we have to be definite about them. What do they look like?" (vii). Indeed, and what do they sound like? Broadly, Milne confines his linguistic class-markers to his "farce" characters, toning down Grahame's nervous undercurrents. The gaoler's daughter's aunt, who is prepared to be bound and gagged, appears in *The Wind in the Willows* only by report: "the only stipulation the old lady made being that she should be gagged and bound and dumped down in a corner. By this not very convincing artifice, she explained, aided by picturesque fiction which she could supply herself, she hoped to retain her situation, in spite of the suspicious appearance of things" (149–50). The late-Victorian ornateness of this example of "indirect tagged speech" indicates a high degree of authorial control and distancing: the old lady's speech is filtered through the author's watchful presence. Milne, of course, cannot share this device, but he makes good use of Grahame's pastiches:

PHOEBE: My aunt thinks she ought to be gagged and bound, so as to look as if she had been overcome. You'd like it too. You wanted to leave the prison in style.
TOAD *(beamingly)*: An excellent idea! So much more in keeping with my character.
AUNT: I brought a rope along, in case like.
TOAD: Splendid!
AUNT *(enjoying it)*: Got a nankerchief?
TOAD *(producing one)*: Yes.
AUNT: Then you gags me first. *(In a hoarse whisper)* Help! Help! Help! Help!
TOAD *(carried away by the realism of this)*: Silence, woman, else I gag thee. . . . Thou has brought it on thyself. [73]

However, as I have suggested, it is in the subtle gradations *within* the closed ruling society that Grahame's linguistic uncertainties and evasions are most striking. For who or what *are* Mole, Badger, Rat, Toad, and Otter? Are they different aspects of Grahame or different aspects of his aspirations? Are they different aspects of children or of adults, different aspects of the same class or of different classes? There is, I think, linguistic evidence (although in dialogue it is somewhat meager) for all these interpretations. If what Grahame has done, as Green suggests, "is to project his own private dream onto a social pattern which he admired, but to which he did not belong" (248), then we might expect to find an uneasy (but complex and fascinating) interleaving of fantasy and reality. As Battiscombe has observed, when Grahame's uncle refused to let him go to Oxford as a student, it "meant that he must forever remain an outsider" (286). The result of his outsider's view is expressed, linguistically, with great ambivalence.

Badger is an excellent example, as multilayered as he is linguistically uneven. We have seen him dismissing Baxter Ferret (or his invisible equivalent) in Olympian tones; later in the book, we see his earthiness being asserted: " 'I want some grub, I do,' he said, in that rather common way he had of speaking" (243). C. S. Lewis described Badger as "that extraordinary amalgam of high rank, coarse manners, gruffness, shyness, and goodness. The child who has once met Mr Badger has ever afterwards, in his bones, a knowledge of humanity and of English Social History which he could not get any other way" (235). Badger represents, in short, a paternalistic society: he is the old squirearchy whose power lies, literally and metaphorically, beneath the wood, and at the same time he is the uncle/grandfather figure, capable of putting Rat in his place (see the epigraph to this essay) and continually treating the others as children (an interesting comment on natural history, too): "He looked kindly down on them and patted both their heads. 'This is not the sort of night for small animals to be out,' he said paternally. 'I'm afraid you've been up to some of your pranks again, Ratty. But come along; come into the kitchen. There's a first-rate fire there, and supper and everything" (66). Geraldine Poss has argued that the "Olympians" of Grahame's earlier books "have been eliminated from *The Wind of the Willows*" (84); I would demur. The Olympians are still there, and, as before, Grahame wishes to be one of them, while at the same time wishing to circumvent them.

Thus while Rat represents poet, aesthete, dreamer, and elder brother, and Toad represents rebel, nouveau riche, fantasist, and "personification of the spoilt infant" (Tucker 161)—all perhaps aspects of Grahame—they are *insiders*, concerned with the codes of their class. (Toad is not criticized for breaking the law, only for breaking ranks.) It is Mole, whose bildungsroman forms the backbone of the book (Hunt 116) who provides the *lens sana* for Grahame's dream world.

Mole is sometimes taken as just another aspect of the upper classes, but although he may be retiring and perhaps middle-aged, he is essentially a Mr. Pooter, of the clerkly, villa-dwelling type immortalized in George and Weedon Grossmith's *Diary of a Nobody* (1892) and pinned down very accurately by his taste in statuary (94), or even, perhaps, a senior official at the Bank of England. He is, of course, also the child learning the shibboleths of adulthood, and, by one of those multiple references that make *The Wind in the Willows* so subtle and resonant a book, he has a special relationship to Badger: " ' . . . but underground to come back to at last—that's my idea of *home!*' The Mole assented heartily; and the Badger in consequence got very friendly with him. 'When lunch is over,' he said, 'I'll take you round this little place of mine. I can see you'll appreciate it. You understand what domestic architecture ought to be, you do' " (78). Mole and Badger are youngest and oldest, but they also represent the curious affinity between the working class and the upper classes in England.

This may be residual in 1987, but it subsists in, say, enthusiasm for the monarchy and certain affectations of dress, notably the flat cap, worn both by dukes and greyhound-racing aficionados from the working class.

Mole's first encounters with the River Bankers are important, for Grahame, as the outsider, sees the way in which one class acknowledges another as a significant (and, no doubt, often painful) indication of their breeding. Thus, in the meeting between Mole and Rat, it is Mole who displays less than good manners: " 'Would you like to come over?' inquired the Rat presently. 'Oh, it's all very well to *talk*,' said the Mole, rather pettishly, he being new to a river and riverside life and its ways" (11). Rat, from a position of social superiority, is naturally polite; Toad, in the full confidence of his own security, "never waits" to be introduced (31). Otter— whose easy familiarity with all classes may well mark him in Grahame's scheme of things as being closest to the nobility—presents the author with a problem. Friendship between the Mole/Grahame "outsider" and some strata of the upper classes, represented by Badger, Rat, and Toad, might be conceivable—but not that stratum represented by Otter. Their friendship, therefore, has to be asserted rather than described: " 'By the way [said the Rat]—my friend, Mr Mole.' 'Proud, I'm sure,' said the Otter, and the two animals were friends forthwith" (18).

Mole's relationship with the classes "below" him is very different from Rat's or Badger's (although he shares the fear/anger response, at least initially, of Toad). When he is at home in Dulce Domum, his friendly treatment of the field mice is a far cry from Badger's relations with the hedgehogs, and it is quite subtly contrasted with Rat's bonhomie: " 'Very well sung, boys!' cried the Rat heartily. 'And now come along in, all of you . . . and have something hot.' 'Yes, come along, field-mice,' cried the Mole, eagerly. 'This is quite like old times' " (101).

Absences in a text are quite as important as presences, so it is striking that such a subtle and accomplished stylist as Grahame should avoid or evade class dialogue in a book so centrally concerned with class. As we have seen, it may well be a reflection of his profound ambivalence toward the class to which he aspired, and the class which he feared. This ambivalence, in combination with the complex class/power/age dialectic of the book, is a central oddity—but it is as deeply embedded in Britain's social and linguistic stratification as *The Wind in the Willows* is in its literary consciousness.

Works Cited

Battiscombe, Georgina. "Exile from the Golden City." *The Cool Web.* Ed. Margaret Meek, Aidan Warlow, and Griselda Barton. London: Bodley Head, 1977. 284–90.

Cripps, Elizabeth A. "Kenneth Grahame, Children's Author?" *Children's Literature in Education* 12 (1981): 15–23.

Crouch, Marcus. *Treasure Seekers and Borrowers.* London: Library Association, 1962.

Grahame, Elspeth, ed. *First Whisper of* The Wind in the Willows. London: Methuen, 1944.

Grahame, Kenneth. *The Wind in the Willows.* Illus. E. H. Shepard. 1908. London: Methuen, 1981.

Green, Peter. *Kenneth Grahame, 1859–1932: A Study of His Life, Work, and Times.* London: John Murray, 1959.

Hunt, Peter. "Necessary Misreadings: Directions in Narrative Theory for Children's Literature." *Studies in the Literary Imagination* 18 (Fall 1985): 107–21.

Inglis, Fred. *The Promise of Happiness.* Cambridge: Cambridge UP, 1981.

Leeson, Robert. *Reading and Righting.* London: Collins, 1985.

Lewis, C. S. "On Three Ways of Writing for Children." *Horn Book* 38 (1963). Rpt. *Children and Literature.* Ed. Virginia Haviland. New York: Scott, Foresman, 1973. 231–240.

Milne, A. A. *Toad of Toad Hall.* 1929. London: Methuen, 1940.

Needle, Jan. *Wild Wood.* 1981. London: Methuen, 1982.

Nesbit, E. *The Railway Children.* 1906. Harmondsworth: Penguin, 1970.

Philip, Neil. "Kenneth Grahame's *Wind in the Willows*: A Companionable Vitality." *Touchstones: Reflections on the Best in Children's Literature*, Vol. 1. Ed. Perry Nodelman. West Lafayette: Children's Literature Association, 1985. 96–105.

Poss, Geraldine D. "An Epic in Arcadia: The Pastoral World of *The Wind in the Willows.*" *Children's Literature* 4 (1975): 80–90.

Tucker, Nicholas. "The Children's Falstaff." *Suitable for Children?* Ed. Nicholas Tucker. London: Sussex UP, 1976. 160–64.

Romantic Echoes in the Willows

Richard Gillin

> *The constant chorus of the orchards and hedges*
> *had shrunk to a casual evensong from a few yet un-*
> *wearied performers; the robin was beginning to as-*
> *sert himself once more; and there was a feeling in the*
> *air of change and departure.*—Grahame, The Wind
> in the Willows

> *Then in a wailful choir the small gnats mourn*
> *Among the river sallows . . .*
> *Hedge-crickets sing; and now with treble soft*
> *The red-breast whistles from a garden-croft;*
> *And gathering swallows twitter in the skies.*—Keats,
> "Ode to Autumn"

The retrospective hymns to natural beauty in "Wayfarers All," chapter 9 of *The Wind in the Willows*, bear tribute not only to departing summer but to Grahame's Romantic predecessors: Keats, Coleridge, and Wordsworth, themselves "by distance ruralized." With surprisingly few explicit verbal echoes, Grahame nonetheless manages to call up for readers familiar with the Romantics—as his Victorian audience certainly was—some central poems of the canon: "To Autumn," "Ode to a Nightingale," "The Ancient Mariner," and *The Prelude*. These subtle allusions serve several functions. The most striking among them reinforce parallels between Grahame's plot and the master plots he found in Wordsworth and Coleridge. Descriptive echoes call attention, by contrast, to Grahame's claim to realism and his humorous narrative tone. And finally, the echoes distinguish Grahame's transcendental vision from that of his predecessors.

"Wayfarers All," the most explicitly Romantic chapter of the novel, describes the Water Rat's restlessness, catalyzed by his encounter with the spellbinding Sea Rat. This "ageing" seafarer, with his "thin and long" paws (152) reminds us of Coleridge's Ancient Mariner, with his "skinny hand" and "glittering eye" ("Mariner," ll. 9, 13). Indeed, Grahame emphasizes his mariner's "eye lit with a brightness that seemed caught from some far-away

169

sea-beacon." The storyteller, hypnotically "leaning towards the Water Rat, compelled his gaze and held him, body and soul, while he talked," "mastered the Water Rat and held him bound, fascinated, powerless" (157). He succeeds in enthralling the Water Rat, who, like Coleridge's stunned Wedding Guest, is left in a "waking dream" (158), "paralyzed and staring . . . like a sleep-walker" (159).

Like Coleridge, too, Grahame stresses the reflexive implications of his theme, the link between the driven wanderer and the compulsion attendant on poetic gifts. The Sea Rat's tale has incantatory power ("was it speech entirely, or did it pass at times into song?" [157]). And his listener (at the encouragement of Mole) strives to translate the experience into poetry, to revive and rebuild the vision he has seen. For Rat, after all, is a bard whom we see "trying over rhymes that wouldn't fit," and who can hear the music of the piper first, before his friend the Mole. All these Coleridgean echoes help Grahame to fuse several of his central themes: the "imperious call" (27) to depart that is both natural and dangerous, the imaginative transcendence of material experience, and the seductions of storytelling.

Allusions serve Grahame not only in the definition of theme but in establishing his own narrative mode. The descriptions in this chapter dedicated to the Romantic imagination blend various Keatsian descriptions of the thirst for escape and transcendence. The swallows who gather among the osiers (river sallows) twittering among themselves transmit to Rat the call of the warm South, with "their intoxicating babble . . . of violet seas, tawny sands, and lizard-haunted walls" (151), "the authentic odour" of what Keats calls "the true, the blushful Hippocrene" ("Autumn," l. 16); not surprisingly, in order to entertain the wayfarer, Rat breaks out "a long-necked straw-covered flask wherein lay bottled sunshine shed and garnered on far Southern slopes" (156), the "vintage of the South." Listening to descriptions of picturesque ports and *dolce far niente*, Rat, like the speaker in "Ode to a Nightingale," dares "to dream a moment in full abandonment," imagining what it would mean to "leave the world unseen" (l. 19).

What distinguishes Grahame's elegiac descriptions from those of Keats, of course, is his humorously practical return to material detail: the field mice examine plans of desirable small flats in

town; the swallows enjoy the planning as much as the trip itself
and fear the hunger of an insect-killing cold. England, like "Nature's Grand Hotel," has its Season, and those of us who stay re-
sent the departures of our more busy companions. In another
example of comic deflation, the Water Rat imagines epic adventures like those of the Ancient Mariner: "Months and months out
of sight of land, and provisions running short, and allowanced as
to water, and your mind communing with the mighty ocean, and
all that sort of thing?" (154). But the Sea Rat quickly sets his host
straight about the "highly-coloured life" (154) he knows. His voy-
ages, it turns out, are coastal ones, dedicated to sensual pleasures
and companionship, not the transcendent visions of the solitary
visionary, not "opening on the foam/Of perilous seas, in faery
lands forlorn" (Keats, "Nightingale," ll. 69–70). The cosmopo-
lite's jolly materialism here is of a piece with Grahame's other
down-to-earth, parodic allusions. If his fancy cheats, it does so in
terms other than those of the Romantics, in the braggadocio of
Toad, for example.

While the Rat, with his intellect and bardic trance, seems Coleridgean, the Mole's progress through stages of self-realization
aligns him rather with Wordsworth and *The Prelude*. When in
chapter 1 he first left his burrow on hearing the imperious call of
spring, touched by "its spirit of divine discontent and longing"
(27), "soft breezes caressed his heated brow" and "the carol of
happy birds fell on his dulled hearing almost like a shout" (28).
What Wordsworth calls "this gentle breeze" that "fans my cheek"
(Prelude 1:1, 3) seems animate, half-conscious of the joyful message of correspondences that it brings.

Most important is the encounter with the river, which as in *The
Prelude* lulls the protagonist murmuringly into rest, points out his
course, tells stories, and shapes the Mole's relationship to the phe-
nomenological world. Giving voice to all of animate nature, the
river's "glints and gleams and sparkles, rustle and swirl, chatter
and bubble" (29) have the same effect on Mole that the mariner
had on Rat, leaving him "bewitched, entranced, fascinated" (3).
The river becomes the focal point of his quest and his reflections.
The Mole's release from habitual order leads him toward perceptions of natural beauty: he "entered into the joy of running water;
and with his ear to the reed-stems he caught, at intervals some-

thing of what the wind went whispering so constantly among them" (39).

But like Wordsworth, Mole must be "fostered alike by beauty and by fear" (*Prelude* 1:306). If the Romantic is taught the inviolate power and life of nature when he steals "a little boat tied to a willow tree" (*Prelude* 1:374), the Victorian Mole learns to chasten his desires when he seizes control of Rat's oars and capsizes the boat. Mole's education through nature's "severer interventions" (*Prelude* 1:370) takes place most fully in the terror of the Wild Wood. There his isolation teaches him about individualist life beyond the restraints of community, a lawless world identified with nature red in tooth and claw, and shows him that the radical individualism of the Romantics is alien to him and his needs.

In the chapter entitled "Piper at the Gates of Dawn," Grahame clearly distinguishes his own transcendental vision from that of his predecessors. The theme of this chapter is perception: Mole's transformation by the keener sense of reality he is granted at the end of his search for the lost otter child, Portly. This night quest leads him finally to Pan's island, where briefly he will glimpse the eternal and the universal in a particular place and embodiment. In a characteristically Romantic identification of moonlight with the imagination, which makes the influence of Wordsworth and Coleridge most palpable, Mole sees his "old haunts" in "other raiment" and "new apparel." As the moon rises, the world loses its disturbing ambiguities: "all softly disclosed, all washed clean of mystery and terror, all radiant again as by day, but with a difference that was tremendous" (120). We see, as Coleridge suggests in Chapter 14 of *Biographia Literaria*, "the sudden charm, which accidents of light and shade, which moon-light or sun-set diffused over a known and familiar landscape" (397). These transformations, as Coleridge notes, "are the poetry of nature."

Grahame marks the threshold of the animal's vision "into the life of things" by stressing the image of suspension. In "Tintern Abbey" Wordsworth argued that we achieve such moments only when

> . . . the breath of this corporeal frame
> And even the motion of our human blood
> Almost suspended, we are laid asleep
> In body, and become a living soul. [ll. 43–46]

Breathless and transfixed, Mole finally joins Rat in hearing the divine piper. "For a space they hung there." Then through their cleansed senses they take in "a freshness and a greenness unsurpassable. Never had they noticed the roses so vivid, the willow-herb so riotous, the meadowsweet so odorous and pervading." Transcendence of self and of the moment permits, paradoxically, the intensest consciousness of the immanent divine. Most finely, Grahame identifies vision with song, in a typical Romantic image of liquid light and sound. "Breathless and transfixed the Mole stopped rowing as the liquid run of that glad piping broke on him like a wave, caught him up, and possessed him utterly" (122). The transcendent speaks, as Wordsworth would put it, in "voices issuing forth to silent light / In one continuous stream" (*Prelude* 14: 73–74).

Yet the animals' vision is not, strictly speaking, Romantic. Wordsworth's genius loci may be a rock, yew, or raving stream. But "personifications," he held, "do not make any natural or regular part" of men's language (Preface to *Lyrical Ballads* p. 162). His visionary climaxes are marked as much by absence as presence, the sublime of negation, as Geoffrey Hartman and Thomas Weiskel have persuasively shown. Furthermore, Grahame's visionary chapter has a communal and practical aspect: Mole shares his moment of ecstasy with Rat, and he finds not only himself but Portly. By contrast to the natural symbols, cult of solitude, and sublime negations in the vision of the Romantics whose work otherwise permeates the language of this novel, Grahame offers us good cheer and fostering companionship.

This distinctive representation of the transcendent moment coincides with a more general difference between Grahame and his predecessors in his representation of psychic growth. Self-understanding in Grahame is progressive and communal rather than retrospective and solitary, as would so often be true in Wordsworth's "spots of time." Significantly, where Grahame does use a return to explore deepened understanding and "recollection in tranquillity," the locus is not some isolated natural spot, not the valley of the Wye or the River, but home. He returns Mole to his burrow in "Dulce Domum" to underscore the love of familiar domesticity, and he chastens Toad with a homecoming feast at Toad Hall minus boastful songs. These distinctively domestic patterns correspond to the genre Grahame chose: the convention of the return home that governs so much of children's literature.

Works Cited

Coleridge, Samuel Taylor. "Biographia Literaria." *Norton Anthology of English Literature*. Gen. ed. M. H. Abrams. 5th ed. 2 vols. New York: Norton, 1986. 2:386–405.

———. "The Rime of the Ancient Mariner." *Norton Anthology* 2:335–52.

Grahame, Kenneth. *The Wind in the Willows*. 1908. New York: New American Library, 1969.

Keats, John. "Ode to a Nightingale." *Norton Anthology* 2:819–22.

———. "To Autumn." *Norton Anthology* 2:844–45.

Wordsworth, William. "Lines Composed a Few Miles above Tintern Abbey." *Norton Anthology* 2:151–55.

———. Preface to *Lyrical Ballads*. *Norton Anthology* 2:155–70.

———. *The Prelude*. *Norton Anthology* 2:229–312.

Kenneth Grahame and Father Nature, or Whither *Blows* The Wind in the Willows?

Lois R. Kuznets

To Teddy Roosevelt, a longtime Grahame enthusiast influential in getting *The Wind in the Willows* published in the United States, Grahame wrote that the book's "qualities, if any, are mostly negative—i.e.—no problems, no sex, no second meaning—it is only an expression of the simplest joys of life as lived by the simplest beings" (Green 274). Had the book been quite as charmingly and thoughtlessly simple as Grahame suggests, perhaps ingenuously, it would probably not have survived until today. For beneath its Arcadian surface lie deeply buried and complex concerns that have saved it from oblivion yet remain troubling for some modern readers.

Whereas Grahame claimed to his editor at Charles Scribner's that the novel is "free of problems, clear of the clash of sex,"[1] I would argue that at the same time as the novel attempts to *repress* the clash of sex, it also *perpetuates* it in the dramatization of certain traditional themes: woman's dangerous power to limit man's freedom, and the male longing to be completely accepted by—and as—the father.

Grahame's contemporaries, like a number of recent critics, found his marriage to Elspeth Thomson a severely troubled one. Many would probably have considered it to be the source of his view of sexuality as conflict. I do not find the subject so simple, since much of Grahame's writing prior to his marriage at the age of forty (that is, *Pagan Papers*, *The Golden Age*, *Dream Days*, and *The Headswoman*) already juxtaposes a romantically idealized image of women with even more prominent fantasies of a comfortable, mildly adventurous life among similarly minded gentlemen, pleasantly free of social restraints—a number of which Grahame depicted as imposed by women, either as a result of their own domineering nature or as agents of a restrictive society.[2]

Central to *The Wind in the Willows* is this vision of a nurturing male society, the idyllic male-only animal world, free of "feminine control."[3] The animal community in turn is linked to a mystical

vision of a male nature god, Pan, as well as to the more subtly
personified, companionable, storytelling River.[4] These two figures suggest Grahame's effort to transform various aspects of nature "herself," so archetypically maternal, into male parents.[5] Set
against that natural world we find in the human domain of *The
Wind in the Willows* three women: the young girl, the servant, and
the dominatrix, all stereotypical figures who lie outside the world
of the protagonists and help define its limits.

Many interpreters have noted the mock-epic features of the
book. Not only is Toad an inept yet convincingly wily Ulysses, but
the Odyssean motif of the journey home is repeated in the adventures of Mole and Rat, who must inevitably return and accommo-
date themselves to their own homes. What we have somehow
taken for granted is that Grahame's Odyssey lacks Penelope, the
faithful wife, waiting at home and guilefully fooling the suitors
while her husband guilefully makes his way back to her.[6] Hitherto, we have probably paid too little attention to the way in which
Grahame eliminates not only wives but mothers as well, *without*
dispensing with their traditional nurturing functions. In the River
Bank world, and even in the Wild Wood that borders it, males
rather than females dispense the hospitality, create the welcoming
atmosphere, and share the oral delights of food and drink and
the talk that goes with them. In the Wide World, it is only the
gaoler's daughter who takes over that function. (Of course, only
the good parts of this function need be paid much attention
anyway—shopping, cooking, cleaning, and maintenance are largely ignored or done by invisible hands, the same hands that
finished Mole's spring-cleaning for him when he left it so precipi-
tously to go live with Rat.)[7]

Not only do males nurture each other by offering hospitality,
but they are actively involved in parenting. Exit Penelope,while
Telemachus remains onstage. Like Joyce in his Irish Odyssey,
Grahame exploits the Telemachan theme, the motif of father and
son in search of each other. He incorporates it as one motivating
force in his vision of a male society. Moreover, he explores both
the positive and negative sides of the relationship. On the positive
side is the scene in which Pan is featured. Otter, the father, rather
than Mrs. Otter, is desperately searching for young Portly, who
has briefly found a heavenly father, the protective Pan. Otter's

good male friends, Mole and Rat, find the child. On the negative side—and Grahame was certainly aware of patriarchy's control over his own life—can be seen Badger's insistence on converting and controlling Toad, locking him in his room so that he cannot indulge his motorcar mania and killing no fatted calf when the prodigal returns from gaol. All this, incidentally, Badger does in the name of Toad's dead father, who was Badger's friend. A muted version of Grahame's resentment towards his own male relatives can be discerned in his portrayal of Badger's bullying ways, although Badger too participates in the good, hospitable nurturing and he is certainly forgiven far more righteous high-handedness in this book than any that Grahame condemns in his earlier writing.[8] Badger's badgering is also more acceptable than the prospect of "more weeks in the hospital, being ordered around by female nurses" (112) with which Mole threatens Toad if he persists in his dangerous sport.[9]

The really important relationships are all between males in this book, with the possible exception of Toad's with the gaoler's daughter. In spite of her function as an agent of the state whose duty is to repress the irrepressible Toad, she also nurtures him, tempting Toad to eat and to abandon despondency with the most mouthwatering, sensually buttered toast I have ever vicariously experienced: "cut very thick, very brown on both sides, with the butter running through the holes in it in great golden drops, like honey from the honeycomb" (145). Such understanding young girls, with certain romantic possibilities, appear elsewhere in Grahame's work, but here Grahame manages to keep the relationship uncomplicated by raising insurmountable class barriers (repressing the subterranean grotesquerie of the notion of this union—not unheard of in fairy tales, of course—of girl and toad): "Toad, of course, in his vanity thought that her interest in him proceeded from a growing tenderness; and he could not help half regretting that the social gulf between them was so very wide" (147).

The second woman to appear, the girl's aunt, the washerwoman, is important largely for her clothes, which fit Toad.[10] She belongs to the class of helpful female servants, who show up often in Grahame's earlier writing. But the "comic" scene in which Toad, in drag, has to endure "the chaff and the humourous sallies" of the prison guards, who plead "with simulated passion for just one farewell embrace" hardly suggests a world clear of "the clash of sex."[11] Toad, the consummate con man, does exploit his feminine role for all it is worth; nevertheless, the dress he wears becomes virtually a flirtatious woman who castrates him: "a strange uncanny thing that seemed to hold his hands, turn all muscular strivings to water, and laugh at him all the time" (153). At the railroad station, this outfit, lacking useful pockets and their content, clearly reinforces his momentary relegation to the status of that being who lacks "all that makes life worth living, all that distinguishes the many-pocketed animal, the lord of creation, from the inferior one-pocketed or no-pocketed productions that hop or trip about permissively, unequipped for real contest" (154)—that is, women.

While the struggles of Toad as washerwoman are certainly comical and, it might be argued, show some sympathy for "the weaker sex" or at least make fun of the "stronger" one, Toad has yet to meet the most threatening of the three women of the Wide World, the bargewoman. She is also the last woman we see in the book, the one who betters Toad in a match in which he calls her a "common, low *fat* barge-woman," after which she throws him from the boat with her "big, mottled arm" (196).[12] She seems to exult in her power to dominate him, to make him—horror of horrors— wash her underthings (194).[13] His cross-dressing, of course, by eliminating both class and sexual distinctions, leaves Toad open to the bargewoman's exploitation and laughter. She can see through his charade at once.

Again, one should note that all of these women reside only in the Wide World, which Toad should have avoided. The problems the riverbankers encounter on their own ground—the invasion of Toad Hall by the inhabitants of the Wild Wood—have more to do with that other buried concern—class conflict—which Grahame ignored when he commended the book to Teddy Roosevelt for its negative virtues.

Looking back over Grahame's writing as a whole, one can see that Grahame rarely personifies natural forces as female. To give the paternal role to Pan can be seen as part of this overall exclusionary pattern. Grahame's desexualized Pan also differs significantly from that of many of his contemporaries. Half-goat, half-human musician, Pan symbolized at the turn of the century the frustrating dualisms of modern society and a divided sensibility, in which the civilized intellectual self was perforce separated from the natural, animal self. Aubrey Beardsley's frontispiece to the first edition of Grahame's *Pagan Papers*, for example, shows Pan in the loose shirt and flowing tie of the 1890s artist, gazing lasciviously at a faun. Grahame's essay "The Rural Pan" in *Pagan Papers* as well as the chapter at the center of *The Wind in the Willows*, "Piper at the Gates of Dawn," emphasizes the god's good-natured sociability rather than his randy goatishness. In the novel, Grahame draws Pan as masculine, with his "stern, hooked nose," beard, "rippling muscles," and shaggy limbs. Yet Pan's "kindly eyes . . . looking down on them humourously" and the "little, round, podgy, childish form of the baby otter . . . nestling between his very hooves, sleeping soundly in entire peace and contentment" (135−36) not only repress Pan's sexuality but exaggerate his paternity.[14]

If there is a choice, Grahame is likely to choose the male image. The river too, despite an archetypal link between water and the feminine, becomes another paternal avatar, another concrete manifestation of masculine divinity. Mole, emerging from his hole at the spring beginning of *The Wind in the Willows*, trots beside the river "as one trots when very small, by the side of a man who holds one spellbound by exciting stories" (4). At the center of this river, as Mole will discover later, is the central figure of Pan, the spiritual ruler of Grahame's alternative, womanless utopia.

Whither blows *The Wind in the Willows*? Toward No−Woman's−Land. Its attractive androgyny of nurturing males is one that can postulate no similar androgyny for females.[15] Women remain, forever, the Other in *The Wind in the Willows*. Its utopian goal is a society that incorporates what are traditionally seen as female values while at the same time excluding females entirely, not just as lovers, wives, mothers, sisters, daughters, or aunts, but also as friends who would be happy to mess about in boats (if they didn't always get stuck holding the baby) or to participate in those wonderful alfresco feasts (if they didn't always have to prepare them). Yet this central spiritual vision is possibly no more patriarchally exclusive than that of any major Western religion.[16] Moreover, Grahame's undeniable artistry and his sincere advocacy of nurturing relationships among male friends, fathers, and sons may continue to weigh the balance of judgment in favor of *The Wind in the Willows* as a good book for children despite the fact that it is indeed permeated by the clash of sex.

Notes

This paper is derived from a longer version delivered as part of the CAL Lecture Series, San Diego State University, November 1986. In its present form, it has benefited from the editorial suggestions of Margaret Higonnet.

1. Letter quoted by Charles Scribner IV in the preface to the 1953 edition of *The Wind in the Willows* (reprinted in the 1965 edition).

2. I trace these themes, which become virtual leitmotifs in the corpus of Grahame's work, in my book. There I also go into biographical detail, inapppropriate here.

3. An expression Grahame uses in one of his last essays, "Oxford through a Boy's Eyes," published posthumously in *Country Life*, 3 December, 1932, and quoted in Chalmers (17–26).

4. Peter Green traces the line of neopaganism in Grahame's work and shows how it is both like and different from the neopaganism which intrigued many of Grahame's contemporaries in late-nineteenth-century England. See especially Green, chap. 4.

5. I have come across only one instance, also in *The Wind in the Willows*, where Grahame pays lip service to the female archetype of Nature. After being thrown off the barge by the nasty bargewoman Toad smells the gypsy's stew; that smell "seemed like the very soul of Nature taking form and appearing to her children, a true Goddess, a mother of solace and comfort" (199). This is certainly not the image that pervades the rest of the book.

6. The only critic I have found who specifically mentions Penelope's absence is Geraldine Poss (Geraldine DeLuca), to whose article I am indebted for much feminist inspiration, although Poss does not attempt to trace the paternal theme or the absence of mothers as well as wives and lovers. Jerome Griswold was the one who really put me on the trail of the missing Penelope and her negative significance.

7. See Chalmers (62–63) for the letter Grahame wrote in response to a query about Mole's spring-cleaning.

8. With some of the gusto of Swift's *Modest Proposal*, Grahame's *Pagan Papers* essay, "Justifiable Homicide," plays with the idea of picking off stingy male relatives.

9. One cannot help being reminded here of Ken Kesey's misogynist nightmare, *One Flew over the Cuckoo's Nest*.

10. Poss suggests that we have here an allusion to the Nausicaa incident in the Odyssey.

11. The original version of this scene, with which Grahame entertained his young son in one of the letters preserved in *First Whispers of* The Wind in the Willows, gives rather full rein to hostility of a class and sexual nature: "Out he marched, past the gaolers, as bold as you please. As he was passing one of them, the man said, 'Hullo mother washerwoman, why didn't you send home my Sunday shirt last week, you lazy old pig?' & took his stick & beat her full sore" (Elspeth Grahame 55).

12. Like a number of Victorians, Grahame seems to make a fetish of women's arms. In *The Headswoman*, Jeanne, the attractive executioner, bares her beautiful white arms as she prepares to behead a man (32).

13. In the final rewriting of the book Grahame went out of his way to depict this dominatrix. In the original version (see note 11), it is a bargeman who asks Toad to wash shirts, and while their exchange includes class-biased insults, it does not add shades of sexual humiliation.

14. We are used to women's sexuality being separated from their maternity, but we rarely see a similar disjunction between sexuality and paternity with men, perhaps because we so rarely imagine men who nurture others rather than aggrandize themselves.

15. Dorothy Dinnerstein, in *The Mermaid and the Minotaur*, points to a similar inability on the part of Norman O. Brown, in his *Life Against Death: The Psychoanalytic Meaning of History*, to imagine androgyny that was not still essentially male (184).

16. It is, however, more elitist than these religions in its exclusion of the "lower classes."

Works Cited

Chalmers, Patrick. *Kenneth Grahame: Life, Letters and Unpublished Works.* London: Methuen, 1933.

Dinnerstein, Dorothy. *The Mermaid and the Minotaur: Sexual Arrangements and Human Malaise.* New York: Harper and Row, 1976.

Grahame, Elspeth, ed. *First Whispers of* The Wind in the Willows. Philadelphia: P.J. Lippincott, 1944.

Grahame, Kenneth. *Dream Days.* London: John Lane, Bodley Head, 1898.

———. *The Golden Age.* London: John Lane, 1895.

———. *The Headswoman.* London: John Lane, Bodley Booklets no. 5, 1898.

———. *Pagan Papers.* London: John Lane, 1893.

———. *The Wind in the Willows.* 1908. New York: Charles Scribner's Sons, 1965.

Green, Peter. *Kenneth Grahame, 1859–1932: A Study of His Life, Work, and Times.* London: John Murray, 1959.

Kuznets, Lois R. *Kenneth Grahame.* Twayne English Author Series. Boston: G.K. Hall, 1987.

Poss, Geraldine D.[DeLuca] "An Epic in Arcadia: The Pastoral World of *The Wind in the Willows.*" *Children's Literature* 4 (1975): 80–90.

Varia

"Plain" and "Fancy" Laura: A Mennonite Reader of Girls' Books

Laura Weaver

As a "plain" girl growing up in a horse-and-buggy Mennonite family of the 1930s and 1940s, I felt the need to read about and observe "fancy" girls in the dominant culture. My upbringing had taught me to perceive the plain as good, the fancy as evil, but my reading showed me that female protagonists who seemed to me fancy were not necessarily wicked; in fact, they were taught values similar to mine. Therefore, what might have been an unbridgeable gap, inhibiting my imaginative identification with these characters, was lessened and my moral vision complicated. As I retrace my early reading of girls' classics—*Little Women, Children of Greycourt, Anne of Green Gables, Pollyanna,* and *Rebecca of Sunnybrook Farm*[1]—I see a version of every child's experience, the projections and self-transformations that flow from observing and participating in a literary world. In my imagination both fancy Laura and plain Laura, I could emulate yet judge, eventually reaching a more complex understanding of femininity and other values.

My Mennonite family and church had taught me to "be in the World but not of the World," to live in the dominant culture without committing myself to it. I became an onlooker in everyday life, a role that affected my reading as well. Because I was brought up without family photographs, my image of myself grew out of observing others, both those nearest me in externals and those closest to my secret images of myself.

Neither text nor illustrations in the girls' classics that I loved offered me models of the "plain" femininity I was expected to cultivate; for those I turned to women in my family and the church, whose plain clothing and braids matched mine. I wore a dress with a yoke, gathers between the yoke and the sewn-in belt, snaps for the back opening, long sleeves, and a long skirt over black stockings. Sometimes my dresses had collars; they might be in solids, small prints, or plaids, but they were never decorated with lace or ribbons. Parted in the middle, my hair was drawn back in twists on the top of my head and braided in back with no

185

ribbons; it could not be cut or worn loose. That my hair was naturally curly I know from school photographs in which curls escape
at my forehead. At twelve, I became a church member and began
wearing my hair in a bun covered by a white cap. Norms of plain
appearance such as these carried moral weight and framed my
perceptions of women outside the Mennonite world.

While the idea of femininity involves many facets of life, physical appearance has special importance for a young girl in our culture. As a child, I made no distinction between my schoolmates
and the heroines of my books; all were "others," whose "worldly"
clothing, cut or curled hair, and jewelry marked them off as different. But in my reading I could become an Other as well.

My books showed me heroines for whom worldly jewelry, clothing, and hairstyles constituted a norm, whether in their daily
experience or as a desired way of life. A conflict between my own
norms and those of these books was one of my first and most vivid
experiences as a reader. For example, Anne, "so plainly and soberly gowned," is, as Matthew observes, "different from her
mates"; and that difference, he thinks, is "something that should
not exist" (AGG 190–91).

Perhaps because jewelry is treated in these fictions as special, I
noted without envy the coral bracelet, brooch, garnet set, and
gold and ebony rosary in *Little Women* (123, 131, 258–59); an
amethyst brooch and a silver bangle bracelet in *Anne of Green Gables* (92,155); a chain of pink coral beads in *Rebecca of Sunnybrook
Farm* (179); and a pearl necklace, a ring, a chain and pendant in
Children of Greycourt (121, 124, 167). Though usually charged with
family memories and love, these heirlooms and gifts were sometimes considered temptations to vanity. Mrs. March, for example,
objects to the Moffat family's placing excessive jewelry on Meg
and to Aunt March's giving a turquoise ring to Amy, who is
"rather too young for such ornaments." Trained as I was in the
rejection of earthly vanity, I saw the irony in Amy's thought that
the ring would remind her "not to be selfish" (LW 139–140,
268–60). My status as outsider enhanced my sensitivity, then, to
distance between the narrator and the foibles of her heroines.

Much more inviting were the dresses of these heroines. Several
began dressed as I was. Marilla, for example, gives Anne dresses
with "plain skirts . . . , plain waists, with sleeves as plain as waist

and skirt," which are "neat and clean and new, . . . good, sensible, serviceable" (AGG 76−77). Anne's opinion, however, of her "horrid old wincey," "snuffy-colored gingham," and "black-and-white checked sateen" is sharply opposed: "they're not—pretty" (AGG 13,76).

With these heroines, who were often impoverished or orphaned, I could dream of dresses with ribbons, ruffles and puffs. I could appreciate the delicacy of Rebecca's green cashmere dress with its tatted collar (RSF 178−79). With Anne, I contemplated each detail of her brown gloria dress:

> Anne took the dress and looked at it in reverent silence. Oh, how pretty it was—a lovely soft brown gloria with all the gloss of silk; a skirt with dainty frills and shirrings; a waist elaborately pintucked in the most fashionable way, with a little ruffle of filmy lace at the neck. But the sleeves—they were the crowning glory! Long elbow cuffs, and above them two beautiful puffs divided by rows of shirring and bows of brown-silk ribbon.[AGG 196]

To be sure, the extravagance of these girls' desires seemed to me comically showy. Rebecca and Emma Jane dream of a ruby dress with "sweeping train and ruffly, curly edges" and contrasting sash (RSF 142−43). And for Anne, "life was really not worth living without puffed sleeves" (AGG 79).

Even more than clothing, hairstyles carried symbolic weight in my reading. Unlike my own braids, Anne's and Rebecca's became ornaments, looped up and tied with big bows (AGG 259, RSF 248). Since "plainness" had meant a struggle to suppress my naturally fancy curls, I probably felt about curls as Anne did about puffed sleeves. Even neutral descriptions caught my attention: "little curls [were] blowing about . . . [Meg's] forehead" (LW 166); and "short, silky curls . . . clustered over Anne's head" (AGG 215). Especially significant to me—and often symbolic within the text—were scenes of liberated hair and curls: "Jo pull[ed] . . . off her net, and . . . [shook] down her chestnut mane" (LW 21). With her wavy hair loosened from pigtails, Rebecca becomes not only "handsome" (RSF 89) but more womanly: "Then a purely feminine touch was given to the hair that waved back from . . .

[Rebecca's] face—a touch that rescued little crests and wavelets from bondage and set them free to take a new color in the sun" (RSF 264).

Equally striking, plain hairstyles like my own were equated in these books with sickness, sorrow, and rigidity. Marilla, "tall, thin, . . . with angles and without curves," wears her hair in "a hard little knot . . . with two wire hairpins stuck aggressively through it." Her appearance reflects "narrow experience and rigid conscience" (AGG 5). Pollyanna's aunt wears her hair in a tight bun as a sign of her rejection of marriage; once Pollyanna loosens and arranges Miss Polly's "softening little curls," she is pretty, but so long as she represses her emotions the curls lie "stretched dead at the ends of her fingers" (P 11–12, 153,155). Such symbolism called up and contradicted that of my own culture, which condemned my curls, and I echoed as a reader Pollyanna's question when she discovers her aunt's naturally curly hair: "*Can* folks have 'em [curls] when you don't know they've got 'em? *Do* you suppose I could?*" (P 148)

Thus these books reversed the symbols of femininity to which I had been accustomed: worldly, fancy jewelry, clothing, and hairstyles were good; plain appearance signaled defects of character and lack of love. Yet in areas other than physical appearance, the fictional world was much like my own, inculcating the values of beauty in character, discipline of children, duty, contentment, and especially work and religion. Since, despite their worldly appearance, the heroines practiced moral virtues, these books shook my belief in Mennonite teachings on dress.[2] Ironically, these heroines taught me to see *behind* appearances.

The moral realm of these novels included a familiar emphasis on discipline. My strict upbringing aligned me with aunts who insisted that children should be "trained up proper" (AGG 6) to patience, obedience, and silence (CG 86–87, 94, 115, 119; AGG 32, 67; P 1–2, 46). Though impatient with many such restraints, my heroines also embraced duty and accepted adversity. Anne "looked her duty courageously in the face and found it a friend" (AGG 293), the March girls model their behavior on *Pilgrim's Progress*, and Pollyanna plays the glad game. For me they exemplified a familiar Pauline model: "I have learned, in whatsoever state I am, therewith to be content" (Phil. 4:11).[3]

But the most significant values in these books for me—

confirming that the heroines' world was good—were work and religion. Taught that I should be "a good worker" and that "if any would not work, neither should he eat" (2 Thess. 3:10), I identified with the characters' will to serve. I noted not just the multitude of chores—the women wash dishes, make beds, clean, cook, iron, sew, feed poultry—but the attitude, as when Rebecca surprises her aunts by preparing breakfast for visiting missionaries (RSF 211–14), or the Marches find in their tasks a "blessed solace" (LW 226).

One of the features of these books least familiar to most modern readers—their biblical echoes—brought them close to me. I recognized immediately the David and Goliath story in *Children of Greycourt*, paraphrases such as "bridle your unruly tongue" (RSF 120), "we have put our hand to the plough" (RSF 255; see also AGG 98), "loving our neighbour better than ourselves" (LW 37), or "denying yourself and taking up your cross" (P 82).[4] The heroines engage in Bible reading, prayer, hymn singing; they confess their wrongdoings and express in various ways their Christian beliefs.

Imitation, it is said, is the highest form of praise. Having vicariously experienced an alternative mode of femininity through my reading, I created a "fancy" Laura in my daydreams. On visits to my non-Mennonite cousin Blanche, I could even dress up in her worldly pink and white beribboned dress with pink socks and let my curly hair hang loose. Once I had left home as an adult, I had even more freedom to decide how I would appear to others and to myself. Gradually I found, however, that the world of fashion also imprisons women in "self-imposed tortures" (RSF 298). Only as an adult have I fully appreciated the irony of Alcott and Wiggin in describing curling irons and "the price" of socially conditioned ideals of beauty (LW 48, RSF 297–98). By reading and then imitating, I have come to understand Anne, who explained "There's such a lot of different Annes in me" (AGG 158).

Reading as an outsider intensified for me the dualities that are embedded in these books and led me to recognize the diversity of values such as plainness and fanciness, moral virtues and worldly beauty. As an adult I am still partially a "plain" outsider observing the World, but I am also a "worldly" observer of "plain" people. I have chosen to live on the hyphen: "Sitting atop the hyphen provides a marvelous view" (Aycock 2).

Notes

1. In parenthetical documentation the following abbreviations will be used: *Anne of Green Gables, AGG.; Children of Greycourt, CG; Little Women, LW; Pollyanna, P; Rebecca of Sunnybrook Farm, RSF.*

2. Simple appearances do figure as an ideal at times: Mr. Ladd prefers Rebecca's "clover blossom" beauty to Huldah Meserve's "gaudy sunflower" beauty (RSF 249); Mrs. March hopes for modesty as well as beauty in her daughters (LW 140); and Anne realizes, when her green dyed hair has been cut off, that she has been "vain" about her "long and thick and curly" hair (AGG 213).

3. Compare the Pennsylvania Dutch saying, "It could have been worse" (Good 25).

4. *Children of Greycourt* even includes biblical verses as epigraphs (Phil. 4:8 and Eph. 6:11).

Works Cited

Alcott, Louisa M. *Little Women.* 1868. Harmondsworth: Penguin, 1953.
Aycock, Wendell. "Hyphen-nation." MELUS 7 (Spring 1980): 2.
Glover, Julia Lestarjette. *Children of Greycourt and Some Things They Learned.* Rock Island, Ill.: Augustana Book Concern, 1928.
Good, Noah G., trans., "It Could Have Been Worse" [a translation of "Es Hett Awwer Schlimmer Sei Kenne," a Pennsylvania Dutch story recorded by Good from memories of a story circulated orally in Brecknock Township, Lancaster County, Pennsylvania, during the early 1900s. *Pennsylvania Mennonite Heritage* 7 (Oct. 1984): 24–25.
Montgomery, Lucy Maud. *Anne of Green Gables.* 1908. New York: Grosset & Dunlap, 1935.
Porter, Eleanor Hodgman. *Pollyanna.* New York: L.C. Page & Company, 1913.
Wiggin, Kate Douglas. *Rebecca of Sunnybrook Farm.* 1903. New York: Grosset & Dunlap, 1917.

Reviews

The History of American Children's Books

Gillian Avery

Dictionary of American Children's Fiction, 1859–1959, by Alethea K. Helbig and Agnes Regan Perkins. Westport, Conn.: Greenwood Press, 1985.

American Childhood: A Research Guide and Historical Handbook, edited by Joseph M. Hawes and N. Ray Hiner. Westport, Conn.: Greenwood Press, 1985.

Children's Periodicals of the United States, edited by R. Gordon Kelly. Westport, Conn.: Greenwood Press, 1984.

Curiously, despite the seriousness with which children's books are treated in the United States, we have so far no comprehensive history of American children's books; and indeed, if contributions to *Children's Literature* are representative, there is far more interest in the history of English books (perhaps due to the appeal of the fantasy in which the English tradition is so strong). The Greenwood Press's *Dictionary of American Children's Fiction, 1859–1959* would seem to provide at last what so many of us have been looking for. The preface claims that "it is intended for the use of everyone who is concerned with children's literature in any way: librarians, teachers, literary scholars, researchers in American studies, parents, booksellers, publishers, editors—those to whom literature for children is a vital interest professionally or personally." But a cursory glance at the index establishes that, despite the title, there is little here to help those with an interest in the pre-twentieth-century book. Inexplicable omissions—for instance, neither *Uncle Remus* nor *Rootabaga Stories* gets a mention—raise the question whether it will be adequate even for parents and teachers searching for worthwhile reading.

It is teachers, however, that the editors seem mostly to have in mind, and librarians in their capacity of information bureaus. To judge by articles about individual fictitious characters and a subject index that ranges from *Customs Inspectors* to *Left-handed Persons,* from *Merry-go-rounds* to *Salt, Mistaken for Sugar,* they seem to envisage a source of topics for school projects or answers to questions about the identification of books—"It was something about a left-handed customs inspector on a merry-go-round"—when the author, the title, and the plot have been forgotten by the inquirer. It makes for dull reading, though. Margery Fisher's *Who's Who in Children's Books* (London, 1975), a compilation with illustrations (which the *Dictionary* lacks) of familiar characters from English and American children's books, is both more lively and more perceptive.

Fisher also has a far keener sense of history. It is baffling to speculate why the editors of the *Dictionary* bothered to include the nineteenth century at all since, out of 420 titles, at my rough count, only thirteen were published before 1900: by Alcott, Aldrich, Burnett (whom the English also claim), Dodge, Lucretia Hale, Washington Irving (well outside the time span of the volume), Jack London, Laura Richards, Stockton, and Twain. The editors appear to be able to assess books only by present-day criteria, and though they say bravely, "We realized that it would be necessary to include fiction which was once thought meritorious, even though changing values have dated it or made it unacceptable by modern standards," they have for all practical purposes abandoned the last century as hopeless.

Those with any feeling for the children's books of the past must feel outraged at all that has been passed over in a particularly rich period, more especially because of the apparently dreary mediocrity of so much of the twentieth-century writing. One searches the preface desperately for a clue to the editors' guidelines. The answer seems to lie in the subtitle—"Books of Recognized Merit." The editors say modestly that "subjective judgement about which books are best or most important would produce a lopsided and idiosyncratic work," and so they have settled for books that have won literary awards. The ephemeral life of award-winners was finely observed by Rosemary Manning in "Whatever became of Onion John," an article in the *Times Literary Supplement*, 4 December 1969. *Onion John*, a Newberry of 1959, had disappeared from memory ten years later without leaving a ripple, as had so many other award-winners. It is the usual fate of children's books well-regarded by the authority of the time; one could cite innumerable examples, from the very start of children's book reviewing in Mrs. Trimmer's little journal, *The Guardian of Education*, at the beginning of the last century. Conversely, those that are going to become classics are rarely identified at first, the obvious example of course being *Alice's Adventures in Wonderland*, which few reviewers of 1865 felt was more noteworthy—except for the distinction of the Tenniel illustrations—than any other book offered that particular Christmas season. If the editors felt unequal to making their own selection, it would have been far better to use Jacob Blanck's *Parley to Penrod* (1956) than to rely on contemporary awards or critics' views. While Blanck's compilation is mainly a bibliographical guide, it is valuable to literary historians since he took pains to ensure that in this list of the most popular children's books in each year from 1850 to 1926, all the major writers were represented. And, contrary to the impression that the *Dictionary* gives, there were scores of good writers in the last century who still merit attention from readers today.

Admittedly, the great majority of children's books, once the generation for whom they were written has grown up, hold interest only for social historians. By concentrating on what critics and educators have deemed meritorious, the *Dictionary* has sadly missed much in the fabric of American childhood of the past. It is no good looking here for Elsie Dinsmore, the Bobbsey Twins, the Hardy Boys or Nancy Drew, or for Katy Carr, Daddy Long-Legs, Mrs. Wiggs of the Cabbage Patch, Penrod, Pollyanna, the Five Little Peppers, Peck's Bad Boy, or Toby Tyler.

Though never scintillating, the *Dictionary* is at least clearly written and accurate, which is more than can be said for Elizabeth Francis's article "American Children's Literature, 1646–1880" in the Greenwood Press symposium *American Childhood*, edited by Joseph M. Hawes and N. Ray Hiner. There are some amazing errors, such as the wrong dates for *Alice* and *The King of the Golden River*, and extraordinary statements such as that Charlotte Brontë wrote for children or that Isaiah Thomas commissioned new children's books. Worse than this are the cloudy oratory, general muddle, and omissions. It is transparently clear that Francis has read few primary works in this area other than some Cotton Mather texts, Hawthorne, and *Little Women*, eked out with various literary histories and a couple of early rarities. Peter Parley, Jacob Abbott, and other educators are never discussed, nor the travelogue genre which is uniquely American; none of the boys' books (not even *Tom Sawyer*) is mentioned nor such Sunday school blockbusters as *The Wide, Wide World*, *The Lamplighter*, or *Elsie Dinsmore*. There is far too much about English publications, often wrong (there was no "Newbery Press"; the author of *The Blind Child* is

Mrs. Pinchard, not Pritchard; Lewis Carroll's writing owed nothing
to the stories of Grimm or Andersen); and the analysis of *Little
Women* is inappropriately long, when so much has been excluded.

The second essay in this volume, by Sally Allen McNall, is as
good as the first is inadequate; indeed it is probably the best account available of the period from 1880 to the present. McNall
analyzes the main trends with commendable clarity and succinct-
ness, threading her way (and never losing it) through scores of
now-forgotten titles. With an unusual feeling for the immediate
past, she summarizes the spirit of each age and produces books
that illustrate her point. What so easily could have become an arid
catalogue is both highly readable and illuminating. There are one
or two errors, even so: it is Henry A. Shute, not Schulte, and his
Real Diary of a Real Boy was published in 1902, not 1903; and
Booth Tarkington's *Penrod* series began in 1914, not 1913.

Children's Periodicals of the United States, edited by R. Gordon
Kelly, is similarly excellent. Together with the editor's *Mother was
a Lady* (1974), a study of the ethic of selected nineteenth-century
children's periodicals), it is probably the best work at present on
the subject of American children's books. Its editor makes modest
claims, saying that the volume is only a beginning, that much remains to be done, that specialists will quickly point out certain
omissions, that ten more years would have made it a better book.
But this work of some fifty different hands is a model of scholarship, and the style of writing is crisp, succinct, and readable.

The earliest American juvenile magazine, *The Children's Magazine,* which survived only for four months in 1789, was, it must be
said, a very prosy affair. Children had done better with Newbery's
Lilliputian Magazine, which in its brief life from 1751–52,
attracted subscribers even in Maryland. There were at least stories
and riddles and, what was more, a Lilliputian Society. We could
hardly guess that *The Children's Magazine* was catering to the same
species, with its advice "on the best methods of recovering from
the dreadful effect of dram drinking" and "rules for a life of business." But until the 1860s, with the honorable exception of *The
Juvenile Miscellany* and Samuel Goodrich's publications *Parley's
Magazine* and its companion *Merry's Museum,* the early periodicals
seemed to be aimed at miniature adults rather than children.
Moreover, these miniature adults on occasion produced their own
journals—not happy-go-lucky, handwritten family affairs like *The*

Rectory Umbrella, which the young Lewis Carroll supervised, but properly printed commercial propositions, like *The Juvenile Port-Folio,* which fourteen-year-old Thomas Condie of Philadelphia ran from 1812 to 1816. A high-minded youth, he went in for philosophical musings on such subjects as "Deceit," "Punctuality," "Bets and Oaths." There was the occasional joke, but he complained of the difficulty in procuring "a sufficiency of *chaste* wit and humour." And such jokes as he does print belong to the bar rather than to the nursery. One of the most chilling publications for the juvenile businessman was *The Juvenile Key,* published from Brunswick, Maine between 1830 and 1833 by Joseph Griffen, whose two sons, aged seven and nine, did most of the typesetting besides being involved with the makeup, promotion, and distribution. This was entirely appropriate since the ideal child of *The Juvenile Key* was the child dedicated to usefulness. Children were told to eschew all games and recreation. As to reading and learning, they should limit themselves to practical matters which would make them good farmers or mechanics, "for these are the hope of our country." There was, surprisingly, little religious content, for although Griffin, like many Protestants, opposed alcohol, tobacco, and holiday fireworks, he did so on the grounds that these inhibited work and wealth.

Many such little-known publications are to be found in Kelly, each with a full account of its publishing history, a lively analysis of its general character and content, and the location of libraries holding files. Southern rarities such as *Acanthus* and *Rose Bud* are included, as well as the obvious favorites like *The Youth's Companion* (with a life span of 102 years, the longest-lived of all), *Our Young Folks, The Riverside Magazine, St. Nicholas,* and *Harper's Young People.* In articles on these and other journals of the 1870s and the 1880s one can find important information about children's writers of the day. An appendix lists 423 titles of publications from 1789 to 1980, of which fewer than a quarter are discussed in detail; the choice of these has been eclectic, ranging from Mennonite and Jewish periodicals to *Ranger Rick's Nature Magazine,* from temperance journals to *Seventeen.* There is an admirable index, as well as chronological and geographical listings. It is a book hard to fault, and it will be a most useful tool to historians working in the field of children's books.

Moralists, but with No Pretense

Janice M. Alberghene

The Moral Life of Children, by Robert Coles. Boston: Atlantic
Monthly Press, 1986.
The Political Life of Children, by Robert Coles. Boston: Atlantic
Monthly Press, 1986.

Children's literature and the didactic impulse are, it seems, inseparable. Although overt moralizing has gone out of fashion in
books for all but the very young, adult readers are as quick to
note the subtle messages in contemporary texts as they are to debate the socialization engendered by cautionary tale and classic
fairy tale alike. The big questions behind this critical investigation
never change. "Is this a good book for children?" and "Is this
book good *for* children?" (two questions that differ only in the
degree to which they announce their didactic concern) prompt as
much interest today as they did in the days when the Good Book
was one of the few books good enough to read. Few questions in
the study of children's literature are more necessary, but the value
of the question is directly proportional to the asker's willingness to
make concrete and particular those most abstract and ideological
of terms—*good* and *children*. What particular "good" and what particular "child" does the critic have in mind?

What "good" and what "child" are the very questions *The Moral
Life of Children* and its companion colume, *The Political Life of Children*, ask the critic of children's literature to consider. For child
psychiatrist Robert Coles, best known for his five-volume *Children
of Crisis* series, such concrete questions have always been embedded in his methodology of long-term direct observation of individual children. His insights derive from the specifics of particular
situations, or as Coles himself says in the introduction to *The Political Life*, "The hope is that a few dozen children, quite intensively
visited, fairly well known (one hopes and prays) will shed some
light on how children grow psychologically, and of course, morally and politically" (17).

Here we need to pause. This last phrase—"and of course, morally and politically"—is, as Coles would be the first to say, a little

misleading taken out of the context of the companion volume's
introduction. It is true that Coles's *methodology* of direct observation has always led him to present questions of value in both the
circumstances in which they arise and in terms which reflect as
faithfully as possible the perception of the child or children with
whom he was speaking. This manner of presenting values should
not be confused, however, with his always having had his present
interest in the moral life of children as a *subject* in its own right.
Coles opens *The Moral Life* with an admission:

> If my wife had had her way, back in 1960, when our work in
> the South with black and white children was just starting, the
> subject matter of this book would have been our major preoc-
> cupation all along. She is a high school teacher (English and
> history), and she has always been interested in the moral side
> of her students' lives: their ideals and values; their sense of
> what is right and wrong, and how they state their reasons;
> and not least, the moral statements they make in response to
> what she teaches. . . .
> I have to say that such was not my inclination. [3]

While it is gratifying for those of us who teach literature to see
the prescience of a fellow English teacher, let me hasten to add
that Coles's coming late to the subject of the moral life of children
means that he has all the more to suggest to adults interested in
either good books for children or books good for children. Consider for instance, the following:

> I hope that my mode of approach to the moral thinking of
> children, my way of regarding their daily life from a moral
> perspective *they themselves uphold* [italics added], gives a boost
> to the tradition of "direct observation" Anna Freud urged
> upon us clinicians who work with the young. "Let us try to
> learn from children all they have to tell us," she said, "and let
> us sort out only later, how their ideas fit in with our own."
> Then she added: "Sometimes the children we see will even
> help us with our own problems, those of theory, because
> there can be many clues for theory in what a child chooses to
> say to an adult listener." [15]

The presuppositions here—that children are capable of forming
and upholding their own moral perspectives; that, as Anna Freud

urges, the adult should learn from children and only then theorize about them—provide a salutary perspective from which to view and perhaps enter into the current debate on teaching values and molding character in our schools. As calls for some teaching of values become more and more frequent (and these calls come from across the political spectrum), the terms of discussion shift ever more resolutely toward determining which values to teach. This framework precludes the possibility that children may be more than characterless, valueless blank pages that need to be filled with the right material from the right books.

The framework Coles provides in *The Moral Life* shows young people as seekers and formulators of codes that shape their actions in daily life. While Coles declares his respect for the theories of moral development articulated by Lawrence Kohlberg and Carol Gilligan, two theorists often cited by critics of children's literature, he also notes that his readers will see his "perplexity that sometimes slides into pique as I compare their ideas about 'moral development' with the thoroughly complicated matter of moral (and yes, spiritual) *behavior* in children, and [readers] will notice irony, at the very least" (286).

Coles lays out his own ideas and observations about moral behavior in seven chapters that begin with an exploration of moral development and psychoanalysis and end by considering children's reactions to the nuclear bomb. Intervening chapters address such issues as moral purpose and the dynamics of the conscience, the meaning of the term *character*, idealism as a moral habit, and, to borrow a phrase Coles uses above, the "thoroughly complicated matter" of social class as a shaper of moral vision. Each of these chapters offers much to think about, but none is more suggestive to the literary critic than that chapter titled "Movies and Moral Energy."

The chapter could have been subtitled "The Mysteries of Viewer/Reader Response." Coles presents both a spectrum of reactions to the same film and reaction to a spectrum of films. Puzzled why one child, Tessie, heeded certain aspects of *Raisin in the Sun* while ignoring others, Coles concludes, "One is left only with the mystery that takes place between each reader and each text, and each viewer and each film: the diversity of stimulation that emerges from several characters embedded in a complex plot, and the considerable latitude of awareness and moral concern in an

audience" (65). Adults who study literature for children and adolescents may be mystified themselves by Coles's surprise that several young people who saw *To Kill a Mockingbird* focused on the
Boo Radley subplot (in which Boo saves the lives of a six-year-old
and a ten-year-old) while adults focused on the "movie's explicit
celebration of a lawyer's decency and rectitude." Reader response
studies in the field of children's literature have made critics aware
of the potentially vast differences between children's responses to
texts and those of adults, but hindsight plays a part as well; Coles
notes that what then caught the children's attention is now "the
most arresting part of the movie for many viewers" (68). At any
rate, Coles's pointing to a text's "diversity of stimulation" and an
audience's "considerable latitude of awareness" avoids psychological determinism and provides reader response critics further incentive to observe actual children.

Coles finds much that is heartening in his own observations of
children's responses to texts. He refers time and again to acts of
"moral imagination," not a few of which derive their energy from
what appear to be unlikely sources: "On some days one wonders
about the use of that word 'moral' in connection with certain
movies—say, those of Clint Eastwood and Charles Bronson," yet
even these movies can offer children the opportunity to exercise
their moral imaginations (88).

Just as Coles sees children's moral lives informed by imagination, so too does he see imagination at work / at play in their
political lives. Authority, the idea of the homeland, religion, ideology, language, culture, race, class, exile, and political morality—all
these are important too and receive careful consideration in *The
Political Life of Children*, but these factors' very importance derives
in part from their relationship to the life of the imagination. Coles
cites the work of Australian social scientist Robert Connell in this
connection: "Among his observations . . . is the notion of 'intuitive political thinking.' Young and not-so-young children, from
four or five to nine or ten, say, not only show evidence of 'socialization,' but of surprisingly outspoken, idiosyncratic, blunt, and
imaginative political opinions. They can poke fun at the self-
important, see through any number of phonies, and wryly take on
subjects the rest of us have learned to skirt or get at only indirectly" (27).

If readers of Coles's book are surprised to learn that five-year-olds have political lives, let alone political lives that are richly imaginative, a quick review of Hans Christian Andersen's story "The Emperor's New Clothes" might be in order. Andersen's fairy tale shows a young child undeterred by the smooth talk of any number of phonies. The child bluntly states what the courtiers and townspeople skirt: the emperor is not wearing any clothes. Children's literature affords many examples of children's intuitive political thinking, yet those critics who discuss children's political lives usually do so in terms of "political socialization." Intuitive political thinking, though not ignored, is perceived subliminally in terms of moral choice; Andersen's child is pure of heart and sees through the moral hypocrisy of his elders.

Although critics have an obligation to think analytically as well as intuitively, this conflating of the moral and political is not exactly an occasion for distress. Coles's companion volumes make clear the inseparable connections between moral life and political life; problems arise precisely when the political is divorced from moral considerations and moral action. No such divorce clouds these two volumes and Coles's portraits of the admirable children Jane Coles calls "moralists, with no pretense."

Playing Hopscotch through Children's Literature

Glenn Edward Sadler

The World Treasury of Children's Literature, selected with commentary by Clifton Fadiman. Illustrated by Leslie Morrill. 2 volumes. Boston: Little, Brown, 1984−85.

Clifton Fadiman's *World Treasury* anthology, which is intended for a popular market, presents a highly selective and personal collection of works centered on the "hidden child" figure in books written for or adopted by children. Fadiman defines the "hidden child" vaguely: "The child, we know, is something more, or less, but in any case other, than an embryonic 'civilized' adult" (598). Supposedly for handling convenience by the real child, the treasury comes in two volumes, and volume 1 is subdivided into two books; but the resulting books are still too big and heavy for a child to carry. The volumes provide an accessible source of well-known materials for home reading, but there is no attempt to present a comprehensive coverage of the field of children's literature.

Fadiman's individualistic approach ends up being a pathless maze of octogenarian literary reminiscences, starting with nursery rhymes (from four nationalities only) and concluding with selections from José Maria Sanchez-Silva and Maurice Sendak. Except for an apologetic attempt to group the selections according to reading age levels (ages 4−8 and 9−14), the editor offers no constructive reading plan for child or adult readers ("Some people like to read *through*. Others like to read *in*").

Even more dismaying is the decision to offer a number of brief selections from long stories or novels. From a child's point of view, the ongoing movement of the narrative itself—its development and ending—is the most desirable element of reading. It is wishful thinking to assume that a child will read two chapters of, say, *The Lion, the Witch and the Wardrobe* by C. S. Lewis or a single chapter of *Tom's Midnight Garden* by Philippa Pearce and then "want to read the whole book," as Fadiman suggests. Adults might take this approach, but children would rarely be so enticed.

The mixture of poetry and prose is not in theory a bad idea, but there should be some apparent pattern, which these volumes conspicuously lack; it is all like so many commercials on television. Poems and illustrations selected by Fadiman are hung like decorations on the anthology tree; for instance, Dorothy Aldis's poem "Alone" is tacked on, like a pictorial caboose, to Piper's fictional story "I think I can." Why not put this poem next to Stevenson's "hidden child" verses, where it would fit?

Certainly one of the main purposes of an anthology is to present fresh materials so that the reader will discover unknown works in the context of familiar ones or be encouraged by unfamiliar anthologized selections to read a whole book elsewhere. Unfortunately, this anthology cannot offer many readers this kind of discovery. Except for minor pieces (the Russian fable by Sergei Mikhalkov and Francelia Butler's folktale "The Blanket") there is very little in the *World Treasury* which is not readily available elsewhere.

Fadiman offers the child reader "grandfather's chats" as introductions. Although these bedtime reveries are chatty enough, they add little to the child reader's knowledge of children's literature; to be told that "comic strips such as 'Peanuts' in a way come from Aesop" adds nothing to one's understanding of the beast fables or the influence of the Aesopian tradition. Even if children do not read these introductions, as Fadiman suggests they may not ("Suppose it turned out to be something 'just for people to skip?' "), at least the adult reader could benefit from informative prefaces, which might be passed on to the child at the right moment.

In "For Grown-ups Only," an appendix to volume 2, Fadiman offers a critical discussion of his "hidden child" theory and his "case for a children's literature." This essay is lucidly written and starts some hares worth pursuing, though it seems impossible to distinguish adult from child literature solely—as Fadiman seems to do—on the basis of the "hidden child" theory; children and adults may discover their different versions of the "hidden child" in the same places but at different ages.

What Fadiman has produced is an adult book of selections taken from the vast field of children's classics, one which may or may not be read by children, depending on adult encouragement. *The World Treasury of Children's Literature* is, finally, a missed opportunity.

Meeting the Twayne: Beatrix Potter and Frances Hodgson Burnett

Louisa Smith

Beatrix Potter, by Ruth MacDonald. Boston: Twayne Publishers, 1986.
Frances Hodgson Burnett, by Phyllis Bixler. Boston: Twayne Publishers, 1984.

During the latter part of the nineteenth century, writing for children became both a viable occupation and a source of livelihood for women. Whether by writing books or contributing to the many new periodicals, female authors with talent and persistence could become part of the publishing world. Two recent Twayne studies examine writers who took advantage of this opportunity.

The reviewer's first question must be what these works add to the biographical and critical material already available on Potter and Burnett. Compared with Margaret Lane's biography, *The Magic Years of Beatrix Potter*, the three Leslie Linder books on Potter, and Ann Thwaite's *Waiting for the Party: The Life of Frances Hodgson Burnett*, the Twayne books, limited to 150 pages, look slight. What these Twayne authors can contribute to the scholarship of their subject is a succinct account of the connections between major works and the autobiographical and topical details which put them in perspective.

Bixler's book is the more successful of the two because it also provides original research, a critical thoroughness, and a conclusion which assesses Burnett's contributions to both adult and children's literature; but MacDonald had the tougher assignment. Although Potter left copious finished artwork and sketches, a journal, and letters to her publisher, she remained an intensely private person; as Lane commented, "Here is a life so innocent, so uneventful that one would have supposed the only difficulty would be in finding something to say."

MacDonald is further hampered by her attempt to evaluate both the written and visual work in a Twayne format which does not allow for illustrations. In her treatment of the drafts of artwork for *Benjamin Bunny*, for instance, MacDonald must first describe the original, then the revision: "Though the rabbit's neck still has a peculiar bend to it, the angle is not nearly as odd as in the original drawing. . . . In her revision she made the rabbits larger, and their ears more flared to their sides. The larger rabbits standing on the wall frame the vista of the garden more emphatically, partly because they are larger and partly because they are drawn in darker shades." A few pictures would have been worth many words to MacDonald. As it is, three of her chapters must follow the awkward pattern of telling the stories of the tales, describing the illustrations, and then commenting on both. Perhaps because of this, the book does not venture far into the realm of art criticism; more often than not, MacDonald merely relates the art to places and interests in Potter's life, without much further critical elaboration, as when she links Potter's home in Sawrey with *The Tale of the Roly-Poly Pudding*: "and her two drawings that include the bannister and spindles on the stairway to the second floor imply her admiration for the carpentry and her affection for the claret-colored curtains which she hung in the window of the landing."

MacDonald does provide material on the sources and revisions of the stories, as well as retelling them; but she adds little which has not been well covered by Lane in her biography (for example, compare her account of the private publication of *The Tailor of Gloucester* with Lane's).

In her chapter on Potter's life, MacDonald does not challenge the Sleeping Beauty legend of her youth, which has her kept a virtual prisoner by overprotective parents. She accuses Potter's parents of "deadening regularity," of keeping their daughter dependent and attentive to their health needs, even of rationing her paper because "the elder Potters saw that artwork was luring their daughter away from them." Yet in Potter's journals, one sees a life filled with outings, visits to art galleries, vacations in Scotland, and contact with artists like Millais, who encouraged her drawing. She had freedom to go sketching with her brother on country holidays and at the Museum of Natural History. By her own admission, she was shy and unscholarly. If, like Kate Greenaway, she had had the formal art education available in that day, with its emphasis on classical form, she might not have profited by it or developed her ability to draw woodland animals and settings. Speculation about the senior Potters' intentions regarding their daughter adds little to an understanding of the mysterious interplay of character and circumstance in the development of her creative work.

But MacDonald's book ends with a series of questions that merit fuller development. MacDonald completely misses new information about Potter appearing in the newsletter of the Beatrix Potter Society, which she does not mention at all. Her last chapter, "The Potter Industry," not only discusses the merchandising of the Potter books and their associated paraphernalia but raises the issue of the recent rewriting or reillustration of Potter books which have entered the public domain. She touches on the topic of reception —why Potter has remained so popular with children. Here we must press beyond conclusions that Potter's animals are true to life and that she does not patronize the child reader.

In Frances Hodgson Burnett, Bixler had a livelier personality to work with; Burnett garnered a good deal of press in her own day, for both her success as a popular writer and her unconventional lifestyle. Transplanted from Manchester, England, to Tennessee as a child, by the age of twenty she was writing five or six stories a month for ladies' magazines to help support her siblings (as later she would write to support her husbands and children). She married, divorced, then married a man ten years her junior, to the accompaniment of headlines proclaiming him "Young Enough to be her Son"; she lost a son to tuberculosis. She crossed and recrossed the Atlantic, establishing homes on both sides; hailed as another George Eliot, she found her family life strained by the social life attendant upon her fame.

Although Burnett is now remembered for her children's books—especially *Little Lord Fauntleroy*, *The Secret Garden*, and *The Little Princess*—the reader of Bixler's study will learn that Burnett was once well known as a playwright and author of adult romances (fifty such novels, according to a recent *New Yorker* article). Not satisfied with standard reference works, Bixler has researched the periodicals of Burnett's day; the resulting and surprising effect is to demonstrate how unfairly neglected the bulk of Burnett's work has been. Such books as *Through One Administration* deal with women's issues far more openly than those of her contemporaries, yet she is not studied as a feminist. Other books make careful use of British and American dialect and social habits, yet she is not studied in the context of nineteenth-century realism. Bixler persuades us that some at least of Burnett's work deserves better.

Bixler pulls together the threads of Burnett's complex life to demonstrate how social and biographical events contributed to the patterns of her fiction. Like her friend Henry James, she recognized and dealt with "the international theme"; an interest in the occult which surfaced after her son's death in works like *The Closed Room* and *The White People* connects these works with George MacDonald's *At the Back of the North Wind*. Burnett's growing interest in Christian Science inspired her best-loved book *The Secret Garden*, but later rehandlings of the theme in *The Head of the House of Coombe* and *Robin*, notes Bixler, "show Burnett at her worst as a popular romance writer. They are sentimental, melodramatic and grossly overwritten." This uneven quality of her popular work may explain the undiscriminating critical neglect of Burnett's books for adults.

But Burnett's reputation as a writer for children remains secure. In the final chapter of her study, Bixler sums up Burnett's place in children's literature, the influences on her work, the interrelationship between children's and popular adult fiction, and the debt which both owed to the Romantic movement. This conclusion could stand on its own as a model for the kind of criticism we need in children's literature. In an astonishingly short space, Bixler provides insight into the creation of Burnett's stories, their lasting appeal, and their relationship to other writings of the period. For Bixler, the constraints of the Twayne series work.

Dissertations of Note

Compiled by Rachel Fordyce

Ambanasom, Shadrach Ateke. "The Adolescent Protagonist in the African Novel: An Analysis of Five African Novels." Ph.D. diss. Ohio University, 1985. 288 pp. DAI 47:1320A.

The novels Ambanasom analyzes are *Weep Not Child, A Son of the Soil, The Dark Child, Without a Home,* and *Houseboy.* Each work is directed toward a secondary school audience and has an inspirational protagonist with strong values and a desire for education. The novels deal with such themes as the struggle for independence and liberation, "the quality of social and economic life . . . the dignity and beauty of aspects of the African culture, the question of education, and the problems posed by broken homes." While the major attraction of the novels is their "readability," Ambanasom observes that the authors are more interested in social, political, and cultural issues than "purely adolescent concerns."

Binkney, Richard Harold. "A Study of the Criteria Adolescents Use in the Selection of Novels for a Recommended Reading "Best" List versus the Criteria Adults Use in the Selection of Novels for a Recommended Reading "Best" List." Ph.D. diss. Georgia State University, College of Education, 1986. 344 pp. DAI 47:1167A.

Using the answers to a questionnaire investigating preferences of adolescent and adult groups Binkney suggests that the groups "have conflicting feelings about the criteria used in the selection of novels in terms of subject matter, appearance, and the critical acclaim of works." He concludes that there is no substantial correlation between children's preferences and adult approval, and he includes recommendations that reappraise "literary standards and criteria for evaluation in terms of the extent to which they foster a meaningful experience for the reader."

Cain, Melissa Augustine. "Children's Functioning in the Pictorial Symbol System as Determined by Responses to a Wordless Picture Book." Ph.D. diss. University of Toledo, 1985. 225 pp. DAI 47:450A.

Cain focuses on children's presumed "ability to transmediate their understanding of the pictorial symbol system into oral language" on the assumption that the "true basics of literacy" are "non-verbal experience and oral language."

Campa, Carlota Josephine. "Using Color Computers to Measure Color: Clothes of Main Characters in Caldecott Award Books." Ph.D. diss. University of Maryland, 1985. 140 pp. DAI 47:511A.

The three purposes of this dissertation are to measure the color of the clothing worn by main characters in Caldecott books, to convert the results to a numerical base, and to "determine if there was a relationship between the color of clothing and gender." Campa determines that the differences are not significant, although men's clothes are more drab in hue than women's.

Doering, Sandra Kay. "The Effects of Children's Literature on Self-Concept of Gifted and Nongifted Students." Ed.D. diss. Oklahoma State University, 1985. 93 pp. DAI 46:3595A.

Doering concludes that self-concept appears to be affected by different types of literary programs: gifted students respond better to a "listening" program

211

than to a "structural literature program or to a control program"; nongifted
students are more receptive to structure.

Evans, Arthur Bruce. "Jules Verne and the Scientific Novel." 2 vols. Ph.D. diss.
Columbia University, 1985. 520 pp. DAI 47:174A.

Evans attempts to ameliorate Verne's reputation which, he believes, has suf-
fered considerably at the hands of poor translators, "Hollywood cinema, university snobbism, and the familiar 'pigeon-holing' effect of literary histories." Evans
notes that "as one of the five most translated authors of all time," Verne has
always been a "popular" author; but within the past twenty years his reputation
has improved appreciably in France and his works should not be ignored in this
country.

Golden, Catherine Jean. "The Victorian Illustrated Book: Authors Who Composed with Graphic Images and Words." Ph.D. diss. University of Michigan,
1986. 290 pp. DAI 47:1333A.

Golden focuses on William Thackeray, Lewis Carroll, Dante Gabriel Rossetti,
and Beatrix Potter. The first chapter deals with the illustrated letter, a form
which all engaged in prior to illustrating their own works. She then discusses
Thackeray's use of his illustrations in *Vanity Fair* and *The Rose and the Ring* "to
develop themes essential to the text and advance his ambiguity as narrator." She
finds Carroll's illustrations, although naive and anatomically incorrect when
compared with Tenniel's, to be arranged on the page in such a way as "to develop themes essential to the text." She notes Rossetti's "visual-verbal" pairing of
word and image that culminates "in physically joining poem and painting within
one frame" in *Proserpine* and other works. Finally, she asserts that Potter deserves critical acclaim for her illustrations and notes that an analysis of the fair
copy of Potter's work "demonstrates that she writes in her sketches separate
from her narrative as a composing heuristic to bring into being her narrative
pictorial compositions."

Graham, Joan Wynne. "The Effects of Reading Ethnic Literature on the Attitudes
of Adolescents." Ph.D. diss. Georgia State University, College of Education,
1985. 276 pp. DAI 46:3636A.

The purpose of this dissertation is to determine the effect of ethnic literature
on white high school students and their attitudes toward the Vietnamese. Graham acknowledges that "attitude changes are both complex and individual."
Nonetheless, her study produced from "marginal to major positive change."

Gray, Fred Allen. "Children's Musicals, 1973–1985: Annotations with Sourcebook
for Production." D.M.A. diss. University of Arizona, 1985. 357 pp. DAI
46:3643A.

Gray collects and annotates musicals published since 1972 for elementary
school children. He chooses those which have a story line, have "dialog interaction between the characters," and use "mostly original music." He includes a
brief history of musicals for children in America since 1735 and a brief analysis
of 210 contemporary musicals.

Karimipour, Zahra. "A Descriptive Bibliography of C. S. Lewis's Fiction,
1938–1981." Ph.D. diss. Oklahoma State University, 1985. 224 pp. DAI
46:3726A.

Karimipour analyzes the criticism surrounding the Space Trilogy, the Narnia
Chronicles, and *Till We Have Faces*. The purpose of the dissertation is "to describe . . . the essential meaning of each work and evaluate it according to its
stated purpose and its quality relative to other works" by Lewis. Karimipour's
concluding chapter assesses the trends in Lewis criticism and his place in the
history of English letters.

Kutiper, Karen Sue. "A Survey of the Adolescent Poetry Preferences of Seventh, Eighth, and Ninth Graders." Ed.D. diss. University of Houston, 1985. 187 pp. DAI 47:451–52A.

Kutiper surveys 375 students to determine what poems they like best, "to analyze the most popular poems [by] type, content, and . . . poetic elements," to compare her results with those of previous studies, and "to compare differences in preference when different modes of presentation are used." Her study shows that students prefer to read poetry rather than be read to and that their preferences are quite traditional: "they preferred rhyme, the humorous narrative form, and content based on familiar experiences. Haiku and free and blank verse were the least popular forms of poetry."

Lin, Huey-Ya. "Moral Development and Children's Literature in Taiwan." Ph.D. diss. University of California, Santa Barbara, 1985. 158 pp. DAI 47:413A.

Lin analyzes 179 Taiwanese stories "concerning morality for children" aged 6–8, 752 for children 9–10, and 659 for ages 11–12 to determine how "moral traits" are presented to children in the literature with which they identified. Lin finds that the same type of moral issues appear in stories for all ages but that the presentation of them varies considerably.

Loges, Mary Kaiser. "The Poetry of Walter de la Mare: A Re-Evaluation." Ph.D. diss. University of Denver, 1985. 283 pp. DAI 46:3349A.

Loges notes that since de la Mare's death in 1956 there has been no major study of his work. She places him squarely in the middle of "modernist" poetry and analyzes his ties to Yeats, Hardy, and Frost. She says that de la Mare's major theme is that "the solipsistic trap of consciousness can only be broken through in early childhood, in dream, or in death."

McGregor, Barbara Ruth. "The American Fiction of Isaac Bashevis Singer: Lost and Found in America." Ph.D. diss. Texas Christian University, 1985. 342 pp. DAI 46:3353A.

McGregor is concerned primarily with the critical reception of Singer or, more exactly, the lack of criticism of his works in this country. She does not focus specifically on Singer's work for children but her observations are generally applicable.

Monseau, Virginia Ricci. "Young Adult Literature and Reader Response: A Descriptive Study of Students and Teachers." Ph.D. diss. University of Michigan, 1986. 223 pp. DAI 47:816A.

Monseau deals with *subjective* responses of high school students and teachers and concludes that students' responses to young adult literature may be rhetorically less sophisticated than those of their teachers but the response itself is essentially the same. She feels that young adult literature is rarely taken seriously in the classroom except for remedial classes.

Phelps, Ruth M. "A Comparison of Newbery Award Winners in the First and Last Decade of the Award (1922–31 and 1976–85)." Ph.D. diss. Miami University, 1985. 158 pp. DAI 47:453A.

Phelps analyzes changes among the books in terms of "sex role identifications of the protagonist, diverse ethnic oriented context, problems of the main character and the social values of family life, importance of education, initiative and loyalty." Although values remained fairly consistent, Phelps notes considerable difference in emphasis and characterization.

Selinger, Bernard George. "Ursula K. LeGuin and the Paradox of Identity in Contemporary Fiction." Ph.D. diss. York University (Canada), 1984. DAI 46:3721A.

Selinger's four major chapters deal with *A Wizard of Earthsea, The Left Hand of Darkness, The Lathe of Heaven,* and *The Dispossessed.* He contends that "the artist has no strong sense of identity, and that the creative state of mind is, among other things, a temporary regression to preverbal days when one's identity *theme* is 'imprinted.' ' He sees each novel as a variation of the theme of identity in which "the artist confronts the origins of her existence, the problems of separation/autism and symbiosis, private language and public language, and human sexuality." He also relates LeGuin's work to that of Lern, Delany, Nabokov, and Barth and applies to her work the studies of Margaret Mahler, Bruno Bettelheim, D. W. Winnicott, Jacques Lacan, and Julia Kristeva, among others.

Shealy, Daniel Lester. "The Author-Publisher Relationships of Louisa May Alcott." Ph.D. diss. University of South Carolina, 1985. 291 pp. DAI 46:3721A.

Shealy emphasizes the difference between late nineteenth-century and twentieth-century editors in terms of their influence on authors and shows how effective Frank Leslie, James Redpath, A. K. Loring, Mary Mapes Dodge, and, especially, Thomas Niles were in molding Alcott's career. The dissertation draws primarily from unpublished correspondence, "focuses on [Alcott's] relationship with her editor," and illustrates how Niles "changed her from a writer of pulp fiction to the author of classic novels."

Shillinglaw, Susan Grace. "The Art of Cooper's Landscapes: Identity, Theme, and Structure in the Leatherstocking Tales." Ph.D. diss. University of North Carolina, Chapel Hill, 1985. 252 pp. DAI 46:3354A.

The Pioneers, The Last of the Mohicans, The Prairie, The Deerslayer, and *The Pathfinder* are the subject of Shillinglaw's dissertation. She emphasizes the differences among the novels, asserting that Cooper "imaginatively discovered meaning in space, not time"—the latter being impossible because of the lack of social sophistication or long national history in America. "In a Cooper novel the landscape generates meaning: characters' identities as well as the structure and the thematic tension of a novel emerge from the setting." In contrast to D. H. Lawrence, who argues that the novels become progressively more mythic, Shillinglaw argues that "Cooper deepens our involvement with Leatherstocking's heroic spirit as we see the hero first defined in a mythic context, then challenged in an allegorical landscape, and finally matured in a scene both wild and domestic." Finally she shows how Cooper, thoroughly disillusioned with American culture, ultimately reconciles himself to his native land and envisions "some hope for the individual . . . whose understanding of civilization is combined with an appreciation necessary to love natural sublimity and the fortitude necessary to survive in nature."

Stone, Mary Ruth Morris. "The Effect of Selected Children's Literature on Children's Attitudes toward the Elderly." Ed.D. diss. University of Alabama, 1985. 161 pp. DAI 46:3597A.

Stone concludes that it is possible to affect children's perceptions of the elderly, both positively and negatively. She bases her conclusion on students' reactions to semantic difference in twenty-five stories for young people.

Suthamchai, Phanida. "The Fusion of Christian and Fictional Elements in C. S. Lewis's Chronicles of Narnia." Ph.D. diss. Oklahoma State University, 1985. 165 pp. DAI 47:916A.

Suthamchai asserts that there has never been a thorough analysis of Lewis's use of the fairy tale form prior to this one. He achieves his critical perspective by blending a discussion of the fairy tale form with a discussion of how Lewis treats setting, characterization, structure of plot, and theme in a Christian context. He believes that "Lewis's fusion of Christian doctrines and these . . . aspects in the chronicles of Narnia provide a basis for his artistic craftsmanship, and his success guarantees his high achievement in the literary world."

Tubman, William Willis, Jr. "The Development of a Children's Book about Learning Disabilities." Ed.D. diss. University of Maryland, 1985. 245 pp. DAI 47:82A.

With the hope that it would foster greater understanding, Tubman created "Revielle" for nonhandicapped middle school students who, prior to the passage of Public Law 94-142, had never been exposed to handicapped children in the classroom.

Wilson, Patricia Jane. "Children's Classics: A Reading Preference Study of Fifth and Sixth Graders. Ed.D. diss. University of Houston, 1985. 200 pp. DAI 47:454A.

Wilson studies the preference of students for books "generally recognized as classics in children's literature" to identify the most and least preferred, "to compare relationships between the children's classics and grade level and sex," to see if the age of the work had any effect on children's preferences, and to analyze the more popular books in terms of content, tone, and literary aspects. She concludes that *Charlotte's Web* was by far the favorite, followed by *Little House in the Big Woods, The Hobbit, The Secret Garden, The Lion, the Witch, and the Wardrobe, Heidi,* and *The Borrowers.*

Young, Beverly Burgoyne. "The Young Female Protagonist in Juvenile Fiction: Three Decades of Evolution." Ph.D. diss. Washington State University, 1985. 205 pp. DAI 46:3276A.

Young examined realistic children's fiction in the 1930s, the 1950s, and the 1970s to determine the "evolution of societal assumptions" concerning young American female protagonists. She discovered that the treatment of young female characters changed significantly over time, that plots and situations became less formulaic, that the works as a whole became "more mimetic of realities in culture," and that characters became "increasingly protest-oriented" even though they tended to move back to a "traditional perspective" at the conclusion of the works.

Zehr, Janet Susan. "Louisa May Alcott and the Female Fairy Tale." Ph.D. diss. University of Illinois, Urbana-Champaign, 1985. 221 pp. DAI 46:3355A.

Zehr states that the primary form for most of Alcott's fiction is the "female-centered fairy tale." Even though Alcott herself scorned the formula, Zehr argues, she used this genre over and over again because it satisfied her audience's desire for romance and excitement.

Also of Note

Bessell-Browne, Thelma Olive. "Literacy Play in Kindergarten." Ph.D. diss. University of Oregon, 1985. 188 pp. DAI 46:3233A.

Beger, Lois Lee Stewart. "John Donahue and the Children's Theatre Company and School of Minneapolis, 1961–1978." Ph.D. diss. Florida State University, 1985. 444 pp. DAI 47:21A.

Bishop, Norma J. "Liminal Space in Travellers' Tales: Historical and Fictional Passages." Ph.D. diss. Pennsylvania State University, 1986. 226 pp. DAI 47:1313A.

Carlsson, G. "Teater för barn: Tre åldersgruppers upplevelser av profesionelle teatre [Theater for Children: Professional Theater as Experienced by Three Age Groups]. Ph.D. diss. Lunds Universitet, 1984. 215 pp. 45:10/1398C. Published by Liber Förlag, 205 10 Malmö, Sweden.

Denise, Susan Ann. "A Study of the Relationship between Children's Literature and Student Writing in an Intermediate Grade Classroom." Ed.D. diss. Columbia University Teachers College, 1986. 182 pp. DAI 47:815A.

Funk, Elisabeth Paling. "Washington Irving and His Dutch-American Heritage as Seen in *A History of New York, The Sketch Book, Bracebridge Hall,* and *Tales of a Traveller.*" Ph.D. diss. Fordham University, 1986. 412 pp. DAI 47:1322A.

Goldstein, Larry Michael. "The Dorothy Heathcote Approach to Creative Drama: Effectiveness and Impact on Moral Education." Ed.D. diss. Rutgers University, State University of New Jersey (New Brunswick), 1985. 207 pp. DAI 47:347–48A.

Lentz, Richard W. "The Effects of Illustrations on Recall of Instructional Text by Good, Average, and Poor Readers." Ph.D. diss. Indiana University, 1985. 96 pp. DAI 46:3666A.

Luther, Alice Hamilton. "Values, Status and Outlook of Children's Drama in the New Brunswick, Canada Junior High School System." Ph.D. diss. University of Minnesota, 1985. 150 pp. DAI 47:22A.

McMillan, Lex O., III. "C. S. Lewis as Spiritual Autobiographer: A Study in the Sacramental Imagination." Ph.D. diss. University of Notre Dame. 1986. 311 pp. DAI 47:913–14A.

Pinter, Karen Ann. "The Effect of Text Simplification and Instructional Procedure on the Inference Generation of Fifth-Grade Disabled Readers." Ed.D. diss. Northern Illinois University, 1985. 296 pp. DAI 46:3668A.

Rohde, R. "Till Eulenspiegel von Volksbuchhelden zur Kinder- und Jugendbuchfigur [Till Eulenspiegel: From the Hero of a Popular Book to a Figure in Children's and Adolescents' Books]. Ph.D. diss. Universität Hamburg, 1982. 274 pp. DAI 46:10/190C.

Rosenfelt, Zell Berman. "Charles Dickens: Attitudes toward Artists." Ph.D. diss. George Washington University, 1986. 198 pp. DAI 47:915A.

Westfahl, Gary Wesley. "The Mote in Gernsback's Eye: A History of the Idea of Science Fiction." Ph.D. diss. Claremont Graduate School, 1986. 395 pp. DAI 47:184A.

Wheeler, Saundra Segan. "Matthew Arnold and the Young Writer." Ph.D. diss. New York University, 1985. 605 pp. DAI 46:3729A.

Contributors and Editors

JANICE M. ALBERGHENE teaches children's and adolescents' literature at Bowling Green State University; she is currently writing a book on the autobiography of childhood.

GILLIAN AVERY teaches for the Department of External Studies at Oxford University, England. She is currently completing a history of American children's books.

FRANCELIA BUTLER, founder of *Children's Literature*, teaches at the University of Connecticut. She has published widely in criticism and has written an adult novel on child abuse and a book for teenagers, *Madame Ghandi*.

PAULA L. CARDINAL is a graduate student of children's literature at the University of Connecticut. She has a particular interest in feminist and deconstructive criticism.

JOHN CECH, review editor for *Children's Literature* and past president of the Children's Literature Association, teaches English at the University of Florida. He is writing a book on the archetype of the child.

RICHARD FLYNN is a poet, teacher, and law librarian in Washington D.C. His reviews and poetry have appeared in *Washington Review, The Reaper, Gargoyle*, and *The Bloomsbury Review*. His work on Randall Jarrell is included in a volume on Jarrell to be published by the Institute for Southern Studies.

RACHEL FORDYCE is assistant vice president for academic affairs at Eastern Connecticut State University.

SARAH GILEAD teaches at the University of Haifa. Her research interests include autobiography, Victorian novels, and children's literature. She has published in *ELH, Critique, Criticism*, and elsewhere.

RICHARD GILLIN teaches English at Washington College. He is particularly interested in the influence of Romanticism on children's literature and in John Clare's work for children. Currently he is working on the influence of fairy tales on children's literature in South Africa and the West Indies.

CECILY RAYSOR HANCOCK studied English at Harvard and the University of Chicago. She has for many years collected children's oral lore and tunes for children's songs. She is currently working on an annotated edition of Rimbault's *Nursery Rhymes*.

MARGARET R. HIGONNET, whose interests include theory and feminist criticism, has recently coedited *Behind the Lines: Gender and the Two World Wars*.

PETER HUNT, who teaches English and directs the Program in Communication Studies at the University of Wales in Cardiff, has written prolifically on children's literature. He has just finished his third novel for children (following *The Maps of Time* [1983] and *A Step off the Path* [1985]).

LOIS R. KUZNETS, who teaches children's literature at San Diego State University, has just published the Twayne *Kenneth Grahame*.

ROBERT H. MACDONALD, who teaches English at Carleton University, Ottawa, has edited the prose and poems of William Drummond of Hawthornden and published numerous essays in *Canadian Literature, Modern Language Review, Journal of the History of Ideas*, and elsewhere. He is currently working on imperialism and the history of scouting.

CYNTHIA MARSHALL teaches English at Rhodes College, specializing in Shakespeare. She has published articles on *Pericles* and *The Winter's Tale* and is currently working on eschatology in Shakespeare's romances. She is also editing a collection of essays on George MacDonald and C. S. Lewis.

MICHAEL MENDELSON teaches children's literature and rhetoric at Iowa State University. He has written on Victorian fantasy and fairy tales, as well as on narrative and rhetorical theory. He is currently at work on the fairy tales of George MacDonald.

FRANK MYSZOR, a secondary school teacher, is at present engaged in research at Southampton University. He is studying graphical means of representing teenagers' responses to short stories, using ethnographic techniques.

BARBARA ROSEN, who teaches at the University of Connecticut, has edited Shakespeare, a book of reports of Elizabethan witch trials, and *Children's Literature*.

GLENN EDWARD SADLER teaches at Bloomsburg University. He is an authority on the works of George MacDonald and C. S. Lewis, and a past co-editor of *Children's Literature*.

M. SARAH SMEDMAN teaches English at the University of North Carolina at Charlotte; she is particularly interested in twentieth-century fiction for children and adolescents.

LOUISA SMITH teaches English at Mankato State University. She is currently working on British illustrator H. R. Millar.

LAURA WEAVER teaches technical and business writing at the University of Evansville, Indiana. She has written on the divided self in the dramas of David Storey and in her own life for the MLA volume *A Road Retaken: Women Reenter the Academy*.

Index to Volumes 11–15

Compiled by Paula L. Cardinal

Essays and Varia

Book Reviews